The Invention of Childhood

The Invention of
CHILDHOOD

HUGH CUNNINGHAM

BOOKS

Published to accompany the radio series
The Invention of Childhood, first broadcast
on BBC Radio 4 in 2006.

Presenter: Michael Morpurgo
Producer: Beaty Rubens

First published 2006
Copyright © Hugh Cunningham 2006
Foreword and *The Voices of Children*
© Michael Morpurgo 2006
The moral right of the authors has been asserted.

ISBN-13: 978 0 563 49390 7
ISBN-10: 0 563 49390 9

Published by BBC Books, BBC Worldwide Ltd,
Woodlands, 80 Wood Lane, London W12 0TT

Commissioning editor: Martin Redfern
Project editor: Christopher Tinker
Copy-editor: Helen Armitage
Designer: Andrew Barron
Picture researcher: Cath Harries
Production controller: Peter Hunt

Set in FF Scala and Scala Sans by BBC Books
Printed and bound in Great Britain by
Clays Ltd, St Ives plc
Colour origination by Dot Gradations,
Wickford, Essex

For more information on this and other
BBC books, please visit www.bbcshop.com

Contents

For Diane

List of Illustrations

Foreword

That we have had to wait so long for a comprehensive book on the last thousand years of British childhood in itself perhaps says something about our attitude to childhood. Prevalent still is the notion that childhood is simply a stage on the road to adulthood, and little more. Hardly worth a book then. Quite why we need to patronize childhood and children I am not sure, but we do. We forget, or want to forget, ourselves as children. Maybe it's because we can only define our adulthood by distancing ourselves from our childhood. Perhaps St Paul is partly to blame here, advising us as he did 'to put away childish things'. The truth is that it has always been adults (grown-up children, that is – and some of them have been saints too) who have sought to define childhood, or more often to negate it, or to exploit it, and sometimes to idealize it. But it was always each new generation of children themselves who reinvented it and lived it.

Hugh Cunningham's book, steeped in learning and insight as it is, has been the foundation of the 30-part radio series that accompanies it. Along with Beaty Rubens, the producer of the programme, guide and mentor and friend, I had the wonderful experience of co-writing it and presenting it. We have attempted, the three of us together, to discover how the concept of childhood came about and how it has developed through the last ten centuries. Central to this story of childhood in Hugh's book are the voices of children. Their voices, when they could be found, sing the theme tune throughout. The accompanying orchestration of parental concerns, of governmental reforms, of ever changing sociological and educational thinking, of psychological insights, combine to create a great symphony of childhood, to explain how and why our concept of childhood may have altered over the years, while the children themselves have not.

As I went on this epic voyage of discovery I realized just how little I really knew and understood, although this was my field. After all I'd been a father, a grandfather, a teacher for 40 years. I'd written several dozen books in which children usually play a central role. What I'd lacked all along, of course, was scholarship, the rigour of historical perspective – and Hugh Cunningham provided both.

Inevitably, the journey was at times a painful one and shameful too. Poverty, neglect, cruelty and exploitation appear all too often in this story. But what shines throughout is the spirit of the child to survive, to cope, to forgive and always to reinvent. At its heart there is a story of the millions of children who have lived in this country over the centuries. It is their story.

This is why, instead of a rambling overture of an introduction, which Hugh Cunningham's marvellously enlightening book simply does not need, I have written a play. I wanted to give the children the last word, which they deserve I think after all they have been through. And this is why you'll find a play at the end of this book. I've called it *The Voices of Children*. Read it and you'll hear their tune. But first here is Hugh Cunningham's full orchestral symphony: *The Invention of Childhood*.

Michael Morpurgo
June 2006

Introduction

'What is a child, or to be a child?' asked Thomas Becon in 1550. It is a question that runs throughout this book. From the seventh century, our starting-point, up to the twenty-first, the answers given have ranged enormously. And they have been given mostly by adults. Occasionally we hear a child reflecting on childhood. 'I ain't a child ... I'm past eight, I am,' said a girl selling watercress in mid-nineteenth-century London, shocking her interlocutor, the investigative journalist Henry Mayhew, who thought childhood ended when you were 15.[1] But mostly what we hear are adults imagining childhood, inventing it, in order to make sense of their world. Children have to live with the consequences.

Babies and children go through certain well-marked stages as they grow: smiling, crawling, walking, talking, teething and so on through to puberty and adulthood. To a very large extent these biological imperatives determine their development. Adult intervention, or the lack of it, will affect what happens only at the margin. Children's minds, too, may develop in predictable ways, as mapped out by the eminent Swiss developmental psychologist Jean Piaget in the twentieth century. On top of these biological universals there are genetic particulars, the inheritance from parents, that help to shape a child as he or she grows up. And, though perhaps more controversially, in their relationship with those near to them – mother, father, siblings, carer, grandparents and so on – children may have emotional responses that have a degree of universality. Fear, anger and jealousy may be as prominent as affection, generosity and love. Children may re-enact those Greek tragedies to which Sigmund Freud alerted us: the boys, like Oedipus, desiring their mothers, the girls, like Electra, their fathers.[2]

Much, then, in the history of children in the past is a given. True, biological development itself has not been immune from change. Improvements in the standard of living, for example, have brought about a significant decline in the age of menarche in Britain, by about three years over a century. Puberty in nearly all societies is one of the markers of the end of childhood, and a change of this magnitude is likely to alter the contours of childhood. But if children themselves have in some ways changed over time, much more subject to change have been ideas about childhood.

Take the question of the age at which someone can be said to be criminally responsible, something also often thought of as a marker of the end of childhood. There have been debates on this from the time of the Anglo-Saxons onwards. In the Middle Ages the age was set at 12. It is therefore something of a shock to move forward to the eighteenth century and find a girl of seven in Norwich being hanged for stealing a petticoat.[3] It tells us, if nothing else, that the history of childhood is not, as has sometimes been thought, a simple story of progress.

Thomas Becon's answer to his question alerts us to how many possible different answers there are to it: 'A child in Scripture', he wrote, 'is a wicked man, as he that is ignorant and not exercised in godliness.'[4] Becon, chaplain to the archbishop of Canterbury, Thomas Cranmer, was writing at the beginning of the Reformation. It is unlikely that any one would answer the question in that way today. Nor would they have done so in the Middle Ages. Nor even would many people have answered it that way in Becon's time. At almost exactly the same date a preacher stressed the innocence of children. The adults who define childhood are rarely in agreement with one another. They differ across time; they differ within their own time.

In the twenty-first century we are uncertain how to answer Becon's question. We don't all agree on when childhood begins. At conception? At birth? At some point beyond babyhood? And we certainly don't agree on when it ends. At puberty? When we leave school? When we leave home? When we cease to be financially dependent on our parents? When we are of an age to be criminally responsible, or to have sex, serve in the armed forces, vote, buy alcoholic drinks or drive a car? All these seem to be markers of some kind for the end of childhood, but there is no one ceremony or ritual, as in some societies, in which we leave childhood and move to something beyond it. And of course we use the word 'child' in different senses: a child can cease to be one with time, but we are always a child of our parents.

If we are uncertain or, perhaps, flexible about the beginning and end of childhood, we are also so with respect to what might be called its contents. We know what we don't like about childhood and children in the present; it is rammed home to us in statistics and news stories: children who are obese, or the 90 per cent of children set to be 'couch potatoes', children who 'terrorize' their neighbourhoods, children who bully other children. We worry about children who seem to be in danger from the adult world, children who grow up too fast, the rising rate of mental illness among children, the one in twelve British children who self-harm.[5] But turn the question round and ask how positively we would like to see childhood, and we are often struggling. And this is in part because we are heirs to so many conflicting views of childhood from the past, so many different inventions. Just as an individual's life, right to its end, will be influenced by often sub-conscious memories and experiences from early childhood, so as a society we, in the present, are a kind of sum of our past. We often think that children ought to be happy, a notion that dates back to the romanticism of the eighteenth century. We also often want them to be obedient to adults, an idea with deep roots in many parts of the past. We sometimes think of children as innocent, but can equally easily lurch into thinking that some of them at any rate are evil, both of them ideas with a traceable ancestry.

In the nineteenth century some observers of children in the slums of the burgeoning towns or in the factories of the Industrial Revolution saw 'children without childhood'. They strove to give such children a childhood, to strip away the stigmata of adulthood that were disfiguring their bodies. They began to talk of a child's right to a childhood. According to Benjamin Waugh, who played a prominent role in the early history of the National Society for the Prevention of Cruelty to Children, 'The rights of a child are its birthrights. The Magna Carta of them, is a child's nature. The Author, its Creator.'[6] Waugh didn't have to pause, as we might, over 'a child's nature'. A child, he would have thought, was innocent, was owed a duty of protection by adults, was entitled to be dependent on adults and had a right to happiness. We also often talk about a child's right to a childhood. And when we do, our thoughts of what it might be may not differ that much from those of Benjamin Waugh, more than a century ago. And yet the conditions in which children live are markedly different. The inventions of the past live on into the present.

In 1842, journalist and writer on art Lady Eastlake wrote that childhood was 'the only truly enviable part of life'.[7] The envy, of course, was that of adults whose childhood lay in the past. Children themselves are quite unlikely to think the same way. They may, when they become adults, look back with nostalgia on their childhoods, even think, as was once fashionable for males, that their schooldays were the happiest days of their lives. But for many people throughout history to think of childhood as the most enviable part of life would have been unimaginable. Childhood was something to be got through on the way, they hoped, to something better.

This history of childhood in Britain sets out to explain how the many different ideas about childhood in the past, the many inventions of it, come together to shape our ideas of it in the present. But the emphasis is not only on the ideas themselves. It is also on the experience of being a child under one or more of these inventions. This is no easy task. Children rarely leave behind them the kind of evidence that would enable us to know what it had been like to be a child in the eighth or the eighteenth century. Even when we come across what looks like the voice of a child, in a diary, for example, we need to be aware that diaries are often written to a formula, the girls (normally) who write them knowing what is expected of a diary writer.[8] Sometimes we can pick up clues from things left behind, a spinning top, perhaps, or a doll. We can also learn much from adults reminiscing about their childhoods, though we need to be alert to tricks of memory or a colouring from nostalgia. Despite the difficulties, there are in fact many ways in which we can recapture the lives of children in the past. We can find out about the families and homes in which they lived, about the nature and quality of their relationships with others, about their play and their education and about their mental world, the stories and beliefs that shaped their lives. Sometimes we encounter adults, like Henry Mayhew, who record for us what children say and do.

The history of childhood has sometimes been written as a history of parenthood, and the relations between parents and children play a large part in what follows. But there is more to a history of childhood than relations between children and parents, or even between children and their siblings or grandparents or any other family members. Children, often at a very young age, are brought into contact with society outside the family and with some key institutions. In the earlier centuries, and for most of our history, the church was by a long way the most important of these. In addition, increasingly important over time, there was school. And children themselves formed a society, a culture, unique to their age group, almost impenetrable to outsiders.

Any history of childhood has to look beyond what would be the known world of most children, beyond their homes and neighbourhoods. There was always a minority of children who had no homes, whose lives were dependent on the support of the community – orphans, foundlings or children whose parents for one reason or another couldn't or wouldn't look after them. There were many children throughout our history in such poverty that their lives (if they survived) were blighted and who came under the care of charitable organizations, the Poor Law or the welfare state. The solution was sometimes drastic, such as the emigration of children to Canada or Australia. For children, little though they might know it, were always of concern to those who held power. They were the future. On the way they were brought up depended the future of state and nation. That rhetoric is still with us.

A history of childhood can easily become a history of what adults have done to children. Children become the victims or the beneficiaries of adult actions. But children can also be agents in the making of their lives and their world. By drawing on sources that show children doing things as well as having things done to them, *The Invention of Childhood* integrates children of the past into the particular world in which they lived. In doing so, it highlights the ways in which childhoods in the past can sometimes seem almost unimaginable and sometimes eerily familiar.

CHAPTER ONE

The Middle Ages

FOR NEARLY A MILLENNIUM, from the coming of Christianity in the seventh century to the dawn of the Protestant Reformation in the mid-sixteenth century, the dominant influence on childhood in Britain was the Catholic church. Its beliefs and rituals shaped the lives of children from the moment they were baptized on the day of their birth.

Politically, the world into which children were born changed out of recognition over these 900 years. In AD 600 what we now think of as Britain was made up of perhaps dozens of kingdoms, some, like Wessex or Northumbria, Strathclyde or Gwynedd, more powerful than others. But, quite rapidly, the more prominent kings had aspirations to rule over a people. King Offa of Mercia (AD 757–96) is described in his charters as 'king of the English', and he also built the famous Offa's Dyke to keep out the Welsh. But it was in the later ninth century, in King Alfred's resistance to the Danes from his base in Wessex, and in the tenth century when his successors overcame the Danes in the south and east of England, that an English identity began to be forged. The Anglo-Saxons never conquered either Wales or Scotland; in each a native power had emerged as dominant by 1066, the year that the Anglo-Saxons fell to the Normans. By then England was a nation state with advanced institutions of local government, tax-gathering and law-making. Edward I in the thirteenth century reduced Wales to a state of dependence, and in 1536 Wales was effectively annexed by England. But Scotland in the thirteenth and fourteenth centuries was forging itself as a separate kingdom, with frequent squabbles over the border with England, but no sense that Scotland would be conquered. 'Britain' in these centuries did not exist.

It is always difficult to know how far children are aware of the political entity in which they grow up. Even though in all of these centuries the vast majority of the population was illiterate and living in rural areas, some of them very remote, some sense of national identity – English, Scottish or Welsh – would probably have been implanted in most children as they grew up, certainly in the later Middle Ages. But a more powerful influence on them would have been the church: its architecture, its services, its wealth and its preaching, and the schooling and careers it offered to the bright. Even more influential would have been the day-to-day economic circumstances in which children lived, nearly all of them, in our terms, very poor.

The common experience of a Catholic church and a struggle for existence means that, even if we cannot speak of Britain, we can speak of childhood in what was to become Britain; of a set of assumptions and practices, varying locally, but having sufficient in common that a child in Cornwall would have a life not hugely dissimilar to that of a child in Caithness.

The coming of Christianity

Grave number 133 in the seventh-century Anglo-Saxon cemetery at Castledyke South, Barton-on-Humber, is less than a metre in length. That is one reason why we know that an infant was buried there. There is another reason. The bones have crumbled away, but, as was the norm for the pagan Anglo-Saxons before the coming of Christianity, the infant was buried with objects associated with it. In the grave, alongside three glass beads, was a feeding bottle, shaped like a breast. Perhaps the mother had not been able to produce any milk. Perhaps, as other Anglo-Saxon graves tell us, the baby had a cleft palate and could not suckle.[1] [Fig. 1] Whatever the reason, the bottle is evidence of a vain attempt to sustain life in a baby, of parental care for a child. That parental care, set alongside its opposite, parental neglect or cruelty, will run through this history of children in Britain.

So too will another message we can take from the grave. Parents all too often had to come to terms with the deaths of their children. We have no figures for death rates of children in the early Middle Ages, but there is no reason to suppose they were any better than in later centuries when probably at least one out of every four babies born would fail to live to their first birthday. If you survived your first hours, days, weeks and months of life, your prospects improved, but perhaps as many as a half of all children born would fail to reach the age of ten. When we look at the history of childhood we are constantly confronted with parents trying to cope with the deaths of their children, and children facing the possibility of their own deaths or those of their siblings. King Alfred asked, 'What sight is more intolerable than the death of a child before its father's eyes?'[2] a pain greater than any he could imagine. But the omnipresence of death could not be ignored. People would have been particularly aware of it during and after the fourteenth-century Black Death, in which one in three of the population died, the young being particularly vulnerable. In a fifteenth-century Dance of Death, in which the living are imagined as meeting their own skeletons, these words were put into the mouth of a baby:

I am ful yong
I was born yisterday
Deth is ful hasty
On me to been wreke
And of his strok
List make no delay
I cam but now
And now I go my way.[3]

And of course it was not only children who died. Parents died too. The rate of break-up of the family through parental death in all centuries up to the twentieth century was roughly equivalent to our twenty-first-century rate of break-up through divorce. The death of a parent meant that many children were brought up by one parent alone or had to adjust to a step-parent; or the loss of both parents meant that some other means of care had to be found.

The infant's grave has one further message. Historians of childhood, particularly in the early Middle Ages, have to exercise considerable ingenuity in order to find out anything about children. There are all too many questions to which there is no answer. But sometimes the most unlikely material can at least give us clues. A survey of Anglo-Saxon burial places reveals that children under 15 constituted just over one-third of all burials, a lower percentage than one would expect. This may have been because children's corpses were disposed of in other ways, an indicator that their status was lower than that of adults. Certainly children were less likely than adults to be buried with grave goods. These are clues, but archaeologists and historians are never likely to be in full agreement about their meaning.[4]

In AD 678, Barton-on-Humber became part of the new diocese of Lindsey, and in that same year a monastery was set up at Barrow, only a few miles from Barton. There seems to have been no concerted effort to force the pagan population to abandon their beliefs or their burial practices, but Christianity was on the move.[5] When the Roman monk Augustine arrived in Canterbury in AD 597 the rulers of all the kingdoms were pagan. A century later they were all Christian. From Ireland to Iona, and from Iona to Lindisfarne, Celtic missionaries spread their influence. The two separate movements for the conversion of England, Roman and Celtic, came to terms at the Synod of Whitby in AD 664. The future would be Christian, the people perhaps slower to become so than their rulers. The chief agents of conversion were monks who based themselves in minsters which themselves often became the nucleus of thriving market towns. Then, from the eleventh century, even before the Norman Conquest, parishes began to be mapped out and in time their stone-built churches became the landmarks we know.

Anglo-Saxon attitudes to children came to be strongly influenced by the new ideas that flowed into the country with the coming of Christianity. In pagan Anglo-Saxon culture, the shards of evidence that survive suggest that children were seen as rather marginal to the adult community. The Christian belief in the necessity of salvation for each individual placed a higher value on children. They were no longer on the margin, perhaps not fully human. An Anglo-Saxon poem from the Christian era describing 'the fates of man' opens with a description of caring family life:

> It very often comes to pass by God's might
> That man and wife bring, by means of birth,
> A child into the world, and provide him with delights,
> Cheer and cherish him.[6]

There was provision in Anglo-Saxon laws in the Christian era for children whose parents had died. King Aethelred the Unready (978–1016) decreed 'that widows and step-children should not always be unhappy but should be readily gladdened'. More down to earth, Kent's most famous king, Aethelbert (597–649), ruled that 'If a wife bears a living child, she shall have half the property left by her husband, if he dies first,' and King Ine of Wessex (693–755), the first king of Wessex known to have issued a code of laws, made provision both for those who had been abandoned and those who had lost their father. 'For the maintenance of a foundling up to three years', he ruled, '6 shillings shall be given in the first year, 12 in the second, 30 shillings in the third, and afterwards according to its appearance.' And, 'If a man and his wife have a child between them, and the man dies, the mother will keep and rear the child: she shall be given 6 shillings to maintain it, a cow in summer and an ox in winter. The kinsman will look after the property until it comes of age.'[7] We cannot be certain that these laws were ever fully enforced. But what they undoubtedly show is a recognition that society needed to make provision for children whose parents had died.

The Anglo-Saxons also had debates that resonate to this day about the age at which a child could be said to be responsible for her or his acts, perhaps by implication the age at which childhood ended. Ine of Wessex thought that 'A ten-year-old child may be regarded as an accessory to theft.' In the tenth century Aethelstan, king of England (893/4–939), ruled that 'no thief shall be spared who is caught in the act, if he is over twelve years old,' but then, becoming more soft-hearted and after talking to his 'witan' (his councillors), sent word to the archbishop 'that he thinks it cruel that such young men are executed and for so little, as he has learnt happens everywhere. He declares that he, and those with whom he has spoken, think that no one should be executed who is under fifteen years old, unless he tries to defend himself, or tries to run away and refuses to give himself up.' But this leniency was short lived. A century later, King Canute ruled that 'everyone over twelve years shall swear the oath that he will not be a thief nor a thief's accomplice'.[8] A thousand years later we are still trying to decide when a child can be said to be criminally responsible, and our answers are remarkably similar to those of the Anglo-Saxons.

Infant baptism was the recognized way to bring a child into the family of God. St Augustine of Hippo in modern Algeria (354–430) had taught that infant baptism cleansed an infant from the original sin inherited from Adam, though it did not remove an individual's own tendencies towards evil. St Augustine himself remembered stealing pears for no other reason than a compulsion to do something bad.[9] An unbaptized child, it was thought, would go to hell, though from the end of the twelfth century this was softened to a consignment to limbo.[10] The importance ascribed to infant baptism is once again evident in the laws promulgated by the Anglo-Saxons. At the beginning of the eighth century Ine of Wessex decreed that 'A child must be baptised within thirty days: if this is not done, 30 shillings to be paid in compensation. If, however, it dies without being baptized, he shall pay as compensation all he possesses,' an incentive if ever there was one to get the baby rapidly to the font.[11] Once there, it has to be said, its chances of a longer life were, at least in a temporal sense, hardly improved. Total immersion in the water three times was the norm, and the water itself, priests were advised, should be replaced only if the baby defecated, not if it simply urinated.[12]

The baptized child, verses in the New Testament suggested, might have a value in God's eyes that placed it above its elders. When his disciples tried to prevent children being brought to him, Jesus rebuked them, saying, 'Suffer the little children to come unto me, and forbid them not; for of such is the kingdom of God.' He went on to warn that 'Whosoever shall not receive the kingdom of God as a little child, he shall not enter therein ... Take heed that ye despise not one of these little ones, for there is a special place in heaven for them.'[13] Verses like these, combined with a veneration for the Madonna, entered deep into the medieval mind. The baby Jesus with his mother was, along with the Crucifixion, the image that people were most likely to be familiar with. There were also frequent depictions of the Massacre of the Innocents by Herod.[14] Through these verses and images, people became sensitized to an emotional response to babies and children.

Our evidence for this sensitivity comes mostly from a period later than the time of the Anglo-Saxons. It may be that this is simply because of a lack of earlier sources, but a more emotional response to babies and infants, reinforced by the increasingly realistic portrayals in art of the baby Jesus and his mother, is apparent from about the twelfth century. This was a Europe-wide phenomenon, and the spread of these new ideas was facilitated by the heightened traffic across the English Channel after the Norman Conquest. One of the most telling pieces of evidence comes from a story of St Hugh, bishop of Lincoln in the twelfth century. Hugh was born in France and first came to England when he was nearly 40.

> Because of his unsullied innocence, which made him set great store by
> sincerity and simplicity, the saint had an unusual affection for children
> because of their complete naturalness ... I saw a child of about six
> months, who, when he made the sign of the cross on its forehead with
> the holy oil, expressed such great delight by the movement of its limbs,
> that it reminded one of the joy of the Baptist, leaping up in the womb.
> The tiny mouth and face relaxed in continuous chuckles, and it seemed
> incredible that at an age when babies generally yell it could laugh in this
> way. It then bent and stretched out its little arms, as if it were trying to fly,
> and moved its head to and fro, as if to show that its joy was almost too
> great to bear. Next, it took his hand in both its tiny ones and, exerting all
> its strength, raised it to its face. It then proceeded to lick it instead of
> kissing it. This it did for a long time. Those present were amazed at the
> unusual spectacle of the bishop and the infant absolutely happy in each

other's company. The sight of the attractive scene between the two of them turned men's thoughts to higher things ... What could the infant have seen in the bishop which gave it so much delight, unless it were God in him? What drew the bishop to the baby and made so important a person pay such attention to so small a being except the knowledge of the greatness concealed in such a tiny frame ... The bishop gave the boy an apple and several other things which children usually like, but he refused to be amused by any of them. He rejected them all and seemed completely absorbed and fascinated by the bishop. Disdainfully pushing away the hands of the nurse who was holding him, he gazed hard at the bishop, and clapped his hands smiling all the time.[15]

The scene of this remarkable encounter, we learn, was Newark Castle, the baby boy born of humble stock on the other side of the River Trent. The chronicler is keen that we should know that it actually happened, that it is not a product of the imagination. St Hugh was of course exceptional and recognized to be so, and we should not for a moment imagine that adult–child encounters in the Middle Ages were routinely of this nature. They were not, otherwise there would have been no need to record so precisely the baby's responses to the bishop. But if an exceptional bishop could recognize what the chronicler called 'the greatness concealed in such a tiny frame', and if the encounter could be celebrated in the way it was, we can conclude that there was in the Middle Ages a sensitivity to the special quality of childhood that later centuries might equal but could not surpass.

Further evidence of new attitudes to children lie in the efforts made by English bishops in the thirteenth century to improve parenting skills. In part this consisted of a resort to legal punishment. Both infanticide, the deliberate killing of a baby, and negligence in overlaying babies put to sleep in the parental bed became included in the category of major sins, reserved to the judgement of the bishop. More positively, priests were told that they must warn women every Sunday against taking children into their beds, tell them that drunkenness often led to carelessness and danger to children and remind them how they must secure children in their cradles so that they could not turn over on their faces – shades of our modern worries about sudden infant death syndrome (SIDS) or cot death, the priest rather than the doctor the source of advice.[16]

There are other accounts from the later Middle Ages of close and loving relationships between adults and children. Take this account of bath time:

> When the ... Infant was seated in the bath, he began to play as is the way of infants. He made noise in the water by clapping hands, and as children do, splashed in the water until it spilled out and wet all those around. He continued to splash while moving all of his tiny body. On seeing the water splashing all around, he began to shout with joy in a loud voice ... and when the bathing was complete, she lifted the child from the bath, dried him, and wrapped him in his swaddling bands. She seated him on her lap and as mothers do, began to play with him.[17]

The baby being bathed here is Jesus. The account is a fourteenth-century vision of St Ida who was permitted to assist at the bath time. What we have is an immediately recognizable account of a young child's behaviour in a bath and of a mother's response. She dried him and, 'as mothers do, began to play with him', the swaddling bands, it is worth noting, in no way impeding this.

A belief in the innocence of children runs through the later Middle Ages. We shall encounter later the boy bishops who in December every year were allowed to take on the role of the adult bishop. Sometimes they preached sermons, written for them by adults. In one of the surviving sermons a boy bishop utters these words:

> Young babes are symple, withowt gyle, innocent, wythowt harme, and all pure wythowt corruption ... Considre well the nature of innocent children, and yow shall perceive in them no maner of malice, no envy, no disdayne, no hurtfullness, no synfull affection, no pride, no ambition, no singular-itie, no desyre of honor, of riches, of carnalitie, of revenginge, or quittyng evyll for evyll; but all the affections quiet, in all pacience, in all simplicitie, in all puritie, in all tractableness, in all obedience, in all humilitie, and in all innocency; and no such synful affections reigning in them as commynly rageth in men and women of years.[18]

Some who heard this sermon must have had experience of howling babies or enraged toddlers, but the image, strongly influenced by thoughts of the baby Jesus, was a powerful one.

Accounts like this provide us with an ideal of childhood that had considerable sway in the Middle Ages, certainly from the twelfth century onwards. We should not imagine that reality matched the ideal. The warnings uttered by the English bishops in the thirteenth century arise precisely out of their concern about what was actually happening rather than what should be happening: there was infanticide, there were parents, drunk and careless, who rolled over on to their young children when they were asleep and suffocated them.[19] But the ideals provide us with a base for exploring thoughts on the nature of childhood beyond babyhood. Was the innocence bestowed by Christianity on the baptized baby thought to survive into later childhood?

'Little adults'? Ideas about childhood in medieval Britain

It has often been said that before the eighteenth century children were regarded as 'little adults'. If contemporaries, it is said, distinguished children from adults, it was, apart from their small size, for their deficiency in adult aptitudes and skills. Making some allowance for this, they could otherwise be treated like adults. There was, if you like, in the Middle Ages and beyond, no territory called childhood that was inhabited by children. Children simply meshed into the adult world. Was this really how it was? Was there no recognition that children needed special care in their upbringing?

We can gain some clues from a conversation between St Anselm, archbishop of Canterbury in the eleventh and early twelfth centuries, and an abbot, 'considered to be a sufficiently religious man', who asked Anselm for advice about the boys in his care.

> 'What, I ask you, is to be done with them? They are incorrigible ruffians. We never give over beating them day and night, and they only get worse and worse.'
>
> Anselm replied with astonishment: 'You never give over beating them? And what are they like when they grow up?'
>
> 'Stupid brutes,' he said.
>
> To which Anselm retorted,
>
> 'You have spent your energies in rearing them to good purpose: from men you have reared beasts.'
>
> 'But what can we do about it,' he said; 'We use every means to force them to get better, but without success.'

'You force them? Now tell me, my lord abbot, if you plant a tree-shoot in your garden, and straightway shut it in on every side so that it has no space to put out its branches, what kind of tree will you have in after years when you let it out of its confinement?'

'A useless one, certainly, with its branches all twisted and knotted.'

'And whose fault would this be, except your own for shutting it in so unnaturally? Without doubt, this is what you do with your boys. At their oblation they are planted in the garden of the Church, to grow and bring forth fruit for God. But you so terrify them and hem them in on all sides with threats and blows that they are utterly deprived of their liberty. And being thus injudicially oppressed, they harbour and welcome and nurse within themselves evil and crooked thoughts like thorns, and cherish those thoughts so passionately that they doggedly reject everything which could minister to their correction. Hence, feeling no love or pity, good-will or tenderness in your attitude towards them, they have in future no faith in your goodness but believe that all your actions proceed from hatred and malice against them.'[20]

Here are two views of children, each with a long future ahead of them. Spare the rod and spoil the child doubtless reverberated through the abbot's mind. But Anselm, his advice frequently quoted in the later Middle Ages, has a quite different sense of the best way to bring up a child. A child is like a young plant, it needs care and attention.

The Bible and the writings of Greek and Roman authorities provided a stock of received wisdom about child rearing. We can see them at work in the writings of John of Wales, an eminent Franciscan scholar of the thirteenth century. John is thought to have come originally from north Wales (hence his name) and studied at Oxford before joining the Franciscan order in about 1250. From 1259 to 1262 he was lector to the Oxford Franciscans but seems to have spent most of the latter part of his life in Paris – he died there in 1285. He wrote prolifically, including what are called *ad status* sermons. These were model sermons, or ideas and material for them, which addressed particular groups of the population, and in the thirteenth century, for the first time, we find substantial attention being given to parent–child relationships. Parents, says John, should train their children with discipline. He backs up this assertion with biblical quotations and an extract from Aristotle's *Ethics*. Boys should be prepared to endure hardship, an example held up being the training of Alexander the Great by his father, Philip, and another the upbringing of the Spartans as related by Cicero and Seneca. The emperor Octavian is another exemplar: he adopted sons and set them to a military career, with training in running, leaping, swimming, bearing a sword and throwing missiles, and had his daughters instructed in the spinning of wool so that they could earn a living if they fell into poverty – all showing, according to John, that sons and daughters ought not to be idle. Further examples from the Bible and from the ancient world of paternal discipline, both harsh and moderate, are weighed in the balance before John gives his own view. Severity in discipline is to be commended, but it must not be to excess, and it should be accompanied by moderate praise when it is earned.

Children, says John, should love their parents, obey them, honour them and help them if they fall into poverty. Readers are urged to turn to the work of Valerius Maximus for examples from the Roman world, and much is made of the Romans' respect for their parents. Failure to behave in the approved way could be fatal, children were warned – and here John takes his example from St Augustine who had a story of some brothers and sisters who spoke ill of their mother and were punished with a palsy. It is from the ancient world that John takes his conventional division of the childhood years into *infancia*, the first seven years, and *puericia*, the second seven. In infancy, care should be taken in selecting a nurse. Avoid chatterboxes, says John, for words are like milk or food if they are good, but like poison if bad. St Augustine is again invoked on childhood sin – 'so small a child, so great a sinner' – but parents are held to be responsible for a child's sins up to the age of seven. Boys from the age of seven are warned especially against lust and covetousness, with further positive reference to the Spartans. For education, John's main sources are Jerome, Quintilian and Augustine, with much emphasis on learning thoroughly and correctly at the outset.

John of Wales had an insatiable appetite for stories from the ancient world about child rearing, and it seems that the examples he cited would have carried quite as much authority as texts from the Bible. From the combination of the two he arrived at advice that we know was taken up or copied by other preachers. Model sermons were much in demand, and we can be confident that John's thoughts and examples would have spread widely.[21]

Medical writings give us further insight into medieval ideas about childhood. Medical thinking about childhood derived ultimately from Greece's most famous doctor, Hippocrates, who in about 400 BC identified 20 diseases peculiar to children, and from the physician and philosopher Galen, the most influential individual in the medical world for the medieval period, who in the second century AD wrote quite extensively about the perfectly constituted child. These ideas were supplemented by Arabic sources that became known in Europe in the twelfth century. The most important of them were the work of two Persians of the eleventh and twelfth centuries, Rasis (or Rhazes), who described measles and smallpox, and Avicenna, whose treatise contained chapters on the hygiene and diseases of childhood. All these sources are evident in the work of the early thirteenth-century Franciscan encyclopedist Bartholomew of England.

Some of the ideas expressed in medieval medical writings may strike us as odd. Here, for example, is an early fourteenth-century account of birth: 'The first age, the age of being born, is a lamentable, miserable, and shameful age ... It is clearly lamentable, because the newborn infant immediately begins to cry and wail ... Birth is also miserable because the infant enters the desert of this present life naked. It is furthermore shameful because he emerges from sordid bilge-water and he is enveloped in stench.' But the advice that follows may strike us as thoroughly sensible. 'The child', we read, 'is to be received in a place as similar as possible to the womb, because any sudden change is harmful.' Everything possible should be done to pacify the baby, offering the nipple, rocking gently, singing 'sweet songs', carrying the baby about, checking whether its clothing is soiled or too tight or too loose.

Most medical advice agreed that there were two key turning-points in the early years. The first came with teething, a hazardous period, and the second, at about the age of seven, with the development of articulate speech. On top of this universal pattern of child development, more and more illnesses of childhood began to be identified. By the end of the fifteenth century over 50 specific childhood ailments had been noted, headed by diarrhoea, sleeplessness and intestinal worms, thrush, vomiting, wheezing and coughing, and fevers. Much of the advice for treatment was thoroughly sensible, vaporubs for coughs for example.[22]

Another considerable body of medieval literature focused on the stages of life. Here again the writers were inheriting ideas from the ancient world. Some, following Aristotle, saw life as falling into three stages, periods of growth and decline, marked by deficiencies as much as positive qualities, sandwiching a middle age that is the summit of life. Others identified four stages, corresponding to the four seasons and the qualities, humours and elements associated with them. Following this scheme, the scholar and saint the Venerable Bede in 725 equated childhood with spring. Then the air is moist and hot, and blood is at its greatest strength. Blood, wrote Bede, 'makes those in whom it most prevails merry, delightful, tender-hearted, and much given to laughter and talk', an entirely positive view of childhood. But other and later versions of the four stages had the first stage lasting up to age 30, with no special mention of childhood. From the twelfth century onwards, perhaps even more popular than three or four stages was the idea of seven stages, itself derived from astrology – infancy associated with the Moon, childhood with Mercury and so on. It is this seven-stage model that is most familiar to us from the morbid view of it presented by Jaques in Shakespeare's *As You Like It*:

> At first, the Infant,
> Mewling and puking in the nurse's arms.
> Then the whining School-boy, with his satchel
> And shining morning face, creeping like snail
> Unwillingly to school.

Painters often depicted the seven stages. Visitors to Longthorpe Tower, near Peterborough, entering the great chamber from the south, would have been confronted by a painted arch over a recess, dating from about 1330. The seven stages start with *infans* in a cot on the bottom left, rising through *puer*, a boy playing with a whipping top, *adolescens* now almost obliterated, to reach *juvenis* at the top of the arch. After that it's downhill through *senior*, *senex* and finally *decrepitus* on crutches.

There was no one consistent medieval view of life's course. Rather, what we can detect is a compulsion to make sense of life by dividing it up into stages. In many of these there is the familiar distinction, derived from classical authorities, of life at its outset divided into seven-year slices, often termed *infans*, up to seven, *puer*, seven to 14, and *adolescens*, from 14 to 21. And a very common way of depicting the life's course was as an arch, marked at one end by the helplessness of infancy and at the other by the decrepitude of old age. The peak of life, at the top of the arch, was in life's middle.[23] Some Victorians came to think of childhood as the best time of life. This would have made little sense to medieval people. They differed, too, from the Victorians and from us, in that they did not think that childhood experiences would inexorably mould adult life. In the rare documents that come near to being autobiographies, childhood receives hardly a mention. In the autobiography of the author and ecclesiastic Gerald of Wales (c. 1146–1220) it takes up two and a half pages out of 325 and then only to pinpoint activities that foreshadowed his future life.[24] But this downplaying of the importance of childhood for the future adult did not mean that medieval people did not recognize childhood at all.

People in the Middle Ages were by no means wholly dependent on ancient sources for their views on childhood. They learnt from their own experience and from each other. If we return to St Anselm, we find him getting quite angry with the abbot for his treatment of his boys:

'But, in God's name, I would have you tell me why you are so incensed against them. Are they not human? Are they not flesh and blood like you? Would you like to have been treated as you treat them, and to have become what they now are? Now consider this. You wish to form them in good habits by blows and chastisement alone. Have you ever seen a goldsmith form his leaves of gold or silver into a beautiful figure with blows alone? I think not. How then does he work? In order to mould his leaf into a suitable form he now presses it and strikes it gently with his tool, and now even more gently raises it with careful pressure and gives it shape. So, if you want your boys to be adorned with good habits, you too, besides the pressure of blows, must apply the encouragement and help of fatherly sympathy and gentleness ... the weak soul, which is still inexperienced in the service of God, needs milk, – gentleness from others, kindness, compassion, loving forbearance, and much else of the same kind.'[25]

Anselm's advice on how children learn was heartfelt. In offering it he was drawing not upon the stock of classical and biblical stories, but the memories of his own childhood in northern Italy. He had been overworked at school, never allowed out to play and returned home so withdrawn and distressed that his shocked mother ordered that he must be allowed to do what he wanted – gradually he was restored to his original happy state.

Anselm was not the only teacher to draw on his own memories or observations. Bartholomew of England wrote of small boys, in words that resonate down the centuries, as 'without thought or care, loving only to play, fearing no danger ... always hungry and disposed to illness as a result of greed, resisting their mothers' efforts to wash and comb them, and no sooner clean than dirty again'. Little girls, he thought, were more careful, more modest and timid, and more easily disciplined. And Thomas Docking, who succeeded John of Wales as lector to the Oxford Franciscans, seems to have been describing his own relatively prosperous and idyllic Norfolk childhood when he wrote:

> Note the characteristics of a little boy. He is not anxious, he does not covet, he occupies himself with simple and innocent games, he values his household so much that, having been transferred to a kingdom, he seeks rather the things of old, and longs to be among his accustomed ones. He knows the property of his father, and runs now in the field, now in the garden, now in the orchard, now in the meadow, now to the stream, now to the vineyard. He has his own particular favourite times of the year; in spring he follows the ploughers and sowers, in summer and autumn he accompanies those gathering the grapes. Sometimes he is restored to his former vigour with a taste of the outdoor meals of the serfs. He takes much pleasure in gathering fruit, rubbing unripe grain, picking bunches of unripe grapes, exploring the nests of birds and bringing home recovered sheep or hens with great rejoicing and leaping. And he prefers hunting with snares to repairing coppices.[26]

In their memories of their own childhoods, in their observations of the childhoods around them, in the intellectual frameworks that they inherited from ancient sources and that they moulded in their own way, medieval writers and painters showed that they distinguished childhood from other ages, divided it up into different stages and invested it with characteristic forms of behaviour and feeling. Children were not simply 'little adults'. Was this reflected in the advice given to parents and in the day-to-day lives of medieval people?

'And child, worship thy father and thy mother'

There are two main ways in which we can hope to find out about how parents brought up their children in the Middle Ages. First, as in later centuries, there is a considerable volume of advice both for parents and for children. And, second, there is some direct evidence of how both parents and children behaved.

The families in which children were brought up were much smaller than we often imagine. It is true that mothers sometimes gave birth to a large number of babies. Eleanor of Castile, Edward I's first wife, had at least 15. But many of these would die in infancy. It is estimated that baronial and knightly families in the twelfth century would typically have only two or three surviving children, and this picture seems to have been true of the later Middle Ages as well. Poor labouring families would have even fewer, on average less than two. As a general rule, a majority of households with children would at any one time have had no more than three. A household would be formed on marriage, which, outside the nobility and gentry, would be likely to be when the groom was 28, the bride 26 and, unless they were wealthy enough to have servants, would in composition come to resemble an early twentieth-century household: father, mother and two or three children – there was no space for grandparents, whose role seems to have been marginal.[27] [Fig. 2]

Parents and children in the Middle Ages were not lacking in written advice as to how they should behave. Few of them would have been able to read this well-intentioned counsel, but it may be that some of it filtered through to the illiterate by word of mouth, in sermon or in conversation. Equally important for our purposes, we can perhaps use this literature, with its strictures against ill-advised behaviour, to learn about the actual lives of parents and children.

The sixteenth-century sermon by a boy bishop provides some useful insights:

> Both boys and wenches, it is for yow most necessary to kepe the inno-
> cency of your childhod, and other vertues proper unto that tendre age,
> and not to learn the vices and evill qualities of your elders, leste yow lose
> the kyngdom which is appoynted unto yow by name. And tyme it is to call
> upon yow this to do, for not only I, but the world, do se in yow that yow
> and the very litill ones that follow yow do grow nowadayes so fast owt of
> this innocent state that it is wonder to me to se amonge yow so many
> childer in years, and so few innocentes in maners. I am not very old my
> selfe to speake by experience; but I have hard say of my elders that a child

was wont to continew an innocent untill he was 7. years old, and untill 14. years he was provyd to be of such vertue and honest nurture that he deservyd the love and prayse of all people; and now we shall not fynd such a one at 7. as was then at 14, nor at 5, as was then at 7, nor scant at 3. as was then at 9. or x. years old.[28]

Here is a constant refrain in the history of childhood: children behaved better in previous generations and remained children for much longer.

And who is to blame for this all too rapid loss of innocence? Parents and teachers for their failure to impose proper discipline. Parents, it is said, mistakenly look for love from their children and think they'll get it if they 'dandill hym and didill hym and pamper hym and stroke his hedd and sett hym a hye bence, and gyve hym the swetyst soppe in the dish evyn when he lest deserve it: this marrs the child, it makes hym to thynke he does well when he do stark nought'.[29] We hear in this literature of mothers who play with their children as if they were puppets or dolls and encourage their children to do what they want. Fathers are no better, and children take extraordinary licence: 'yf thei hape to call the dame "hoore" or the father "cockolde" ... thei laff therat and take it for a sport, saynge it is kynde [natural] for children to be wanton in ther youghe'.[30]

Such a relaxed parental attitude is perhaps hardly what we imagine of centuries gone by. In face of it, there was a simple message: discipline had to be imposed. In *How the Good Wife Taught Her Daughter*, dating from about 1430, and almost the only advice offered to a daughter rather than a son, the mother imagines her daughter already married and with children: 'And if thy children be rebel and will not bow them low, / If any of them misdo, neither curse them nor blow; / But take a smart rod and beat them in a row / Till they cry mercy and their guilt well know.'[31]

Or in another version of the same theme, this time from about 1500:

> And as men say that learned be,
> Who spareth the rod, the child hateth he;
> And as the wise man saith in his book,
> Of proverbs and wisdoms, who will look:
> 'As a sharp spur maketh a horse to move
> Under a man that should war prove,

Right so a yard may make a child,
To learn well his lesson and to be mild.'
Lo! Children, here may ye all hear and see,
How all children chastised should be.
And therefore, childer, look ye do well
And no hard beating shall you befall.

If they were to avoid the beating, children should behave towards their parents in a very different way to that outlined by the critics: 'And child, worship thy father and thy mother; / Look that thou grieve neither one nor other, / But ever, among them thou shalt kneel down, / And ask their blessing and benison.' It goes on: 'And child, keep thy clothes fair and clean; Let no foul filth on them be seen.'[32]

Well-born children often left home, perhaps from the age of seven upwards, to become servants in another rich person's household. A considerable, and repetitious, body of literature told them how to behave, particularly at table. Here is one version from the second half of the fifteenth century:

Now must I tell you shortly what you shall do at noon when your lord
goes to his meat. Be ready to fetch him clear water, and some of you hold
the towel for him until he has done, and leave not until he be set down,
and ye have heard grace said. Stand before him until he bids you sit, and
be always ready to serve him with clean hands ... Look ye be not caught
leaning on the table, and keep clear of soiling the cloth. Do not hang your
head over your dish, or in any wise drink with full mouth. Keep from
picking your nose, your teeth, your nails at meal-time – so we are taught.[33]

And here is another:

Nor shalt thou spit over the table, nor down upon it ever,
Nor scrape nor scratch thine own flesh with thy fingers.
Be thy hand ever clean; let it avoid to wipe the nose.
At table beware of cleaning thy teeth with thy knife.
When thou holdest in thy mouth meat, beware of superadding drink.
Beware of touching ever at table what may offend your companions,
Of stroking ever the cat and the dog.[34]

Books of this kind – *The Little Children's Little Book, The Young Children's Book, The Babees' Book* – were, as their titles indicate, aimed directly at children. They would surely have little purchase unless children in these noble homes were at least sometimes picking their noses, scratching themselves, spitting and, we might think more innocently, stroking the cat and dog. The manuals aimed to teach manners and behaviour, perhaps what was called chivalry. And beneath the details of table manners lay one clear message: defer to your elders, and be considerate of your equals. Five centuries on, inspired by such manuals, in 2005 police sergeant Gary Brown set up a Knight School in Spilsy, Lincolnshire, a course to train children, aged between six and eight, to improve their manners and to smarten their appearance. Children who complete the course are 'knighted' by the lord-lieutenant and receive a set of armour, a wooden shield and a sword. Youth crime in Spilsby has apparently halved.[35]

Did the advice have such beneficial outcomes in the Middle Ages? It is hard to know. We have very little direct knowledge of parenting in the mass of the rural and illiterate population of medieval Britain. To find out anything about it requires some ingenuity. Two of our best sources centre round children who died or were injured in accidents. We learn about the deaths in coroners' inquests and about the injuries in accounts of miracles at the shrines of saints. If a child were injured, parents might invoke the name of the saint, perhaps St Thomas à Becket at Canterbury or the thirteenth-century St Thomas Cantilupe, bishop of Hereford, and promise that if the child recovered they would give thanks at the shrine where a chronicler would record their stories. What do these sources tell us?

Children were most likely to die in accidents when they were under four. In their first year of life they spent much of their time lying swaddled in a cradle near the hearth. Death by burning was by a long way the most common cause of death. Often the child must have been left alone otherwise an adult or older child might have saved it. Frequently the fires seem to have been caused by a hen or pig wandering in and moving burning straw or an ember.[36]

Once they were mobile, from their second and third years upwards, water was the main danger: children fell into wells, ponds and ditches. A brief parental absence or distraction could lead to disaster or, in the case of miracles, near disaster. William Faunceys, aged three and a half, fell into a ditch at Robert Wreng's house while his mother was in Robert's house getting ale.

A girl, aged two and a half, came out of her father's house holding a piece of bread. A small pig tried to take it off her and pushed her into a ditch where she drowned. A pig was to blame, too, for pushing a boy into a harbour. Agnes, aged two, the daughter of William Wrighte of Fordham, was tagging along with other children and playing in the king's highway. She tried to follow her playmates across a stream and drowned. A three year old trying to pick watercress flowers in a neighbour's ditch fell in and drowned. Edith Drake sent her 18-month-old son John out to play in the street with other children, but John wandered off and fell into a watering pond. Another mother, washing and bleaching her best clothes in preparation for the feast of St James, failed to notice that her two year old had gone out of the house; he fell into the pond of a neighbour.[37]

Were these children exceptionally unlucky, or was the perhaps brief lack of parental or other oversight common? We don't know for sure, though there is in some of the reports remorse on the part of parents or criticism of the parents for neglect. A mother whose five-year-old daughter had apparently drowned begged St Thomas à Becket to bring her back to life: 'If anyone is guilty, I alone, her mother, must bear the blame. I, who did not order supervision of her childish wandering. I should have had a servant accompany my child, but I was blind.' A mother and father who had gone off to vespers leaving their 15-month-old son in front of a burning hearth were lucky that he recovered through the saint's help, but the chronicler drew a lesson for all parents: 'May those who look after little children ... be warned by this example which shows how much danger and distress carelessness of parents can bring ... For they certainly were not unaware of an infant's weakness and of the fact that babies of that age can scarcely get around by leaning on benches and stools unless they crawl or walk.'[38]

Sometimes the parents had child-care arrangements – though in the case of Maude, the daughter of William Bigge, with fatal consequences for she wandered off and drowned while left in the care of a blind woman. But often parents had pressing or strong reasons for being away from home, and children were left alone. Mothers go out to thresh the barley or shear a sheep and come back to find some disaster. William Claunche's daughters, Maud almost six and Beatrice rising three, were left alone at home in Great Barford while William and his wife worked in the fields. A fire broke out and young Beatrice was not able to escape. On Christmas Day 1345, William Senenok and his wife went to church leaving their infant daughter Lucy in a cradle in the care of three-year-old Agnes. Agnes drifted outside to play, and Lucy died in a fire.[39] Or take the extraordinary case of two-year-old Roger, whose father was one of the cooks at Conway Castle. Roger's parents were attending an all-night funeral service in a nearby church. Roger wriggled out of his cradle, escaping from his restraining bonds and his nightclothes. He went out into the street, leaving behind his sleeping sisters and headed for the castle, his father's work-place. Sometime before dawn he tumbled into the dry moat – the drawbridge that he usually crossed to go to see his father had been raised. At daybreak some of the castle staff saw Roger lying naked and covered with frost. When his mother arrived on the scene she tore open her dress, holding Roger close to her skin to warm him up, and he was soon happy and laughing.[40]

Once they reached the age of four, children were much less likely to die in accidents, perhaps because they were spending more time with their parents. But they still seem to have had some four years of play ahead of them before the focus of the accidents switches from play to work. But even if they con-tinued to play, as soon as they were reasonably mobile, young children would be learning by watching their parents. A three year old was watching his father cutting wood. The axe blade broke off from the handle, hit the young boy and killed him. Boys were much more likely than girls to be killed in acci-dents, and the deaths of girls were most likely to be in or near the home, as they started to learn the domestic tasks that would dominate their lives. All too often their curiosity or lack of coordination led to a scalding pot tipping its contents over them.[41]

A negative finding, from which one can draw positive conclusions, is that very few children died from domestic violence. A mother in a fit of rage whipped her ten-year-old son so severely that he died from the wounds, but this is an exceptional case.[42]

Our fullest account of child life and adult responses, drawn up some years after the event, comes from a miracle attributed to St Thomas Cantilupe:

One Sunday in late April, 1292, Adam and Cecilia went to a nearby alehouse to spend the afternoon with friends. They sent their daughter, Joan, aged five, home with her brothers and sisters. Joan broke away from her siblings and followed her parents into the tavern. Seeing that there were other children of her age about, they allowed her to remain.

Eventually Joan, along with John, the son of her godmother, and two other children went out into a garden behind the tavern to play. They threw pebbles into a fish pond from the bank six feet above the surface of the water. John pushed Joan in order to frighten her, and she fell into the pond. John and the two other children ran off. Joan clutched at the grassy bank for a while, but her cries for help were unheard and she sank. A group of young adults came out of the tavern into the garden to dance. Seeing the child's body lying at the bottom of the pond, they assumed it was the daughter of Christina, a beggar woman who they thought had drowned her child in a fit of rage and despondency at her wretched existence. The dancers, wishing to avoid appearing at an inquest, decided not to send for the coroner, and they planned to put the body secretly in a nearby river at nightfall. One among them, a servant, wanted to tell his master, the tavern keeper, but the others would not let him leave.

Meanwhile John went into the tavern to tell Joan's mother what had happened. Just as he was beginning to describe the accident, his father, who had led the dance, thinking he was about to disclose the presence of a corpse, pulled him away and took him home. John, however, returned to the tavern as soon as he could and told Cecilia that Joan had fallen into the fish pond. Cecilia and his mother, who was Joan's godmother, rushed out to the water. Cecilia, eight months pregnant, could only weep, but John's mother, spying the body on the bottom of the pond, jumped in, pulled her up, swam to the shore and handed the apparently dead child up to bystanders on the bank. Joan's face was so swollen that her mother did not recognize her at first but soon identified her by her newly-bought shoes with red thongs.

Forty men and women then gathered to pray for Joan. Many of them on bare knees kept up a vigil until midnight. Joan, warm in her mother's arms, revived, and was asked by her mother what had happened: '"John pushed me," she replied.'[43]

Change a detail here and there, and it is a story that might come from any century. The Sunday afternoon drink in the pub, the children out playing in the garden, the prank that goes wrong, the young adults whose first thought is how they might be inconvenienced, the persistence of young John, the mother who can swim (something very rare in the Middle Ages), Joan's new shoes and her simple telling of what had happened: 'John pushed me.' What does not belong to all centuries, of course, was the communal prayers to St Thomas Cantilupe.

The children we know most about in the Middle Ages are those who died or nearly died in accidents. They were, thankfully, a minority. But their lives and accidents make them sound as if they were simply unlucky rather than unusual. And the stories we hear about them give us a vivid insight into the lives of children and their relationship with their parents and other adults. Perhaps there were also parents who behaved in the ways that the conduct books lamented, exercising no discipline and teaching their children no manners. But the very existence of the careful record of child deaths in the coroners' reports and of parental resort to the help of the saints when disaster happened suggest to us an expected level of care for children. They also indicate that society as a whole was felt to have a responsibility for children.

Did children themselves feel this, or did they live in a world of their own making? An exploration of how they played may give us the answer.

'For joy they sing and hop'

In their famous book, *The Lore and Language of Schoolchildren*, Iona and Peter Opie built up an extraordinarily vivid picture of a culture peculiar to children and one that, when the Opies wrote in the 1950s, could be shown to have been handed down from one generation of children to the next. Did children have such a culture of their own in the Middle Ages, or was it so tied up with the culture of the rest of society as to be indistinguishable?

Our earliest records of possible answers to these questions lie, rather oddly, in the lives recorded of saints. In their childhood saints were expected either to be perfectly normal or to show very early signs of the destinies that lay ahead of them. St Nicholas, it was said, stood up on the day he was born and observed fasts by taking the breast only once on Wednesdays and Fridays.[44] But there are rather more plausible childhood stories of saints than this. Bede in his life of St Cuthbert, the seventh-century bishop of Lindisfarne, recorded how Cuthbert 'loved games and pranks, and as was natural at his age, loved to play with other children ... He used to boast that he had beaten all those of his own age and many who were older at wrestling, jumping, running, and every other exercise.'[45] Another, anonymous, biographer gives an even more graphic account of the young Cuthbert: 'Many youths were gathered together one day on a piece of level ground and he too was found among them. They began thereupon to indulge in a variety of games and tricks: some stood naked, with their legs stretched out and pivoted skywards, and some did one thing and some another.'[46] Of the rather more virtuous St Guthlac, again in the seventh century, it was said that he 'did not imitate the impudence of the children ... nor the different cries of the various kinds of birds as children of that age are wont to do'.[47]

Gerald of Wales, not exactly a saint, but a man of the church nevertheless, recorded in his autobiography in the twelfth century how he had been born into a noble family and brought up near Pembroke with three older brothers. 'When the other three, preluding the pursuits of manhood in their childish play, were tracing or building, in sand or dust, now towns, now palaces, he himself, in like prophetic play, was ever busy with all his might in designing churches or building monasteries.'[48] It doesn't really matter whether or not these stories are entirely true. What is important about them is the assumptions they make, assumptions they know their contemporary readers will understand and share: that children naturally like to play with one another, that they engage in games and sports – and pranks; that they build in the sand, if not, as we might, castles, then more ambitiously towns, palaces, churches and monasteries. We are immediately, as early as the seventh century, taken into a world where children have their own well-known games and pastimes – their own culture.

The world of childhood play was structured by a calendar. We have a description of one such calendar – doubtless there were variations in detail – in poet and scholar Alexander Barclay's description of the play of young boys in the early sixteenth century:

> Eche time and season hath its delite and joyes,
> Loke in the stretes beholde the little boyes
> Howe in fruite season for joy they sing and hop;
> In Lent is eche one full busy with his top,
> And nowe in winter for all the greevous colde,
> All rent and ragged a man may them beholde.
> They have great pleasour, supposing well to dine,
> When men be busied in killing of fat swine.
> They get the bladder and blowe it great and thin

With many beanes or peasen put within;
It ratleth, soundeth and shineth clere and fayre
When it is throwen and caste up in the ayre.
Eche one contendeth and hath a great delite
With foote and with hande the bladder for to smite.
If it fall to grounde they lifte it up agayne,
This wise to labour they count it for no payne,
Renning and leaping they drive away the colde.[49]

Barclay identified three periods in the year when boys were most visible in play: in the summer and autumn fruit season, in Lent and in early winter when the pigs were killed. The singing and hopping in the fruit season may have been the accompaniment to a good deal of scrumping: there is a fourteenth-century illustration of a boy up a tree [Fig. 5], apparently picking cherries, with an angry man underneath. Rather more legitimate was nutting. In the 1560s the boys of Eton College had a recognized nutting-day holiday in September.[50]

In Lent, Barclay tells us, boys played with their tops, probably driving them along with whips. Perhaps it was some kind of re-enactment of the scourging of Jesus or of penitent sinners. Archaeologists have found an eleventh-century maple-wood top of this kind at Winchester. There were also finger-spun tops, 'scopperils' they were called, and an early fifteenth-century source mentions both kinds of top 'that children play with'.[51]

And then there was the football season. The killing of animals traditionally began on All Saints' Day, 1 November, and the pigs' bladders provided them with opportunity for sport. Football was also popular on the afternoon of Shrove Tuesday, the last day before Lent. In the morning, according to William FitzStephen, the biographer of Thomas à Becket, describing London at the end of the twelfth century, 'boys from the schools bring fighting cocks to their master, and the whole forenoon is given up to boyish sport; for they have a holiday in the schools that they may watch their cocks do battle.' There is evidence of the same custom in Gloucester and Ely in the fifteenth century, though in the early sixteenth century it was specifically forbidden in the statutes for St Paul's School in London and Manchester Grammar School. After dinner on Shrove Tuesday, it was time for football. 'All the youth of the city', FitzStephen tells us, 'goes out into the fields to a much-frequented game of ball. The scholars of each school have their own ball.' They were joined by the workers of each trade with their balls, and elder men and the rich who came on horseback to watch, reliving the sports of their youth.[52]

Through football and via a multitude of other customs, children were taking part in activities that had the sanction and presence of their elders. The fighting cocks, and the nuts that the Eton boys collected, were handed over to their masters.

There was another annual custom in which children took on adult roles, displacing their elders for the season. In cathedral towns on St Nicholas's Day, 6 December, a boy was chosen by other children to become the boy bishop and retained office until Innocents' Day on 28 December. Dressed as a bishop, with staff and mitre, he, and other boys dressed in clerical garments, would go round the neighbourhood, giving blessings and soliciting gifts. Then, in the cathedral itself, the boy would lead the service, give the blessing and sometimes preach a sermon. York was the centre for the most elaborate boy-bishop ceremonies, accounts being kept of the money and gifts the boys extracted. They went on journeys through the county lasting a week or more, calling on 15 abbeys and priories, and seven lay lords and ladies. The menu at their feast included ducks, chickens, woodcocks, fieldfares and a plover.

The boy-bishop ceremonies are usually understood as a kind of temporary role reversal, a period of licence, in which the brief authority given to boys acts as a means of reconciling them to their normal subordinate role. The two sermons that survive from the Tudor period reinforce this interpretation.

With the dawn of the Reformation in the sixteenth century, the boy-bishop ceremonies, like the cock-fighting on Shrove Tuesday, came under attack. A royal proclamation of 1541 complained that 'children be strangelye decked and apparelid to counterfaite priestes, bysshopps and women, and so ledde with songes and daunces from house to house, bleasing the people and gatherynge of monye'. It forbade the practice, and although boy bishops reappeared briefly under Queen Mary, their days were numbered.[53]

If the licence granted to the boy bishops and their acolytes retained the approval of adult authority through the Middle Ages, there were, and this is hardly surprising, some aspects of children's play that failed in this respect. A *Lesson of Wisdom for All Manner of Children*, dating from about 1500, advises:

> Child, climb not over house nor wall,
> For no fruit, birds nor ball.

Child, over men's houses no stones fling,
Nor at glass windows no stones sling ...

And child, when thou goest to play,
Look thou come home by light of day.[54]

Children doubtless failed to heed this good advice, otherwise the warnings would have been pointless. Yet there is in fact confirmation that the warnings were needed. In London, John atte Noke fell to his death when he climbed out of a window to retrieve a ball from the gutter. Robert, the seven-year-old son of one John de St Botolph, was playing with two other boys on a pile of timber, when a piece fell on him and broke his right leg. The six-year-old son of another man, John de Turneye, a boy called Philip, was walking by a ditch after sunset, slipped, fell in and drowned. Was it children, we may wonder, whom the City of London proclaimed against in 1397 for 'shooting pigeons and other birds perched on St Paul's or on the houses of citizens, with stone bows and arbalests, because the missiles frequently break the windows and wound passers-by'?[55] We know with certainty of a ten-year-old boy who was shooting at a dunghill with his bow and arrow. Missing his inoffensive target he shot and killed a five-year-old girl.[56] We know also that in 1448 the dean and chapter of Exeter Cathedral had 'young persons' in view when they complained of them entering the cloister and playing at 'the toppe, queke, penny prykke and most at tenys by which the walles of the saide cloistre have be defowled and the glas wyndowes all to-brest'.[57] Queke was played with a chessboard, so perhaps was not responsible for the broken windows, but penny prykke involved shooting arrows at a penny target with some predictable outcomes, and doubtless the same was true of the apparently popular tennis.

It is often difficult, as we have seen, to know the precise age of participants in many of these records. FitzStephen, for example, tells us how 'In the holy dayes all the Summer the youths are exercised in leaping, dancing, shooting, wrestling, casting the stone, and practising their shields; the Maidens trip in their Timbrels, and daunce as long as they can well see.'[58] Probably these youths and maidens were in their late teens or early twenties, beyond the age at which they would have been considered children. Fifteenth-century Scotland does provide us with a source that distinguishes play by age.

Between three and seven, we learn, children love to 'play with flowers, to build houses with sticks and branches, to make a white horse of a wand or a sailing ship from broken bread, a spear from a ragwort stalk or a sword from a rush, and to make a beautiful lady from a cloth, decorate it with blossoms and cherish it'. Between seven and 15, among other things, they play chess, backgammon and dice.[59] Another source describes the ages seven to 14, surely with boys in mind, as 'the age of concussion' as 'in that age they begin to run and jump and to hit each other'.[60]

Most of the material we have looked at so far is focused on the play and culture of boys. There is very little mention in any source of girls' play. We do read of a nine-year-old girl who was running around in a field with other girls, 'as girls do' – unfortunately she was carrying an open knife.[61] [Fig. 3] If there were a culture specific to girls, it is likely that it centred on the home and was only rarely visible in public. Even in the home their presence was, desirably, visible but not audible. 'Girls should be instructed', so the advice went, 'first in chastity, then in humility and next in piety, but foremost and especially in taciturnity.' Or, in the words of 'an old Englysch sawe', 'A mayde schuld be seen, but not herd.'[62]

We know from Chaucer's *The Physician's Tale* how a well-born girl should comport herself. Virginia, aged 14, is the daughter of a knight:

> And if her beauty was beyond compare,
> Her virtue was a thousand times more rare ...
> Chaste of her body and of her soul was she,
> And so she flowered in her virginity
> With all humility and abstinence
> In temperate and patient innocence,
> With modesty of bearing and of dress
> And showed in speech a modesty no less.
> Though I dare say as wise as Pallas, she
> Was simple in her words and womanly;
> She used no fancy term in affectation
> Of learning, but according to her station
> She spoke; in all and everything she said
> She showed that she was good and gently bred.
> Shamefast she was, in maiden shamefastness,

And constant in her heart. She was express
In conquering sloth to fill the busy hour;
Over her mouth had never Bacchus power,
For wine and youth swell Venus and desire,
Much as when oil is cast upon the fire.
Indeed her native goodness unconstrained
So prompted her that she had often feigned
Some sickness to escape from company
Where there was likelihood of ribaldry,
As well there may be; junketings and dances
Are good occasion for lascivious glances.
Such things as these may soon too easily
Make a child bold and ripe, as one can see.[63]

Virginia is steadfast in resisting such temptations. But other adolescent girls, as Chaucer tells us, drinking, junketing and dancing, may well have broken the taboos of good breeding and become 'bold and ripe'.

Children in the Middle Ages certainly played among themselves independent of adults. Boys, and less certainly girls, sometimes got into trouble for the nuisance they caused. Outside the home, boys probably followed a calendar of play, one generation after another doing the same things at the same time, in accordance with the season and the festivals of the church. [Fig. 4] And it was in adherence to this calendar of play, and most of all in the boy-bishop ceremonies, that children were part of the culture of the society as a whole, playing a recognized role that their elders before them had played.

There were also other ways in which children were prepared for their adult roles and integrated into the larger society, above all in their education.

'I would my master were a hare': education in medieval Britain

In the early sixteenth century, Richard Hill, a London merchant, inscribed these verses in his commonplace book, a notebook of miscellanea:

Hey! hey! by this day!
What availeth it me though I say nay?
I would fain be a clerk [scholar].

But yet it is a strange work;
The birchen twigs be so sharp,
It maketh me have a faint heart.
    What availeth it me though I say nay?

On Monday in the morning when I shall rise
At six of the clock, it is the guise [practice]
To go to school without advice [without being told] –
I would rather go twenty miles twice!
    What availeth it me though I say nay?

My master looketh as he were mad:
'Where hast thou been, thou sorry lad?'
'Milking ducks, as my mother bade':
It was no marvel that I were sad.
    What availeth it me though I say nay?

My master peppered my tail with good speed,
It was worse than fennel seed,
He would not leave till it did bleed.
Much sorrow have he for his deed!
    What availeth it me though I say nay?

I would my master were a hare,
And all his books greyhounds were,
And I myself a jolly hunter;
To blow my horn I would not spare,
For if he were dead I would not care!
    What availeth it me though I say nay?[64]

The anonymous, unhappy schoolboy is expressing a view heard quite often in the late Middle Ages – we have already encountered him in Shakespeare's boy going 'unwillingly to school'. What is remarkable about this boy is that, though he is resigned to his fate – 'What availeth it me though I say nay?' – he also inhabits a different world of the imagination. When his master asks him where he has been, his cheeky answer, 'milking ducks', probably ensures that he is beaten and beaten hard. And then he imagines his master as a hare, the books the hounds, himself the 'jolly hunter'.

Most children in the Middle Ages didn't go to school. At the end of the period, in the sixteenth century, after considerable recent expansion in the number of schools, probably only one in eight of the population of northern England would have had any experience of school. More were literate, perhaps 15 per cent, the figure being much higher for males, at up to a quarter, than for females. In London, the situation may have been much better with perhaps half the adult population literate.[65]

Attendance at school was not the only way of acquiring an education, of learning. It was in the home and its surrounds that children learnt the skills they would need as adults, and they learnt by observation and doing: helping in all the domestic jobs, or out in the fields, performing ancillary tasks. Educating children, in manners, morals, behaviour and skills, was a job for parents, not schoolteachers. It was parents, too, who introduced children to some understanding of the world through the songs they sang and the tales they told. Most of these were passed on from one generation to another by word of mouth, but we encounter them only when they began to be written down in the later Middle Ages, as in Richard Hill's commonplace book. In the later fifteenth century some of them began to appear in print. If we try to imagine the mental world of the medieval child, it will for some be dominated by the Latin they have learnt at school. But for most it will be made up of three parts: a growing awareness of what adulthood is likely to hold for them; a familiarity with the basics of the Christian doctrine, accompanied perhaps by devotion to a local saint; a stock of sayings, stories and songs that they have learnt from their families or from other children.

But let us start with school. King Alfred the Great (849–899), a great warrior and social reformer, plays a large part in the early history of schooling in Britain. As a young boy he was not taught to read until he was 12 or older. As his biographer, the monk Asser, bishop of Sherborne, put it, 'by the shameful negligence of his parents and tutors he remained ignorant of letters'. But he did learn by heart many English poems, and he learnt how to hunt – the latter, linked to warfare, an essential training for a king. And it was his educational ambitions as king that gave him lasting fame. He was determined that 'All the youth of England's free men who have the means so that they may apply themselves to it, be set to learning as long as they can not be set to any other employment, until such time as they know how to read English writing well. Afterwards let those chosen for further education to be brought to higher office be taught Latin as well.'[66] What may strike us about this is not only that Alfred seemed to be in advance of his time. It is also that his ambitions for schooling were quite limited. It was for a minority only – for boys of free birth. And for most it was to be continued only until other employment became more urgent, and restricted to learning to read English.

In the early medieval centuries there were schools in monasteries, at court and in some great noble households, but only in the twelfth century do we find schools open to anyone who could afford them and run by the secular clergy rather than monks and nuns. The principal reason for the foundation and spread of these schools right up to the sixteenth century was the need for a literate clergy. In an ideal world the clergy would be able to read, to sing plainsong and to know Latin grammar. From the thirteenth century onwards bishops were encouraging them to read the Bible. Not all achieved these goals, but the constantly asserted need for them was a stimulus to schooling. In addition, there was a need for literacy in the royal household, in other departments of royal administration, in noble households and in the administration of the law. Kings were literate by the twelfth century, the nobles and gentry by the fourteenth.[67]

The lowest level of schooling was the song school, or petty school, attended by those aged between seven and ten. There is a brief description of such a school in Chaucer's *The Prioress's Tale*, where, admittedly set in Asia, and just outside a Jewish ghetto,

> A little school stood for the christian flock
> Down at the further end, and it was here
> A heap of children come of christian stock
> Received their early schooling year by year
> And the instruction suited to their ear,
> That is to say in singing and in reading
> – The simple things of childhood and good breeding.

In the *Tale*, 'A little chorister of seven years old', beavering away at his primer, is much taken by hearing older children sing 'O Alma Redemptoris'.

He had no notion what this Latin meant
Being so young, so tender too, so green;

So he asks an older boy who tells him that it is a hymn to the Virgin Mary, though even he doesn't know much: 'I can learn singing, but my grammar's slow.' The young chorister determines to learn the song by heart by Christmas.

Though they should scold me when I cannot say
My primer, though they beat me thrice an hour,
I'll learn it in her honour, to my power.[68]

This little vignette introduces us to some of the characteristics of the song school. Children would start by learning the alphabet. As Robert Holcot, a Dominican friar who died in 1349, put it: 'You know that boys when they are first instructed are not able to learn anything subtle, but only simple things. So they are first taught with a "book" of large letters affixed to a piece of wood, and progress afterwards to learning letters from a more advanced book.' Later, by the end of the fifteenth century, a hornbook was commonly used. This was a piece of board about 23 × 13 cm (9 × 5 inches) with a handle and a transparent sheet of horn covering it. Sometimes, as with Chaucer's little chorister, the alphabet, together with some prayers to learn, would be contained within a short book, a primer. Letters, words and prayers would be learnt by rote, with, as Chaucer notes, much use of song though in some schools reading and singing may have been seen as quite separate disciplines. Writing was a much more advanced skill than reading and was taught later and separately.[69] And, as Chaucer also noted, if the child failed to learn properly, then there could be recourse to beating. In all pictures of medieval schoolteachers, they are seen brandishing a whip. Corporal punishment was universal in the schools of medieval Britain. [Fig. 7] In December 1301 the body of John Newshom, an Oxford schoolmaster, was found in the River Cherwell, near the present Magdalen Bridge. He had fallen out of a willow tree while cutting rods with which to beat his pupils and had drowned.[70]

There were song schools throughout Britain attached to the cathedrals and collegiate churches, training choristers. They, or something very similar to them, were also found in other towns, but of all the schools they are the ones that have left least trace. Many of them may have been short-lived.

After the song schools, children, somewhere between the ages of nine and 12, might progress to grammar schools, accurately named for the emphasis was on learning Latin grammar, and on writing and speaking Latin prose and poetry. Schooling there would typically last five or six years. Latin was the language of the church, of the law and of much administration. If someone were described as *literatus* or 'literate', it almost certainly indicated a knowledge of Latin.[71] Some of the grammar schools must have provided a first-rate schooling. Duns Scotus, who died in 1308, perhaps the foremost philosopher of his day, started a career that took him to Oxford and Paris, at Haddington Grammar School. But there were also at the time some critical comments on the quality of the education on offer. From Exeter in the middle of the fourteenth century Bishop Grandisson complained that pupils learnt Latin prayers by rote without knowing anything of the grammar and then passed on to more advanced books of poetry. The outcome was that 'grown to man's estate, they understand not the things which they daily read or say ... moreover ... they discern not the Catholic Faith'.[72] The famous Elizabethan humanist teacher Roger Ascham in the sixteenth century remembered how when he was at grammar school at Kirby Wiske in northern England, there were hardly any books. The pupils' 'whole knowledge, by learning without the book, was tied only to their tongue and lips, and never ascended up to the brain and head, and therefore was soon spit out of the mouth again'.[73]

There was a major expansion of grammar schools in the fourteenth and fifteenth centuries, before the Reformation, mainly through the spread of the practice of endowing schools. Rich people would set aside land or money to endow a school, providing a building, a salary for a teacher, often scholarships for poorer boys. The most famous of these benefactors was William Wykeham. Born in comparatively humble circumstances in 1328, he rose to become bishop of Winchester and chancellor of England – and also very rich. At the school he founded at Winchester, there were to be 70 scholars under a master and usher. Children were to be admitted between the ages of eight and 12, having shown competence in reading, song and elementary grammar.[74] Winchester was the major foundation of the later Middle Ages, unsurpassed until the royal foundation of Eton College in the fifteenth century.

The free grammar school of Wotton-under-Edge in Gloucestershire, founded by Lady Katherine Berkeley in June 1384, was typical of many endowed schools. Lady Katherine's endowment provided for a schoolmaster but for only two poor scholars receiving free board, lodging and education. Beyond that, there was free education but not board and lodging, which was the major expense, for anyone who might wish to attend. The master, who was to be a priest, had, in addition to teaching grammar, to sing daily Masses for the souls of the foundress and her relatives.[75] This concern was undoubtedly one of the motivations for the charity that established so many endowed grammar schools in the later Middle Ages.

The endowment of schools was not confined to the rich and noble. Lancaster Grammar School was endowed by John Gardyner, who in 1472 turned over the profits of a mill to support the school. In Nottingham, Agnes Mellers, the widow of a mayor of the town, endowed the grammar school. And in wills and bequests there were many more minor gifts to individual scholars or to the poor of the neighbourhood.[76]

The outcome, together with new initiatives by the church, was an enormous increase in the provision for schooling in the later Middle Ages. In England the number of grammar schools in York diocese nearly tripled in the first half of the sixteenth century.[77] If in England the initiatives in the expansion of schooling came from local benefactors, in Scotland there was central direction. In 1496 it was enacted that all barons and freeholders of substance put their eldest sons and heirs to school. Boys were to be sent at eight or nine and remain at grammar school 'till they be completely founded, and have perfect Latin, and thereafter to remain at the Schools of Arts and Law, so that they may have knowledge and understanding of the Laws, through which Justice may reyn universally through all the realm', perhaps the first example of a government investing hope in the social and political consequences of educational reform.[78]

What was it like to be a child in the schoolrooms of medieval Britain? We have seen the omnipresence of the whip. But there was perhaps a more humane side, and it is known to us through what are called *vulgaria*. These were collections of sentences in English that schoolboys had to translate into Latin. These collections, largely, one must assume, the work of the masters, incidentally tell us much about school life and culture. They include proverbs, tongue-twisters, riddles and nonsense. Here, for example, was a tongue-twister to be translated into Latin: 'Thre gray gredy geys [geese] / Flying over three greyn gresy furs [furrows]; / The geys was gray and gredy; / The furs was greyn and gresy.'[79] These *vulgaria* suggest a degree of humanity and liveliness in the medieval schoolroom that might otherwise be unknown to us. One of the *vulgaria*, from Magdalen College in Oxford in about 1500, also contains what is almost the only account we have of how a child may have felt about school – and it makes painful reading for anyone who thinks schooldays are the best days of one's life:

> The worlde waxeth worse every day, and all is turnede upside down, contrary to th'olde guyse, for all that was to me a pleasure when I was a childe, from iij yere olde to x (for now I go upon the xij yere), while I was undre my father and mothers kepyng, be tornyde now to tormentes and payne. For than I was wont to lye styll abedde tyll it was forth dais [late in the day], delitynge myselfe in slepe and ease. The sone sent in his beamys at the wyndowes that gave me lyght instede of a candle. O, what a sporte it was every mornynge when the son was upe to take my lusty pleasur betwixte the shetes, to beholde the rofe, the beamys, and the rafters of my chamber, and loke on the clothes that the chambre was hanged with! There durste no mann but he were made [mad] awake me oute of my slepe upon his owne hede [responsibility] while me list to slepe ... But nowe the worlde rennyth upon another whele, for nowe at fyve of the clocke by the monelyght I most go to my booke and lete slepe and slouthe alon, and yff oure maister hape to awake us, he bryngeth a rode stede of a candle.[80]

Here, from 1500, is a lament for a cosseted and privileged childhood, now only a memory as the 11-year-old boy strives to endure the rigours and discipline of a boarding school. It is a type of writing that had many successors, but if we look back into the earlier Middle Ages we find no surviving records of how children felt about their schooling.[81]

Latin sources on schools in the Middle Ages usually refer to the pupils as *pueri*, a word that could encompass both sexes. But in fact girls seem to have been excluded from most of the schools we have been considering. Girls in nunneries were taught to read, and in wealthy households there would probably have been a teacher. Even so, it seems to have been very rare for a girl to advance to Latin – her learning was confined to vernacular English and perhaps French, and often to reading without proceeding to writing. In the Paston family in Norfolk, the women seem not to have been able to write letters, though they could read them. Occasionally we hear of a schoolgirl. Elizabeth Garrard, aged eight, was at school in London towards the end of the fifteenth century. How do we know? Because her teacher, a priest, was accused of having 'ravysshed' her within three weeks of her arrival. He had promised, he said, to 'instructe and teache ... Elizabeth ... the *Pater Noster, Ave,* and *Credo* with ferther lernyng as at that tyme he taught other yong chyldren to the nowmber of xxx'. Presumably some of the other 30 were girls. Very occasionally we hear of schoolmistresses, Matilda Maresflete in Boston in 1404, Elyn Skolemastre in Taunton in 1494. But what cannot be doubted is that the schooling of girls lagged far behind that of boys.[82]

If girls were at a disadvantage, so also were the poorer members of society. Serfs had to pay a fine for a licence to enable their sons to attend school. Theoretically this ended with the Statute of Laborers, 1405–6, under which serfs were to be 'free to set their Son or Daughter to take Learning at any manner school that pleaseth them within the Realm'. In practice the lord of the manor did not always allow this. And the hurdles in the way of a poor child seeking education were likely to be formidable. Take the case of William Green, the son of a labouring man from Wantlet in Lincolnshire. After two years at the village school, he started work helping his father for five or six years. Next he went to Boston where he lived with an aunt, working and going to school, and getting some help from one of the Austin friars there. He then moved on to Cambridge but without any dependable support, earning a bit by picking saffron, reliant on alms for meat and drink. He eventually received a licence to collect subscriptions for one year towards completing his education, but only collected enough for eight weeks. Desperate, he forged a new licence, and that is why we know of him in the Norwich corporation records of 1521.[83]

Schooling, if you could get it, opened the door to some of the key professions: the church, most of all, the law and administration of any kind. There were even schools in Oxford that prepared you for a career in business. Increasingly the more prestigious trades expected their apprentices to be able to read. But outside school there was an imaginary world open to all children. We know of it chiefly through what was written down, first of all in manuscripts, but it had flourished, and continued to do so, by word of mouth. Then, in the later fifteenth century, what had been laboriously copied in manuscripts could be put into print.

William Caxton was born in Kent, lived in Bruges for much of his life and then, in 1476, returned to England to set up the first printing press. He was fully alive to the demand for stories and fables. *Guy of Warwick*, for example, a tale of sturdy deeds, had been available in English from the thirteenth century – it was to continue in print until the nineteenth century. The amount of reading matter available in English began to escalate from the later fourteenth century. Grubby and tattered manuscripts were being passed from hand to hand, read and re-read. Caxton saw the commercial opportunity. There was no clear dividing line in the Middle Ages between adult and children's literature: ballads (Robin Hood was especially popular), saints' lives, fables and romances appealed to people of all ages. Caxton put this material into print. Some of it had a specific readership in mind. *The Book of the Knight of the Tower* (1484) and the romance of *Blanchardyn and Eglantine* were designed to appeal especially to women and girls.[84]

A male readership was doubtless the primary target for *The Friar and the Boy*, a poem in six-line stanzas, first known to us in a fifteenth-century manuscript, printed in the early sixteenth century in a small, folded pamphlet of eight leaves and proceeding through many editions up to the early nine-teenth century. Jack, the boy, is the eldest son of a farmer. His mother dies, and his stepmother dislikes Jack, urging her husband to send him away to service. The farmer refuses, saying Jack is too young and instead puts him in charge of the cattle. Jack is out with the herd and opens up the dinner that his stepmother has prepared. It is a paltry meal, and, disgusted with her, Jack gives it to a poor, old man, who turns out to have magical powers. He gives Jack three gifts: a bow that always hits its target, a pipe that makes everyone dance and a charm that makes his stepmother fart when she is angry. Jack comes back home hungry, but armed with his three secret weapons. Here is how he uses the third of them:

> His father tooke a Capons wing,
> And at the Boy he did it fling,
> Bidding him eat his fill.
> This griev'd his Stepdames hart full sore,
> Who loath'd the Lad stil more and more
> She stard him in the face:
> With that she let go such a blast,
> As made the people all aghast,

It sounded through the place.
Each one did laugh and made good game
But the curst wife grew red through shame
    And wisht she had been gone:
Pardy (the Boy said) well I wot,
This gun was both wel chargd and shot,
    And might have broke a stone.
Full curtly she lookt on him tho,
That looke another crack let goe,
    Which did a thunder raise:
Quoth the Boy, did you ever see,
A woman let her pellets flee
    More thick or more at ease;
Fie said the Boy unto his Dame,
Temper thy telltale bum for shame.[85]

This is perhaps the first story appealing directly to children, the beginning of what we now call children's literature. We are in the late Middle Ages taken into a world that would have appealed to Roald Dahl, children in their imagination asserting their powers against ridiculous adults. And the world in which Jack lives would have been immediately realistic: the death of a mother, the unloving stepmother, the possibility of being sent away to service, the job looking after the cattle.

If *The Friar and the Boy* is the beginning of children's literature, it comes to the accompaniment of something that we will hear repeated through the centuries: an anxiety that the new media are corrupting the young. In 1528, William Tyndale, the translator of the Bible into English, complained that the clergy were allowing the young to read 'Robin Hood and Bevis of Hampton, Hercules, Hector, and Troylus, with a thousand histories and fables of love and wantons and of ribaldry, as filthy as heart can think, to corrupt the minds of youth withal'.[86] The 'thousand histories and fables' may surely be as good a guide to the mental world of medieval children as the primers and Latin grammars that formed the staple for that minority of children who went to school.

CHAPTER TWO

The Reformation and Its Aftermath

IN 1676, GRISELL HUME, aged 11, was entrusted by her father, Sir Patrick Hume, with delivery of a letter to Robert Baillie, who, like Sir Patrick, was in gaol in Edinburgh. Hume and Baillie, staunchly Presbyterian, had been imprisoned for their opposition to the policies pursued by Charles II and his ministers since the Restoration in 1660. Grisell not only gained admittance to Baillie's cell but also smuggled out a message. Later, she hid her father in the family vault at Polwarth church, then excavated a new hiding-place for him under the family home. We don't hear of many children who were so actively engaged as Grisell was in the civil wars and disturbances that were such a marker of Britain's history in the sixteenth and seventeenth centuries. But at some level it affected them all.

If Catholicism were the leading influence on children in the Middle Ages, Protestantism took its place in the Reformation and its aftermath. But Protestantism came in many different forms, and the history of Britain from the mid-sixteenth to the end of the seventeenth century is a story both of continuing resistance to Catholicism and of disputes among the different versions of Protestantism. It ended with the 'Glorious Revolution' of 1688–9, with Protestantism firmly established and the Stuart flirtation with despotism and Catholicism defeated. But, even so, the disputes within Protestantism shaped childhoods. In England, anyone brought up outside the Church of England was conscious of the discrimination against them. For while the Church of England in its beliefs and ceremonies was not far distant from the Catholicism it had replaced, the Puritans in England and Wales, and the Presbyterians in Scotland, had thrown off the influence of Catholicism much more decisively. Children could be actors in the dramas of the ensuing conflict.

'Live in Gods fear, and dye in his love'

On Christmas Eve 1580, 11-year-old William Withers, from the small Suffolk town of Walsham-le-Willows, fell into a deep trance. William was the second and perhaps oldest-surviving son of a family of tenant farmers. After ten days in a coma he regained consciousness and began to denounce the sin and immorality of the age. Unless, thundered William, his bed trembling with the vehemence of his speech, there was 'spedie repentance', the Lord would shake the villagers' houses and cause the earth to open up and swallow them alive. William picked on a fashionably dressed serving man, inveighing against his 'great and monstrous ruffes', advising him that 'it were better for him to put on sackcloth & mourn for his sinnes, then in such abhominable pride to pranke up himselfe like the divels darling'. Mortified and ashamed, the man ripped the ruffs from his neck and cut them up. News of William's prophesying spread rapidly, and soon there was 'mutche resort of people' from neighbouring villages and from further afield. From Bury St Edmunds, ten miles away, came James Gayton, the godly preacher at St Mary's Church. Also present at the boy's bedside were three zealous Puritan magistrates, Sir Robert Jermyn, Robert Ashfield and Sir William Spring, themselves engaged in a running battle against immorality.

Someone must have taken the story to London, for within a month there appeared from a printing house in the Strand a short pamphlet on *The Wonderfull Worke of God shewed upon a Chylde*, a 'Prodigall child', a 'second Daniel'. Soon the story featured as a popular broadside ballad, and it spread far and wide, reaching the Welsh borders. William seemed to be eloquent testimony to the Psalmist's vision that strength would come 'Out of the mouth of babes and sucklings'.[1]

The world into which William had been born was wracked with dispute. Since the 1530s the Catholic church of the Middle Ages had been legislated from above by Henry VIII and undermined from below by ardent Protestants. It had recovered under Queen Mary, only to be finally shorn of any official or legal standing by the young Elizabeth I. A world shaped and ordered by the Catholic liturgy, by its sacraments, by its calendar of rituals and saints' days, by the sculptures and paintings and stained glass of its churches, by its Corpus Christi plays, had disappeared. In its place was a less colourful religion, based on a text, the Bible, its adherents themselves sharply divided between a moderate majority and more far-reaching reformers. In Scotland, Presbyterians had gained control in the 1560s, the state aligning itself with them. In England, Presbyterians or Puritans – James Gayton, the Bury St Edmunds preacher was one – were fighting a battle to impose their ideas on villages and towns throughout the country.

Ezechias Morley was another who may have been preaching Puritan doctrines in Walsham-le-Willows before he was driven out, and William may have picked up the language of denunciations from his sermons. Perhaps William, like many others, had been disturbed and traumatized by the earthquake that had shaken that part of Suffolk on 6 April 1580. Perhaps he was manipulated by adults, for his utterances were suspiciously similar to those of a German girl, reputedly resurrected from the dead, her story in print in England the previous summer. Or is it possible that William was taking part in an elaborate hoax, a child's revenge on an adult world that was trying to make childhood rather joyless, an individual attempt to recreate the world turned upside down that had been safely embodied in the boy-bishop ceremony of the Middle Ages?[2]

We may never know exactly what was happening in Walsham-le-Willows in 1580, nor what lay behind William Withers's trance and recovery. But the response to it is of a piece with other evidence that some children were thought to be gifted with prophetic powers, or, alternatively, possessed by the devil.

In 1647, 15-year-old Sarah Wight took to her bed in London and lay there blind, deaf and motionless. After 75 days without food and expected to die, she at the last moment recovered and started prophesying. Born into a godly gentry family, she had become convinced of her own sinfulness and had frequently tried to commit suicide. It seems likely that she felt particularly guilty over her failure to fulfil the fifth commandment, to 'Honour your father and your mother that it may be well with you and that you may live long on the earth'. Failure in such honour and obedience bespoke an early death. Youthful sins weighed heavily upon a child like Sarah, brought up in a world divided between the elect and the damned. 'I walked continually in fire and brimstone for rebelling and murmuring against God, and against a Parent,' she proclaimed. While still blind and deaf, Sarah cried out, 'Have I not a Mother somewhere?' and 'Her Mother ... took her Daughters hand, and put it to her own neck, where her Daughter felt a skare, that was there through the enemy: whereby her Daughter, knowing her, cast her head into her Mothers bosom, and wept greatly and kissed her, and stroaked her face, and said, "I know you Mother, and I love you with another love, than I loved you before."'[3]

If a child now displayed symptoms like those of Sarah Wight, or the rather similar ones of 11-year-old Martha Hatfield in Yorkshire – 'The Wise Virgin', as she was called – they would probably receive 'treatment' in some degree of privacy, the family and medical profession alone privy to what was happening. But we know about Sarah Wight and Martha Hatfield because scribes sat at their bedsides writing down their words, and they were visited by eminent divines. They were thought to be possessed of divine truths, their recovery from seemingly inevitable death a sign of God's providence.

These child-prophets nearly all displayed a close knowledge of Bible stories and of the Christian faith. This they had acquired through catechisms, the early training that was thought appropriate for all children in godly families. The catechism was a question-and-answer way of instilling Christian doctrine. For Protestants it was not enough that a child could repeat the words of the Lord's Prayer or the Creed. The child needed to have an inward understanding that would lead to a realization of the need for salvation. In the first phase of the Reformation in England from 1536 to 1553, before the accession of Queen Mary, there was a massive attempt to provide religious instruction for children across the land. Royal injunctions in 1536 instructed the parochial clergy to press on parents and schoolteachers the necessity to teach children 'even from theyr infancy'. This was followed up by official catechisms in 1545, 1549 and 1553. Archbishop Thomas Cranmer claimed editorial responsibility for three English editions of the Nuremberg catechism, and there were many other private initiatives. By the mid-seventeenth century over 350 catechisms had been produced. Catechisms weren't all addressed to children, but some were for very young children. It is an 'idle concept', insisted the Church of England clergyman and scholar Thomas Gataker, that 'Religion and Godlinesse is not for children', and he proceeded to produce a catechism for children 'that are not past the breast yet'.⁴ Thomas Becon's son was 'past the breast' – he was five – when his father produced a catechism 'set forth Dialogue-wise in familiar talk between the father and the son'. After some preliminaries, it opens with the father putting some testing questions:

Father: Declare now unto me of how many parts the doctrine of the catechism consisteth.

Son: Of six parts.

Father: Which are they?

Son: Repentance, faith, law, prayer, sacraments, and the offices of all degrees.

Father: Is the whole sum of Christ's doctrine contained in these six parts?

Son: Yes, verily.

Father: And is repentance the first part of that doctrine which is taught in the catechism?

Son: So have I learned. For our catechist declared unto us, that, when John Baptist, Christ, and his apostles began to teach, they preached first of all repentance ...

> *Father:* What is repentance?
>
> *Son:* Repentance is an inward and true sorrow of the heart, unfeignedly conceived in the mind by earnest consideration of our sins and wickednesses, which heretofore most unkindly we have committed, against the Lord our God, of whom we have freely received so many, so great, and so noble benefits, with a perfect detestation and utter abhorring of our former wicked life; whereunto is also added a fervent and inward desire from henceforth to live godly and virtuously, and to frame our life in all points according to the holy will of God expressed in the divine scriptures.

And so on for 410 closely printed pages.[5] We can only speculate what a five year old would have made of it.

Teaching through the catechism was perhaps the main way in which the authorities of church and state sought to wean people away from Catholicism and towards one or another version of Protestantism. And in the Protestant vision, there was a particular focus on the young. In Catholic doctrine, once a baby had been baptized it was relieved of the burden of original sin and was thought of as innocent. But in Protestantism the sacrament of baptism no longer carried this power. Even in the womb, proclaimed the Nuremberg catechism, unborn babies had 'evyll lustes and appetites'.[6] In religious families, exercises in godliness loomed large, driven by the parental urgency to bring the child to a sense of its sin and of the necessity of faith. With child death all too common, there could be no delay in starting the teaching. The belief in predestination that Calvin had taught, which had taken root in Scotland, did nothing to relieve this parental anxiety, for parents still hoped to see in the behaviour of their children some sign that they were among the elect. The testamentary inventory of Henry Charteris, an Edinburgh bookseller who died in 1599, contained 5400 copies of Calvin's catechism, intended for children up to the age of about eight and at a cost of only 2d. By contrast there were fewer than 100 Bibles, for it was not until the mid-seventeenth century that the day of the small-size and abridged Bible suitable for children made its mark. But by the early eighteenth century the widow of the king's printer in Scotland had almost 28,000 Bibles of various sizes in stock.[7]

Protestantism downgraded the importance of the sacraments and also of the priest who administered them. There was no longer any intermediary between God and a human being. This placed an extra responsibility on parents. 'To have children and servants is thy blessing, O Lord,' said the English Primer of 1553, 'but not to order them according to thy word deserveth thy dreadful curse.'[8] Fathers in particular took on an onus of responsibility. It was a commonplace of the time that fathers stood in relation to their families as the king did to the country and as God did to humanity as a whole. Their rule was expected to be absolute, but just. Obedience to paternal rule had to be enforced. 'Foolishness is tied in the heart of a child,' parents read in the Old Testament, 'but the rod of discipline shall drive it away.' Puritans were taught in the conduct books written for them that the rod should be an instrument of last resort, to be used only after rational arguments had failed to bring about a change in the child's behaviour.[9] But to fail to use it in those circumstances was a dereliction of duty. Thomas Cawton, a minister in London, who 'took a great deal of pains to instruct and catechise [his children], to bring them up in the nurture and admonition of the Lord', nevertheless sometimes felt obliged to resort to corporal punishment, but he 'was often so moved with compassion, his fatherly bowels did so yearn over [his children], that the tears would trickle apace from his eies when he was correcting them: nothing ever wrought upon me like this sight, which did plainly convince his Children of his unwillingness to chastise, but that he was forced to it.'[10]

William Gouge, an influential mid-seventeenth-century Puritan minister in London and a father of 13 children, set out the ideal relationship between parents and children. In his 'A Prayer for a Childe to Use', children were told that their parents were 'as Gods to their children' and acknowledged to the Lord that 'in obeying them, I obey thee: in rebelling against them, I rebell against thee'. In practice they should show their reverence for their parents,

in refraining much speech before them, in patient hearkoning to them, in giving reverend titles to them, and humble and ready answers, without pride or stoutnesse. And when in absence of my Parents, I have occasion to speake of them, give me wisedome, so to order my speech, as it may testifie a reverend respect of them to all that heare me. Keepe me therefore from discovering their infirmities, and from broaching any untruths of them. To my reverend speech, let my dutifull carriage towards my Parents, be answerable, by hasting to meete them when they are comming to me, by rising up to them, by standing before them, by yeelding all due obeisance to them, by giving place to them, and by asking them blessing: Avoiding all unmannerly rudenesse, disdainfull statelinesse, toyish wantonnesse, over-much boldnesse, and high-mindednesse.

This was matched by 'A Prayer for Parents to Use', though most of it is for a father, urging on him the duty to provide properly for his children, with 'neither too-much niggardlinesse and neglect, nor too-much lavishnese and dotage', to train them in a suitable calling, 'to provide fit marriages' for them, but, above all, to be 'conscionable in training up my children unto true piety ... Exercising them to read the Scriptures, catechizing them daily', and 'so long as there is need, without wearisomenesse, to whet instructions upon them: adding reproofe, yea, and correction thereto, as just occasion is offered, and that wisely, so as I neither make my child to despise me through too-much lenity, nor to hate me through too-much severity'.[11]

If we are looking for a time when the level of parental anxiety about children matches that in the early twenty-first century, it is perhaps among the Puritans of the sixteenth and seventeenth centuries that we will find it. Conscious that they stood to their family in the place of God, they worried incessantly about the state of their children's souls. And what raised the anxiety level was the omnipresence of death. 'Learn to die', wrote Thomas Becon in 1560, should be one of the earliest sentences taught to a child. Imagine yourselves on your death-beds, in your coffins, in your graves, John Norris told his children in his *Spiritual Counsel* of 1694.[12] Nowhere is parental anxiety more apparent than in the books the Puritans wrote or recommended for children. Of over 260 books from the seventeenth century written for children, all were religious with the exception of two books of riddles, one or two on sport and a few more on polite manners.[13] 'When thou canst read,' Thomas White, a Nonconformist divine, told children, 'read no Ballads and foolish Books, but a Bible, and the *Plain mans pathway to Heaven*, a very plain holy book for you; get the *Practice of Piety*; Mr Baxter's *Call to the Unconverted*; Allen's *Allarum to the Unconverted*; read the Histories of the Martyrs that dyed for Christ ... Read also often treatises of Death, and Hell and Judgement, and of the Love and Passion of Christ.'[14]

The most famous seventeenth-century book treating of these themes, 'probably the most influential children's book ever written', as it has been described,[15] was James Janeway's *A Token for Children, being an Exact Account of the Conversion, Holy and Exemplary Lives, and Joyful Deaths, of several young Children*. Published in 1671 and 1672, it gives accounts of 13 children who died young. Janeway was a Nonconformist, educated at Christ Church, Oxford, who eventually had his own meeting house in Rotherhithe. A book for children focused on the death of children is likely to seem to us morbid and certainly not, as it was described in the early nineteenth century, 'the most entertaining book that can be'.[16] But Janeway, who had devoted himself to pastoral work in the last great plague year, 1665, knew about child death. London was a particularly deadly environment for children, and in plagues they were the age group hit hardest of all. 'Did you never hear of a little Child that died?', asks Janeway. 'And if other Children die, why may not you be sick and die? And what will you do then, Child, if you should have no grace in your heart, and be found like other naughty Children?' The deaths of the 13 children, 'God's works of Wonder', as Janeway described them, show children often wiser than their parents, more confident than they that they are going to heaven. But it is children, not parents, whom Janeway is addressing. He concludes:

> And now dear Children, I have done. I have written to you, I have prayed for you, but what you will do, I can't tell. O children, if you love me, if you love your Parents, if you love your Souls; if you would escape Hell fire, and if you would live in Heaven when you dye, do you go and do as these good Children, and that you may be your Parents joy, your Countreys honour, and live in Gods fear, and dye in his love, is the prayer of your dear Friend, J. Janeway.[17]

Janeway addressing his child readers in this way brings us back to the transforming impact of the Reformation on children and their centrality to it. Protestants, and especially Puritans, agonized endlessly over children. They were the first to write extensively for children. And they could imagine children not only as infant sinners but also as prophets to an adult world. Sarah Wight and Martha Hatfield both seem to have recovered from their prophetic moments to become reverential members of their congregations. William Withers, a bright lad, was educated at Corpus Christi College, Cambridge, and for some 50 years was a rector in Suffolk, apparently retaining his strong

Puritan sympathies.[18] We know less about the impact of a Puritan upbringing on the majority of children who experienced it. Indeed, the only children whose voices we can hear are those on their sick or death-beds.

The godly saw themselves as, and were, a minority movement in danger of persecution. Their influence, however, stretched way beyond those who with pride saw themselves as 'the godly', or as Puritans or as dissenters from the established Church of England. In power in local communities they could exercise considerable control over the lives of everyone. Few children would have escaped some contact with one or another version of the catechism.

'A pretious child, a bundle of myrrh, a bundle of sweetness'

Most of the family groups in which children were engaging with their catechisms were nuclear units of parents and their children. On average a marriage that lasted 25 years was likely to produce six or seven children, though it would be rare for all the babies born to live through their childhoods. Upper-class women were more likely than others to marry early, to put their children out to wet-nurses and, because of the contraceptive effect of breast-feeding, to have more frequent births, but even with them very large family units were unusual.[19] As in the Middle Ages, households with two generations, parents and children, were the norm. The wealthier the family the larger the household, swollen by servants.

What was the nature of the relationship between parents and children in this post-Reformation society? In the sixteenth and even more in the seventeenth century, letters and other personal documents begin to give us some idea of family relationships in the literate upper and middle classes. [Fig. 9]

If children were being exhorted to 'learn to die', it was the death of their children that brought out most movingly the way parents felt about their children. It was once thought that parents shrugged off the death of children. When infant and child mortality was so high, it made psychological sense, it was thought, to protect yourself against too much grief. Certainly we can find evidence of that, but the dominant tone in the writings of the literate was of anguish and of a struggle to make sense of their loss.

Richard Evelyn, Dick as he was known in the family, died on 27 January 1658. His father described how:

We sent for Physitians to Lond, while there was yet life in him; but the river was frozen up, & the Coach brake by the way ere it got a mile from the house; so as all artificial help failing, & his natural strength exhausted, we lost the prettiest, and dearest Child, that ever Parents had, being but 5 yeares & 3 days old in years but even at that tender age, a prodigie for Witt, & understanding; for beauty of body a very Angel, & for endowments of mind, of incredible & rare hopes ... At 2 yeare and halfe old he could perfectly read any of the *English*, *Latin*, french or *Gottic* letters; pronouncing the three first languages exactly.

We know about the prodigious learning of young Dick, his 'wonderful disposition to Mathematics', his knowledge of Euclid's propositions and his reading of *Aesop's Fables*, because his father was the famous seventeenth-century diarist John Evelyn. The father tried to comfort himself: 'God having dressed up a Saint for himselfe, would not permit him longer with us, unworthy of the future fruites of this incomparable hopefull blossome: ... for such a child I blesse God, in whose bosome he is: May I & mine become as this little child, which now follows the Child Jesus ... Thou gavest him to us, thou hast taken him from us, blessed be the name of the Lord.' Evelyn's resignation to the will of the Lord didn't prevent him from trying to find out why Dick had died. Doctors performed an autopsy, discovering an enlarged liver and spleen.[20]

A lot of children in the sixteenth and seventeenth centuries are known to us mainly because they died young and their fathers wrote about them. Dramatist and poet Ben Jonson wrote poems on the loss of both his first daughter and his first son, Mary only six months old, the boy seven years:

> Farewell, thou child of my right hand, and joy;
>> My sinne was too much hope of thee, lov'd boy,
> Seven yeeres tho'wert lent to me, and I thee pay,
>> Exacted by thy fate, on the just day.
> O, could I loose all father, now. For why
>> Will man lament the state he should envie?
> To have so soone scap'd worlds, and fleshes rage,
>> And, if no other miserie, yet age?

Rest in soft peace, and, ask'd, say here doth lye
Ben: Jonson his best piece of *poetrie*.
For whose sake, hence-forth, all his vowes be such,
As what he loves may never like too much.[21]

Nowhere is the attempt to assuage grief through trying to see it as the will of the Lord more painful than in the tortured lamentations of the Essex clergyman Ralph Josselin on the illness and death of his daughter, eight-year-old Mary:

My little Mary, very weake, wee feared shee was drawing on, feare came on my heart very much, but since shee is not mine, but the Lords, and shee is not too good for her father, shee was tender of her mother, thankefull, mindefull of god, in her extremity, shee would cry out, poore I, poore I ... It was a pretious child, a bundle of myrrh, a bundle of sweetnes, she was a child of ten thousand, full of wisedome, woman-like gravity, knowledge, sweet expression of god, apt in her learning, tender hearted and loving, an obedient child to us. It was free from the rudenesse of little children, it was to us as a boxe of sweet ointment, which now its broken smells more deliciously then it did before, Lord I rejoyce I had such a present for thee.'[22]

It often seems that it was the fathers whose grief was uncontrollable. Nehemiah Wallington, who was a godly wood turner in seventeenth-century London, records the death of four of his five children; the death of Elizabeth in October 1625, just short of her third birthday, was particularly harrowing, her last words, 'Father, I go abroad tomorrow and buy you a plum pie,' engraved in his memory. Nehemiah who, conventionally, had resolved to be 'as a head and governor' towards his wife, Grace, now records this conversation:

Grace: 'Husband, I am persuaded you offend God in grieving for this child so much. Do but consider what a deal of grief and care we are rid of, and what a deal of trouble and sorrow she is gone out of, and what abundance of joy she is gone into. And do but consider, it is your daughter's wedding day and will you grieve to see your daughter go home to her husband

Christ Jesus, where she will never want, but have the fullness of joy forevermore?'

Nehemiah: 'Do you not grieve for this child?'

Grace: 'No, truly, husband, if you will believe me, I do as freely give it again unto God, as I did receive it of him.'[23]

Grace, seven months pregnant, may have had to force herself to look to the future, but her apparent coolness may look to us like denial.

Not all mothers seem to have been so emotionally detached. Anne, Countess of Arundel, wrote about her grandson, James, Lord Maltravers, aged about seven months in 1607, who was making a gradual recovery after having been quite seriously ill: 'He was sometimes at the first distemper of heat and would groan so in his sleep as if I had not remembered his father's hard breeding of teeth I should have been more grieved, but my good daughter I did find to shed tears though she made the best show before me that she could.' Baby ill, mother in tears, grandmother taking comfort from the family history.

Or take another teething child, Susanna Hatton, who, her pregnant mother tells Susanna's father, 'is very ill about her teeth ... [but] she bears it with a great deal of patience ... I hope her teeth will come at last but I am afraid she may be inclined to the rickets. Oh my Lord if I should die, show particular kindness to that child for if I have ten thousand sons I can not love them so well.'[24]

Anxiety did not end once teething was past. Alice Thornton, from a minor Yorkshire gentry family and very religious, described a scene in 1660 with her two daughters Katy and six-year-old Alice:

My dear Katy was playing under the table with her sister (being about three years old, but a very brave, strong child, and full of mettle ... and indeed apt to fall into dangers), as she was playing with pins, and putting them into her mouth, her sister see her, and cried out for fear she should do herself hurt. But she would not be counselled with her, and at last she got a pin cross her throat. By God's pleasure I was just near her, and catched her up in my arms, and put my fingers immediately into the throat, and the pin was cross, and I had much to do to get it out, but with all the force I had, it pleased God to strengthen me to do it.[25]

The anxiety over illness, their own or their child's, is sometimes laid aside, and parents can express their simple pleasure in their child's development. In July 1623 the Duchess of Buckingham sent her husband a detailed description of their daughter. She responded in a different way to each dance tune that was played and would cry, 'hah hah,' when danced. Put her down on her back, and she would kick her legs over her head. 'I wood you were here but to see her for you wood take much delight in her now she is so full of pretye playe and tricks.'[26]

An absent mother, Jane Cornwallis, was similarly reassured in the 1620s when her husband wrote to her about Nicholas, aged three, and Jane, 18 months: 'Our children are well, and little Nick hath cast his coat, and seemeth metamorphosed into a grasshopper. Jane is a very modest maiden, and is wholly taken up with travelling by her self which she performeth very handsomely and will be ready to run at your command when you return.' A year later, perhaps not as attentive a father as he might have been, he writes that 'For little Jane in particular, I should have been glad to have understood some of her new language'.[27]

Another father, Adam Martindale, had proud memories of his son John: 'We had a wanton tearing calfe, that would runne at children to beare them over. This calfe he would encounter with a sticke in his hand, when he was about two yeares old ... stand his ground stoutly, beat it backe, and triumph over it, crying, *caw, caw,* meaning he had beaten the calfe. I doe not think one child of 100 of his age durst doe so much.'[28]

There have survived a scattering of letters from children to their parents that give us some feel for the quality of the child's relationship with parents and family. Here is Justinian Isham, aged about 11, in 1622:

Most deare father though I am u[n]sckilful in writing of epistles never
the lesse I thought it good to write something to you although it will
abounde with many faults where in I will certifie you what I have profited
you in the studie of good letters for now I am newly entred in the exercise
of making s[c]hoole epistles but I pray you accept of it beeing the first
epistle that ever I made. My grandmother and my mother and all the
rest of the household are veri well hoping that you are well too but
I praye you remember my dutie to my aunt denton and to my unkle
Washucton and my aunt and all the rest of my kindred. I have obeayed

your comanndiment which you tooke order with my mother and maister
that I shoulde keepe mee within the compose [compass?] of the yards.
I shoulde bee very glad to see you at home and there I lave you with god
　　Your obeydient son
　　Justinian Isham
I woulde have written this epistle in latin but time would not serve mee.[29]

Writing a letter is a novel and strange medium for the young Justinian. He observes the conventions of this new means of communication, but this does not hide his closeness to his father and family.

These pictures of good relations between parents and children can be matched by cases where the opposite seems to be true. Take the childhood of Sir Simonds D'Ewes, his father a successful London barrister, his mother the daughter of a wealthy Dorset landowner. Simonds was born in December 1602 and spent his first few months with his mother at her parents' Dorset home. Then father, mother and child set off to the D'Ewes's estate in Suffolk. But the young Simonds was so badly affected by the journey that he got no further than Dorchester, where a wet-nurse was found for him. After a few months with her, Simonds moved back to his grandfather's house where he remained for the next seven years, his parents visiting him only twice. At the age of eight he was returned to these parents whom he hardly knew, but was then almost immediately sent off to a boarding school. There was a brief six months when his mother stayed with him, and he became deeply attached to her and adopted her Puritan faith, but for most of his childhood his parents were conspicuous by their absence.[30] Or take William Blundell, an impoverished Lancashire Catholic gentleman, who in 1653 reported that 'My wife has much disappointed my hopes in bringing forth a daughter, which, finding herself not so welcome in this world as a son, hath made already a discreet choice of a better.'[31]

Blundell was not alone in preferring sons. They alone could carry on the name and line. 'If it be thy blessed will', wrote the pregnant Lady Mordaunt in her diary in the 1650s, 'let it be a boy.'[32] Thinking of this kind is often the unspoken signature on paintings of families and children in the seventeenth century. [Fig. 8] Potentially they can tell us something about the quality of family relationships. Yet there is usually more to the painting than we might expect from a family snapshot today. In Anthony Van Dyck's painting of Philip Herbert, 4th Earl of Pembroke, and his family, in about 1635, we see the proud parents with their surviving children spread over the canvas, the ones who have died touchingly represented as putti floating in the sky. And yet the occasion for the painting, and its purpose, was to celebrate a dynastic alliance with another aristocratic family. Similar concerns underlie Van Dyck's *Three Eldest Children of Charles I*. We see the future Charles II, Queen Mary and James II at the ages of five, four and two, the individual portraits sensitive and touching, the two youngest looking up to their elder brother, but here again there was a dynastic agenda. Indeed Van Dyck here failed to satisfy his patron, for Charles I did not want his heir to be portrayed in a child's clothes.[33] Paintings, it seems, can give us what seem to be real-life portraits of children, yet they also suggest that, for royalty and the aristocracy, the family was more important than any individual child. [Fig. 6]

One of the parental duties that all the advice books insisted on was the necessity to set up your children, or at least your sons, in a suitable occupation. William Perkins, an influential and widely read Elizabethan preacher, wrote: 'Now touching children, it is the duty of parents to make choice of fit callings for them, before they apply them to any particular condition of life. And that they may the better judge aright, for what callings their children are fit, they must observe two things in them: first, their inclination, secondly, their natural gifts.'[34]

We can see this advice being put into practice in the account given by John Shaw: 'My parents having no other child but me, and some competent estate to leave me, were very loath to have me depart from them ... but they observing my eager desire ... after knowledge and learning, my good God so overruled their hearts as to incline them ... to send me to Cambridge.'[35]

Even when the choice had been made, and parental duties in some senses were at an end, parents might still worry. Henry Newcome, a seventeenth-century Lancashire minister, was never free of worry about his son Daniel who was serving an apprenticeship in London:

November 20th 1669. This night I had a letter from my friend Mr Ashurst, which brought me the saddest news that ever I had in my life, viz., of the miscarriage [ill-conduct] of Daniel; and in such general terms, that we had sorrow without bounds. It is a great sorrow, bitter, reaches to the very heart; and it is a sorrow I can see no end of. It is a sorrow that many precious men have in the very kind. Mr Angier, Mr Goodwin, Mr Harrison.
And I am sure they have done more for their children's education than

ever I did, or could do. And who am I, that I should not taste of this kind of sorrow? November 21st (being Lord's day), I kept in; and a sorrowful day it was. I wrote to Dr Davenport, as my friend I could best trust, and desired him to acquaint me with the full of the thing. The next day, (November 22nd), I received a letter from him, which gave some general account of what I had heard before, but it was not so dreadful as the other. [But, on the following Saturday] I received a woful account of particulars from Dr Davenport; far above all my fears. [On the 28th] I was wofully cast down in expectation of the post; and unexpectedly he brought me a letter from Daniel, wherein he expressed some sense of his folly, and I seemed secured from the danger of his running away, which was a great ease to me, for that I dreadfully feared.[36]

And so it goes on, the father, far away in Lancashire, endlessly worrying about the misbehaviour of his son and clearly not the only parent to be so doing.

Margaret Evelyn, wife of the diarist, was another worried parent. In 1670 her son John, aged 15 and studying in London, received this stinging warning and rebuke:

I have received your letter and request for a supply of money; but none of those you mention which were bare effects of your duty. If you were so desirous to answer our expectations as you pretend to be, you would give those tutors and overseers you think so exact over you, less trouble than I fear they have with you. Much is to be wished in your behalf; that your temper were humble and tractable, your inclinations virtuous, and that from choice, not compulsion, you make an honest man ... You are not too young to know that lying, defrauding, swearing, disobedience to parents and persons in authority, are offences of God and man: that debauchery is injurious to growth, health, life, and indeed to the pleasures of life; therefore, now that you are turning from child to man, endeavour to follow the best precepts, and choose such ways as may render you worthy of praise and love. You are assured of your father's care and my tenderness; no mark of it shall be wanting at any time to confirm it to you, with this reserve only, that you strive to deserve kindness by a sincere honest proceeding, and not flatter yourself that you are good whilst you only appear to be so.[37]

'[T]urning from child to man', John Evelyn would at least have known that his parents were concerned about him. His mother's advice either took effect or was unnecessary, for Evelyn went on to enjoy a successful career as a writer and civil servant.

We can find examples among Tudor and Stuart parents of coldness, even callousness towards their children. We know that, particularly among the upper classes, the reputation and future of the family was more important than meeting the needs of any particular child. But the overriding impression is of parents loving their children and bereft if they died. Amid a widespread anxiety, there shine through shafts of parental pleasure in their children and their achievements.

'The vast usefulness of Reading'

What was it like to grow up as a boy in this society? Much depended on where you were in the social scale, but we can get a good idea of the boyhood of the moderately prosperous from the autobiography of William Stout. Born in 1665, Stout was the son of a yeoman in Lancashire. While his sister 'was early taught to read, knit and spin, and also needle work', he and his brothers went first to a dame school – a school for young children, usually run by a woman – and then, at the age of seven, to the Boulton free-school – a school where no tuition fees were paid. He remained there until he was 14 and he remembers how,

> from the age of ten or twelve years, we were very much taken off the schoole, espetialy in the spring and summer season, plow time, turfe time, hay time and harvest, in looking after the sheep, helping at plough, goeing to the moss with carts, making hay and shearing in harvest, two of us at 13 or 14 years of age being equall to one man shearer; so that we made small progress in Latin, for what we got in winter we forgot in summer, and the writing master coming to Boulton mostly in winter, wee got what writing we had in winter.

But young William Stout's education was not over. His father in 1678 took him to school to Heversham in Westmorland, and he was there for some 18 months before moving, with his teacher, to a school in Lancaster, where his Latin and Greek were not as good as they might have been, and his writing much criticized because he was left-handed. His father, ill and with death approaching, sensibly sought to get William apprenticed, reaching terms with an ironmonger in Lancaster, Henry Coward, Stout's father paying £20 and agreeing to keep William in clothes for the seven years of his apprenticeship. As he entered his apprenticeship, Stout left his childhood behind him.[38]

For all boys, except those in the upper classes, schooling had to be juggled with the requirement to contribute to the family economy and to earn a living. Most children who had the opportunity to go to school until they were seven had probably learnt to read. They would start either at home or in a rudimentary village school. Oliver Sansom, born in 1636 in Beedon in Berkshire, the son of a timber merchant, recalled that 'When I was about six years of age, I was put to school to a woman, to learn to read, who finding me not unapt to learn, forwarded me so well, that in about four months' time, I could read a chapter in the Bible pretty readily.' James Fretwell, eldest son of another timber merchant, this time from Yorkshire, born in 1699, was sent by his mother 'to an old school-dame who lived at the very next door ... But I suppose I did but continue here but a few days, for growing weary of my book, and my dame not correcting me as my mother desired, she took me under her pedagogy untill I could read in my Bible, and thus she did afterwards by all my brothers and sisters.'[39]

If a boy remained at school until he was eight, he would probably by then have learnt to write. But it was a year earlier, at seven, that a boy became of some economic use to the family, so reading was a skill much more likely to have been acquired than writing. Thomas Tryon, the son of the village plasterer and tiler at Bibury in Oxfordshire, recalled how 'About Five Years old, I was put to School, but being addicted to play, after the Example of my young School-fellows, I scarcely learnt to distinguish my Letters, before I was taken away to Work for my Living.' Thomas's father put him to work spinning and carding, and he was so good at it that he was soon earning two shillings a week. Then he started to help local shepherds with their sheep and eventually persuaded his reluctant father to buy him a few sheep of his own.

> All this while, tho' now about Thirteen Years Old, I could not Read; then thinking of the vast usefulness of Reading, I bought me a Primer, and got now one, then another, to teach me to Spell, and so learn'd to Read imperfectly, my Teachers themselves not being ready Readers: But in a little time having learn't to Read competently well, I was desirous to learn

to Write, but was at a great loss for a Master, none of my Fellow-Shepherds being able to teach me. At last, I bethought myself of a lame young Man who taught some poor People's Children to Read and Write; and having by this time got two Sheep of my own, I applied myself to him, and agreed with him to give him one of my Sheep to teach me to make the Letters, and Joyn them together.[40]

Thomas's fellow shepherds, who could teach him, if imperfectly, to read, but not to write, must have been among many who had attained one skill but not the other. Perhaps shepherds had more time than others to practise reading. Samuel Pepys, on a Sunday jaunt out to Epsom Downs in July 1667, came across a flock of sheep,

and the most pleasant and innocent sight that ever I saw in my life; we find a shepheard and his little boy reading, far from any houses or sight of people, the Bible to him. So I made the boy read to me, which he did with the forced Tone that children do usually read, that was mighty pretty; and then I did give him something and went to the father and talked with him; and I find he had been a servant in my Cosen Pepys's house, and told me what was become of their old servants. He did content himself mightily in my liking his boy's reading and did bless God for him.[41]

The world of the book was in ways like this becoming open to people who could not themselves read. As for Thomas Tryon, he went on to become an apprentice in London, a vegetarian and the author of many books. In one of these he promulgated 'Laws and Orders proper for Women to Observe', which assume that mothers will teach their children to read and write.[42]

So much depended on parental attitudes, the size of the family (the smaller the better) and the lottery of life and death. John Bunyan, whose father was a husbandman and tinker in Bedfordshire, was lucky: 'notwithstanding the meanness [poverty] of ... my Parents, it pleased God to put it into their Hearts to put me to School, to learn both to read and write.'[43] Others, particularly if their father died, and as many as one-eighth of all children may have lost their father by the time they were seven, might have their schooling immediately curtailed. Arise Evans, born in 1606 or 1607, the son of a prosperous yeoman on the Welsh borders, was put to school with his father's friend the curate and his reading much admired, but when his father died when he was six, Arise was withdrawn, subsequently lived with his mother and stepfather 'and then put away from all, and tossed from place to place', ending up at the age of eight or nine in an informal apprenticeship with a tailor.[44] Josiah Langdale, born in 1673 in Nafferton in the East Riding of Yorkshire, was another who had to give up school on the death of his father, when he was nine.[45]

Attendance at school might well involve leaving home to 'table' or board near the school. Adam Martindale, aged seven in 1630, was sent to the free-school of St Helens in his own parish of Prescot in Lancashire, but the school was 'almost two miles from my father's house, a great way for a little fat short legged lad (as I was) to travel twice a day', though he managed it. But for James Fretwell, not quite five when he went to school at Sandal, the distance was too far. 'At my first going to Sandal, I walked it every day, but was not able to hold it long, it being too far for such a child to go daily.' So the young boy was placed with a widow in Sandal, 'usually coming home every Saturday'. At the age of nine he moved to Stoney Stainton where he boarded with the schoolmaster; at 13 he attended Doncaster free-school, again placed with a widow, and after about a year was transferred to Pontefract where he boarded with a mercer, who taught him some account-keeping and arithmetic.[46]

Most boys in the dominantly rural society of Tudor and Stuart times would know that at about 14 they would probably leave home to become servants in husbandry on some neighbouring or distant farm. By this age they could be of some distinct use on the farm, and there would often be neither room nor role for them at home. At this point their childhood ended, for the contract would last a year and be repeated by a succession of further one-year contracts to work on farms until they could expect to marry in their mid-twenties.

Boys slightly higher up the social scale might attend grammar school for a few years, but without any intention that they would go on to university. A common career pattern, like that of William Stout, was to leave at about 14 to become apprenticed. Apprenticeship dates back to the thirteenth century. The Statute of Artificers, 1562, made a seven-year apprenticeship compulsory for all who wished to engage in a craft or trade.[47] The prospect of an apprentice-ship drew many young people to London or to some provincial town. Apprentices made up about one in ten of the population in London and such large towns as Bristol, Norwich or York. Most of them were migrants, in London as many as 90 per cent in the mid-sixteenth century, and half of these came from Scotland, Ireland, Wales, the western counties and the north of England – they travelled considerable distances. It took William Lilly in 1620 six days to travel from Leicester to London, 'cold and uncomfortable'. Edward Barlow, travelling over seven days from Manchester to London, also remembered the hardships of his journey, the 6 shillings the journey cost eating up nearly all his savings – and this despite the fact that he, as well as William Lilly, had walked all the way. The mercantile and more lucrative distributive trades, such as drapers, grocers, mercers and merchant tailors, attracted the sons of gentlemen and yeomen: there were high and rising premiums to pay. But most apprentices were recruited from the sons of craftsmen and husbandmen, even a few labourers, and many of the premiums paid were £10 or less. Urban apprentices in the sixteenth century often started at 16, 17 or 18, and many of them are likely to have been in agricultural service from the age of 13 or 14, and perhaps able in the intervening years to save enough for the premium if their families were not able to help.[48]

At the age of 14 some boys were certainly able to negotiate the terms of their departure from home. Richard Davies was born in North Wales in the 1630s. When he was 14, his father, a small farmer, decided to apprentice him in the shopkeeping trade. Richard was sent to a shopkeeper for a period of trial to see whether the trade and the master suited him. In the course of the trial, young Richard became convinced that 'the conversation of [his] intended master was not right, and that the fear of the Lord was not there', and so returned home. Soon he heard about a feltmaker 'who was very zealous', and performed all 'that which we call family duties', travelled to see him, offered to become his apprentice, discussed the matter with his parents and, with their consent, bound himself apprentice some 40 miles from his parents' home in Welshpool. Parents often, it seems, listened to what their sons wanted. Adam Martindale's father, probably in the building trade, wanted Adam to follow him in the business, but 'he frankely put it to my choice, whether I would go on as I did at present, or returne to schoole againe', and Adam chose the latter, becoming a schoolmaster.[49]

The minority of boys who stayed on at grammar school into their later teens perhaps felt that they were being kept in a state of dependence longer than was appropriate. Certainly that is one way of understanding the disorder that afflicted many schools. In Scottish burgh schools in the late sixteenth century it was the custom for the pupils to petition the town council for their holidays. The reformed Kirk wanted to abolish the Christmas holidays as remnants of superstition, and in 1580 the town councils of Edinburgh and Aberdeen duly refused the petition they received for the Yule vacation. The 'disordered bairns', as they were called, then shut out their master and occupied the school buildings, 'meaning to have the old privilege which was wont to be granted to them'. From 1580 onwards this happened again and again, sometimes at Christmas, sometimes in the summer, for the councils wanted also to shorten the summer holidays. The boys, heavily armed, damaged school furniture, doors and windows, and robbed neighbours in sorties to gain themselves supplies. In Edinburgh in 1587 the provost and baillies recaptured the school by force, but when they attempted to do this again in 1595 a baillie was shot dead by the young son of the chancellor of Caithness. Edinburgh was peaceful after that scandal, but in Aberdeen the struggle went on into the seventeenth century, the council struggling against what it called 'the insolencies and disorders that fall out almost yearly within the burgh by taking of the school about the superstitious time of Yule ... [thereby] breeding in the scholars' hearts a contempt and misregard of their master, and furnishing to them occasion of boldness to rebel against his discipline'. These rebellious scholars were mostly the sons of lairds, willing to take up arms against their schoolmasters.[50]

In schools in the north of England this barring-out of the master at the approach of holidays often became a ritual, boys and masters agreeing how each side would behave. At Hull in 1662 the master of the grammar school and his scholars came to an agreement that was approved by the mayor and aldermen and posted up in the school 'to prevent the disorderly exclusion of the masters of the same school for the future'. Customary holidays and play days were set out, and it was agreed to suspend punishment during the 'time of Orders' that lasted through to the end of the Christmas holidays.

> that always from Martinmas Day, being the eleventh day of November, the master of the said school shall lay aside all rods and ferulas and suspend all manner of correction from the said Martinmas Day during the time of Orders. [If during this period there shall be any irreverence towards the master], it shall be lawful for the masters ... to take special cognizance thereof and to correct such disorderly behaviour in time convenient, but not in Order Time.

But the ritual was not always so tamed. In Manchester Grammar School in the 1690s, it was said, the boys held the school for a fortnight, with supplies of food and firearms from the townsmen. At Market Harborough in 1672 the boys shut out the master, wedged the door and from their first-floor school-room threw squibs at the market stall-holders, frightening women, breaking crockery and scattering chickens.[51]

These barring-out rituals, whether peaceful or not, were, like the boy-bishop ceremonies of the Middle Ages, a moment in the school year when the world seemed turned upside down. For what characterized the schools of the sixteenth and seventeenth centuries was the discipline they imposed. This is not simply a twenty-first-century view. Contemporaries never pretended that school was any-thing other than a regime where boys were subjected to a fierce discipline. The master, perhaps with one or two ushers to help him in the larger schools, was 'an absolute monarch'. 'At country schools', said Richard Baxter, 'your masters drive you on by fear.' And of course it was the rod, the symbol of the master's authority, that was the instrument that inspired the fear. Adam Martindale's teacher at Rainford 'would whip boys most unmercifully for small or no faults at all'. At least from the boys' perspective, that was not at all unusual. Parents, gov-ernors and educational thinkers protested against the excessive beating, and there was even a promising-sounding Children's Petition in 1669, allegedly pre-sented by a boy to the speaker of the House of Commons. This exposure of the sexual perversions involved in corporal punishment is, however, more probably a piece of pornography than a genuine petition from a schoolboy.[52]

The harsh discipline of the schools was in large part needed if the master were to have any hopes of putting across the syllabus during the long hours of school: from six or seven in the morning until 11, starting again at one and going on to five or darkness in winter. During these long hours, boys learnt Latin grammar, and as they advanced up the school, Greek also. In the higher classes boys had to converse in Latin alone. Latin was no longer, as it had been in the Middle Ages, crucial for the professions. It was the discipline imposed in the learning of it that gave it such importance. In the eighteenth century it was still being defended by Sir John Eardley Wilmot, chief justice of Common Pleas, in these terms:

Obedience is one of the capital benefits arising from a public education, for though I am very desirous of having young minds impregnated with classical knowledge, from the pleasure I have derived from it, as well as the utility of it in all stations of life, yet it is but a secondary benefit in my estimation of education; for to break the natural ferocity of human nature, to subdue the passions and to impress the principles of religion and morality, and give habits of obedience and subordination to paternal as well as political authority, is the first object to be attended to by all schoolmasters who know their duty.[53]

The grammar schools had expanded by leaps and bounds in the sixteenth century. The ex-monastic cathedrals were reconstituted as secular cathedrals, and each of them obliged to maintain a grammar school, the king's schools, as they were called. But these were essentially continuations of old schools. Much more important on the national scale were schools founded or supported by the charity of individuals or such bodies as the Merchant Taylors Company in London. Many of these schools were Puritan in their aims. Thus the statutes of Wakefield Grammar School in 1607 declare that 'this school is principally ordained a Seminarie for bringing up of Christian Children to become in time Ambassadors of Reconciliation from God to his Church, and generally is intended a School of Christian instruction for vertue.'[54] New foundations of this kind meant that the gentry, most men in the professions, farmers, merchants, the better-off tradesmen and artisans, and shopkeepers sent their sons to school. School could open up careers, particularly, as had always been the case, in the church. William Laud, archbishop of Canterbury, was a clothier's son, Samuel Harsnett, archbishop of York, a baker's. The schools, nevertheless, were socially exclusive; boys from the lower social ranks could not even aspire to them. Colchester Free Grammar School in the mid-seventeenth century was typical: nearly one-third of the boys were from aristocratic backgrounds, a mere 12 per cent were the sons of yeomen, and there were no sons of husbandmen or labourers.[55]

In the reign of Henry VIII, the Earl of Surrey, a poet, had suggested that school-days were the happiest days of one's life. But a much commoner picture of a schoolboy was, as with Shakespeare, of someone going 'unwillingly to school'. The idea that school-days should be happy did not become a commonplace until the mid-eighteenth century, and even then many protested against it.[56] Having survived the ordeal of school, some chose to think that it had done them good; for many schoolboys, however, an unhealthy cocktail of boredom and fear must have been the dominant emotions they experienced. The barring-out ceremonies provided some release, perhaps the only way in which adolescent boys could have been kept under the regime of discipline imposed on them. For most of their contemporaries, schooling, if they had had any, would have ended at some point between the ages of seven and 14, and with that ending they would probably no longer have thought of themselves as children. But many of them had learnt at least to read. They might, like Pepys's shepherd boy, use the skill to read the Bible or they might, like the young John Bunyan and like their medieval predecessors, immerse themselves in the fables and stories that poured from the presses, particularly in the late seventeenth century. They would have experienced, as Thomas Tryon did, 'the vast usefulness of reading'.

'Let not your girl learn Latin'

On 21 May 1645, Elizabeth Isham, aged about ten, wrote a letter to her sister:

> Sweete sister
> Uppon the sight of your letter to my Lady I could not rest untill I had obtayned her favour to learne to wright. And such is her Motherly care of us, as she will incourage and further our desiers for attaynning any good quallitie; And although I have practised but three weekes, yet I have presented these poore lynes to your view, hoping that as I mend, wee shall often converse by letters being the cheifest means of absent friends. And so you shall indeere mee (as I am)
> > your most affectionate sister
> > Elizabeth Isham[57]

Elizabeth's letter is written in a beautifully clear, italic hand, her achievement, if she had indeed had only three weeks of writing practice, extraordinary. Both in the permission from 'my Lady'(probably her aunt) that she had to gain and in the desire to 'converse by letters' that had prompted her to seek permission, Elizabeth was typical of many girls of the upper and middle classes in the sixteenth and seventeenth centuries. Elizabeth's mother had died in 1642, and her father, Sir Justinian Isham, a Northamptonshire gentleman, had promptly written a code of conduct for his four daughters, Elizabeth the second of them:

Prayers, meditations, and such like holy treatises, I rather commend
unto you than knotty disputes; and although your sex is not so capable
of those stronger abilities of the intellect, to make you so learned and
knowing as men ought to be; yet be sure to keep your hearts upright
and your affections towards God unfeigned and there is no doubt but that
will be more acceptable unto him than all the wisdom of the whole world
besides ... You ought more especially to have regard unto [the virtues and
graces] which the sacred scriptures direct you as most proper for your
sex. As these more especially:

holiness	meekness	discretion
chastity	modesty	frugality
obedience	sobriety	affability
charity	silence[58]	

Many men and women in the seventeenth century frowned on girls' educational ambitions. In the sixteenth century, in Tudor times, there had been a
greater willingness to regard with favour, even to celebrate, the learning that
some women had acquired. This had its roots in the new ideas that spread
northwards from Italy in the Renaissance. The rediscovery of classical
sources, and an accompanying emphasis on the centrality of human beings in
the world, led a handful of men to encourage learning in their daughters. Sir
Thomas More, who in his *Utopia* of 1515/16 had argued for a national system
of education for men and women alike, was the most famous example, the
learning of his three daughters well known way beyond the More household.
Some Protestants also argued the case. Thomas Becon asked in 1559 why, if
there were schools for 'the youth of the male kind', there should not also be
schools 'for the godly institution and virtuous upbringing of the youth of the
female kind?'[59]

This kind of advocacy never made very much headway. So far as girls were
concerned, the impact of the humanism of the Renaissance was confined to a
few exceptional households, and to royal circles. Lady Jane Grey had delighted
in learning, and Queen Elizabeth, the 'learned princess', as she was called,
continued to read Greek and Latin with the famous humanist teacher Roger
Ascham until his death. William Harrison, writing about the court of Queen
Elizabeth, commented:

> And to saie how many gentlewomen and ladies there are, that besides
> sound knowledge of the Greeke and Latine toongs, are thereto no lesse
> skilfull in the Spanish, Italian and French, or in some one of them, it
> resteth not in me; ... [of the women of the Court] some [occupy their
> time] in continuall reading either of the holie scriptures, or histories of
> our owne or forren nations about us (and diverse in writing volumes
> of their owne, or translating of other mens into our Englishe and
> Latine toongs).'[60]

But these highly educated women were always the exception. Most upper-class girls in the sixteenth and into the seventeenth century were educated either at home, or placed for a period of service in someone else's household with, in both cases, marriage as the desired outcome.

Grace Sherrington, born in 1552, and the second of the three daughters of Sir Henry Sherrington of Lacock Abbey, Wiltshire, was brought up at home by her parents and by a governess, Mistress Hamblyn, her father's niece. Grace records that her mother beat her, especially if she lied, and that her governess kept her always occupied:

> And when she did see me ydly disposed she wod sett me to cypher
> with my pen, and to cast up and prove great sums and accompts, and
> sometimes to wryte a supposed letter to this or that body concerning
> such and such things, and other tymes let me read in Dr Turner's Herball
> and Bartholomew Vigoe, and at other tymes sett me to sing psalmes, and
> other tymes sett me to soe curious work; for she was an excellent work-
> woman in all kinds of needlework.[61]

All this prepared Grace for marriage at the age of 15.

Margaret Dakins, by contrast, born in 1571, was at an early age received into the household of the Countess of Huntingdon, well known for her skill in raising upper-class girls. Margaret was married first, at the age of 18, to the son of the Earl of Essex, who was also being brought up in the countess's house-hold, and then, when he died, to the countess's own nephew. Margaret had been prepared by her period in service for her life as a wife. She learnt writing and keeping of accounts, acquired a knowledge of household and estate man-agement, and of what for the time must have been advanced first-aid. During her third marriage, as Lady Hoby, she described how she acted as a midwife and attended to the minor injuries of 'poore folkes'; she 'dressed apoore boies legge that came to me'. She herself trained other girls for this role. In 1603 a cousin brought his daughter Jane, 'beinge of the age of 13 yeares auld, to me, who, as he saied, he freely gave me'.[62]

Often parental death led to a girl being sent off to another household. Lady Bridget Manners was only 11 when her father died. She was promptly sent to be brought up in the household of her step-grandmother, the Countess of Bedford. She had apparently a tendency to stoop and only one accomplishment, an ability to play the lute. The Countess of Bedford, however, was very taken with her and decided to obtain for her a vacancy in the queen's Privy Chamber, and this was achieved when Bridget was 13, to the accompaniment of a letter of advice from her grand-uncle, who enjoined her to 'applie yourself hollye to the service of her majestie with all meekness, love and obediens ... [and] That you use moch sylens, for that becometh maydes, especially of your calling'.[63]

Silence, as we have seen, was one of the virtues held up for his daughters by Sir Justinian Isham in the 1640s, and he was in fact simply voicing what by then was the orthodoxy. 'A maid should be seen, and not heard,' wrote Thomas Becon in his *Catechism*, repeating the old medieval saying.[64] Men had come to think that women were, by nature, sexually voracious. Eve, the seductress, replaced the Madonna as the archetypal woman. On top of this, Britain in the mid-seventeenth century was being torn apart by war and revolution, freeing up some women to become street preachers or to claim a political role. Most male commentators could see only danger in too much learning for women: they needed from an early age to be made to feel subordinate. An advanced educational reformer, John Amos Comenius, had to hedge his advocacy of more education for girls with caution. He could see no reason:

> why the weaker sex ... should be altogether excluded from the pursuit
> of knowledge, whether in Latin or in their mother tongue. They also are
> formed in the image of God and share in his grace and in the kingdom of
> the world to come. They are endowed with equal sharpness of mind and
> capacity for knowledge (often with more than the opposite sex) ... [But]
> we are not advising that women be educated in such a way that their

tendency to curiosity shall be developed, but so that their sincerity and contentedness may be increased, and this chiefly in those things which it becomes a woman to know and to do; that is to say, all that enables her to look after her husband and to promote the welfare of her husband and family.[65]

Women were as likely as men to advocate only a limited education for girls. Elizabeth Joceline had been educated by her maternal grandfather, Bishop Chaderton of Lincoln, and learnt Latin and history, as well as how to live piously. In 1622, aged 27, fearing that she might die in childbirth, which she did, she wrote a treatise for her child's upbringing: '[If I have a daughter] I desire her bringing up to be learning the bible, as my sisters do, good housewifery, writing and good works; other learning a woman needs not, though I admire it in those whom God hath blest with discretion. Yet I desired not so much in my own, having seen that sometimes women have greater portions of learning than wisdom.'[66] Elizabeth Joceline has some hankerings after a learned daughter but clearly feels that it should be secondary to the other skills and aptitudes that a girl needed to acquire.

A strong sense of what was appropriate, or not, for each sex seems to have structured the way siblings spent their time. Margaret Cavendish, born in 1624, described how: '[My brothers'] practice was, when they met together, to exercise themselves with fencing, wrestling, shooting, and such like exercises, for I observed they did seldom hawk or hunt, and very seldom or never dance, or play on music, saying it was too effeminate for masculine spirits ... As for the pastimes of my sisters when they were in the country, it was to read, work, walk, and discourse with each other.'[67] Work, of course, meant needlework, the never-ending occupation of women and girls.

Girls did not always conform to expectations. In 1651, the landowner and politician Ralph Verney wrote to Dr Denton about the education of Denton's daughter Nancy, Verney's god-daughter, advising she should not learn Latin or shorthand, that the difficulty of the former 'may keep her from that vice, for so I must esteem it in a woman; but the easiness of the other may be a prejudice to her; for the pride of taking sermon notes, hath made multitudes of women most unfortunate. Doctor, teach her to live under obedience, and whilst she is unmarried, if she would learn anything, let her ask you, and afterwards her husband, *at home*.'

When Nancy refused to buckle, Verney again set out his advice, this time to Nancy herself:

> My dear child, – nothing but yourself could have been so welcome as
> your letter, nor have surprised me more, for I must confess I did not think
> you had been guilty of so much learning as I see you are; and yet it seems
> you rest unsatisfied or else you would not threaten Latin, Greek, and
> Hebrew too. Good sweetheart be not so covetous; believe me a Bible
> (with the Common Prayer) and a good plain catechism in your mother
> tongue being well read and practised, is well worth all the rest and much
> more suitable to your sex; I know your father thinks this false doctrine,
> but be confident your husband will be of my opinion.[68]

Nancy had the support of her father. But Verney was only, if in a pointed way, uttering a platitude: education for girls should be designed to fit them to become wives and to conform to the restrictions of that role.

Lucy Apsley was another girl with paternal support. She could read English perfectly when she was four and was famous for her ability to memorize sermons:

> When I was about seven years of age, I remember I had at one time eight
> tutors in several qualities, languages, music, dancing, writing, and needle-
> work, but my genius was quite averse from all but my book, and that I
> was so eager of, that my mother thinking it prejudiced my health, would
> moderate me in it; yet this rather animated me than kept me back, and
> every moment I could steal from my play I would employ in any book
> I could find, when my own were locked up from me. After dinner and
> supper I still had an hour allowed me to play, and then I would steal into
> some hole or other to read. My father would have me learn Latin, and
> I was so apt that I outstripped my brothers who were at school ... My
> brothers who had a great deal of wit, had some emulation at the progress
> I made in my learning, which very well pleased my father, though my
> mother would have been contented, I had no so wholly addicted myself to
> that as to neglect my other qualities; as for music and dancing I profited
> very little in them and would never practise my lute or harpsichords but
> when my masters were with me; and for my needle I absolutely hated it.[69]

Both Nancy Denton and Lucy Apsley were unusual and lucky in having the support of their fathers. At school level, the grammar schools, growing rapidly, offered girls few if any opportunities. Some excluded them formally. The founder's statutes for Uffington School in Berkshire in 1637 stated that sending daughters to be taught 'amongst all sorts of youth' was 'very uncomely and not decent' and they were excluded. Occasionally they might be allowed to attend for a year or two. In the early seventeenth century there were private boarding schools for girls on the outskirts of London, notably in Hackney. They taught reading, writing, music, dancing, needlework, household skills and perhaps some French and Latin. By the mid-seventeenth century all towns of any size were likely to have some kind of girls' academy, their curriculum geared to parental demand.[70] In 1647, Unton Dering wrote to his cousin Henry Oxinden, a Kent gentleman, recommending a school kept by a Mr Beven in Ashford for his daughters. Dering's own daughter had been there and done very well, and Beven received his endorsement: 'Besides the qualities of music both for the virginals and singing (if they have voices) and writing (and to cast account which will be useful to them hereafter) he will be careful also that their behaviour be modest and such as becomes their quality; and that they grow in knowledge and understanding for God and their duty to Him, which is above all.' Oxinden's daughters Elizabeth and Margaret, aged 11 and 12, duly went to Beven's school.[71]

Much more ambitious and unusual were the schools kept by one of the most learned women of her day, Mrs Bathsua Makin, at Putney and later Tottenham. She had been tutor to Charles I's daughter Elizabeth and deplored what she called the 'barbarous custom to breed women low'. She wanted to restore the standards that she felt had existed in the past. Her syllabus extended to optional Greek, Hebrew, Italian and Spanish, astronomy, geography, history and arithmetic.[72] Bathsua Makin was voicing a view that has some plausibility: that educational opportunities in the higher echelons of society may have been greater for women in the mid-sixteenth than in the seventeenth century.

The boarding schools existed only for a tiny minority of Stuart society. For the mass of girls the norm was to become servants of one kind or another in order to prepare them for the only vocation open to them: marriage. Some learnt the skills at home. But many left home in their mid-teens to enter into a succession of annual contracts as servants. This was the moment in effect when they put childhood behind them. They were not yet adults – that would come only with marriage, typically in their mid-twenties. A few became apprentices, but, as with schooling, the opportunities for girls seem to have been greater in the early sixteenth century than they were later, and the range of occupations open to them narrowed over time. In a town like Bristol only two or three in a hundred of the apprentices were female, and as many as two-thirds of these were orphans; apprenticeship seemed to offer the best chance of security for a girl without family support. Smaller towns might have a higher percentage of apprentices than Bristol, but formal apprenticeship was only for a small minority of girls.[73]

'Overburdened with children'

At their midsummer sessions held at Canterbury in 1601 the Kent Justices of the Peace considered the case of Constance Highwood. Their decision, recorded with the full majesty of the language of the law, was as follows:

> Item where the parishioners of Bethersden in this county by vertue of an order longe since made by the justices of peace assembled att the generall Quarter Sessions of the peace houlden for this county, have contributed towards the sustentacion and bringinge upp of Constance Highwood, an infante, one of the daughters of John Highwood, late of Woodchurche, deceassed, and have duly payd the same to the hands of one Burton of Woodchurche, aforesayd, who had the keepinge and bringing upp of her the sayd Constance from her infancy unto this tyme that she hath atteyned the age of (twelve yeres) and ys by the sayd Burton placed in service where she ys maynteyned and kept for her service; therefore att the humble request of the sayd parishioners of Bethersden, ytt ys ordered that they be no further charged with the sayd weekely contribucion but that the same shall cease from hencefourthe.[74]

Constance Highwood in this way leaves her tantalizingly light imprint on history. We know from it that her father had died, but nothing of her mother, or whether she had any brothers or sisters. Assuming her mother outlived her father, as a widow she would have struggled to bring up a child. As it was, Constance was raised from her infancy to the age of 12 by another inhabitant of Woodchurch, who was paid for her or his services by a rate charged to the wealthier inhabitants of Bethersden, the parish in which Woodchurch lay. Now, with Constance put out to service and earning her keep, the parishioners of Bethersden were relieved of any further payment.

Or take another typical case, this time from the Easter sessions held at Maidstone in 1634, where the 'court is well given to understand that a poore child conceived to bee about the age of 4 or 5 yeares, whoe affirmed it's name to bee Sam Clerke, was left and found in the church porch of Strowde in or about the beginninge of December last, the certeine parents thereof not being any wayes to bee as yet discovered or found out, nor the place of birth thereof.' We might guess that Sam Clerke's mother, perhaps a widow, had left him there, knowing that he would be found and then looked after. In this case the justices relieved the parish of Strowde, 'a poore parish', of financial responsibility for maintaining the abandoned little boy, but made provision 'as is meete and convenient' for looking after him.[75]

In these two little histories, which could be multiplied by many thousands in the parish and county records throughout England, we see the beginnings of two things that remain with us to this day: first, a recognition that children are particularly likely to feature among the poor, constituting up to a half of all those who were poor; and, second, a sense of obligation on the part of the community to do something about it. And alongside these two foretastes of a welfare state, we will find something else: a fear of what will happen if the state doesn't take care of children.

The poverty of children was nothing new in the sixteenth and seventeenth centuries, though it may have worsened, particularly in the sixteenth century. But the Middle Ages had known poverty. William Langland in *Piers Plowman*, written in about the 1360s, had described the hunger suffered by peasants and labourers in the early summer:

> 'I have no penny', quoth Piers, 'pullets to buy,
> Neither geese nor pigs, but two green [unripe] cheeses,
> And a few curds and cream and an unleavened cake,
> And a loaf of beans and bran baked for my children.'

Later, in the 1380s, he wrote of mothers making meal and milk porridge, 'To satisfy their children that cry for their food.' Langland took it for granted that families 'charged with children' would be in want.[76]

The formal proceedings on behalf of children that took up so much of the time of the Kent Justices in the seventeenth century had their origin nearly a century before, in the early sixteenth century. Population rise (England's population doubled between 1520 and 1680, Scotland's rose by about 50 per cent), and accompanying inflation and unemployment, seem to have led to an increase in vagrancy and begging that much alarmed both local and central authorities. Children were among the vagrants. An Act of Parliament of 1547 allowed for children of recalcitrant vagabonds and any beggar children aged between five and 14 wandering on their own to be taken away from their parents by 'any manner of person' who promised to keep them occupied up to the age of 20 for women and 24 for men. And should the apprentice run away and be recaptured, the master might put the child in chains and 'use him or her as his slave in all points until it came of age'. Slavery was thus made legal in England, and it was children who could be enslaved. True, the legislation was withdrawn two years later, slavery removed from the English statute book, but the principle of removing children of beggars from parental care remained.[77] And begging children there were. A group of 30 vagrants in Essex included 26 children, who had come from as far afield as Yorkshire, Lincolnshire and Cambridge. In Ipswich in 1597 two children aged six and three were sent out begging to add to the 6d a week that their mother earned by spinning, their father being unemployed.[78]

But it was not only adult men who were unemployed. So also were children. Children were much more numerous and visible than they are now, nearly one-third of the population being under 15. And there was a persistent concern that there were not enough jobs for them, and hence they drifted into begging. In 1536 an Act of Parliament included provisions that allowed parish authorities to take healthy but idle begging children aged five to 14 and apprentice them to masters in husbandry or other crafts.[79] In Salisbury, nearly a century later, the Orders for the Poor of 1626 included a rule 'That no child be suffered to beg but that all the children of the poor that are not able to relieve them be set to sewing, knitting, bonelace-making, spinning of woollen or linen yarn, pin-making, card-making, spooling, button-making, or some other handiwork as soon as ever they be capable of instruction to learn the same.'[80] You couldn't begin too early.

In these laws and policies rank social fear seems the dominant motif. Children are dangerous. They need to be put to work. But alongside this fear there is a concern for children. The two concerns, to bring order to every community and to provide care for impoverished individual children, are the two sides of a coin much in evidence in the sixteenth and seventeenth centuries. Spin it, and it might come down on the side of order. Spin it again, and anxiety for the child shines forth. Here, for example, in 1575 is John Hooker, the city chamberlain of Exeter, exhorting his fellow citizens to make provision for those he called the 'poor destituted and helpless children': 'It is lamentable to see what troupes and clusters of children, boyes and elder persons, lye loitering and floistering in every corner of the Citie, but more lamentable is that no care, no order nor redresse is had thereof, which if it be not looked unto in time, it will rebound to the peril of the publique state of your Citie.' Hooker was one of many in the sixteenth century who drew attention to the visibility of poor children. Thomas Anguish, a former mayor of Norwich, suitably named one feels, wrote desperately of the need for a place for the 'keeping, bringing up, and teaching of young and very poor children', especially, 'such as for want, lie in the streets, vaults, doors, and windows, whereby many of them fall into great and onerous diseases and lamenesses, as that they are fit for no profession, ever after'.[81]

The concern about poor children reached its legislative apogee in 1597 with a comprehensive Act for the Relief of the Poor, which was re-enacted with only slight modification in 1601. From the end of the sixteenth century until 1834, when it was amended and became known as 'the Old Poor Law', it determined the lives of countless children. Under it, the churchwardens and overseers of the poor in every parish were required to take measures to set to work and apprentice, not merely vagrant and destitute children but all children whose parents were thought not to be able to keep and maintain them. And the costs of such apprenticeship were to be paid for from a parish rate. It was under this Act that the Kent magistrates dealt with the cases of Constance Highwood and Sam Clerke. All these Acts of Parliament were confined in their scope to England and Wales. The Scottish parliament had passed an Act almost exactly similar to the English one of 1572, but did nothing to implement it. It was not that Scotland suffered less from poverty, but that it did not have the linkage of national government, county administration and the parish to enable it to do anything as comprehensive as was done in England, whose Poor Law was indeed unique in Europe. The Scots, like most Europeans, relied for help on charitable institutions and *ad hoc* fundraising.

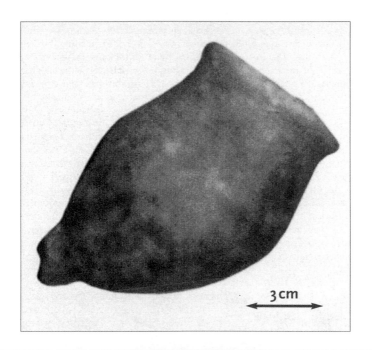

1 This bottle was found in a grave at Castledyke South on Humberside. It dates from the seventh century, shortly before Christianity arrived. Pagan Anglo-Saxons were usually buried with some grave goods. This bottle, with its perforated teat, provides evidence that there were alternatives to breast milk, though they were probably resorted to only if the mother had died or had difficulty in feeding.

2 A domestic scene from sixteenth-century France: mother with the swaddled baby, a toddler in a walking frame and another child tempting the dog. Fires were normally in the centre of rooms and coroners' records reveal that babies or toddlers left on their own all too frequently had accidents. Godparents at baptisms were told to ensure that parents safeguarded their child from fire and other dangers.

3 Very little is known about the recreations of girls, so this fourteenth-century picture of them playing blind man's buff is an invaluable glimpse into a shrouded world. The girl on the right, entering wholeheartedly into the game, is a far cry from the ideal behaviour set out for girls in conduct books or advice for parents.

4 A sixteenth-century image of boys enjoying themselves in a snowball fight that might come from any century. The boy in the middle, down on his right knee, looks as if he may be being set upon, even bullied, by the others, one of whom has an armoury of ready-made snowballs in his pouch.

Dominus sapientia fundavit terra est.

5 A boy in a cherry tree from the Luttrell Psalter (1335–40). The boy, having left his rather elegant pointed shoes down on the ground, is helping himself to the abundant fruit on the cherry tree, but is perhaps about to have a blow inflicted upon him by the angry adult. Alexander Barclay wrote: 'Behold the little boys/How in fruit season for joy they sing and hop.'

6 *Edward VI* by Hans Holbein the Younger. Painted in about 1538, when Edward, son of Henry VIII and Jane Seymour, was some 15 months old, this is a dynastic portrait. The gilt rattle that Edward holds is more like the sceptre of an adult king than something suitable for a young child. Translated, the Latin verses underneath begin: 'Little one, emulate thy father and be the heir of his virtue; the world contains nothing greater. Heaven and earth could scarcely produce a son whose glory would surpass that of a father.'

7 An illustration from *A Text Book in Ye History of Education* (*c.* 1600). From the earliest records through to its abolition in 1987, corporal punishment was a feature of the classroom. Schoolmasters in medieval and early modern times were always depicted with their instruments of chastisement. Boys, if they were not being actually beaten (left), were always aware of what might be their fate (right).

8 *The Capel Family* (*c.* 1640) by Cornelius Johnson. With its elaborate gardens in the background, this painting seems as much concerned to draw attention to the social status of the family as to depict the individuality of its members. The boys are with their father, the girls and baby with their mother – though she is looking away from them towards the son and heir.

LEFT

9 Monument of Thomas Andrews (d. 1590), Charwelton, Northamptonshire. Tombstones often portrayed the children of a deceased parent. However, this one perhaps suggests a new sentiment about children. The youngest daughter (left) is not kneeling but standing to keep a watch on her youngest brother, should he fall.

BELOW

10 *The Graham Children* (1742). Hogarth's painting of the children of Dr Daniel Graham, apothecary to George II and the Chelsea Hospital, picks up the individuality of each child. Richard plays an organ, Anna Maria is dancing, while her elder sister, Henrietta, looks after Thomas, seated in a go-cart. By the time the painting was completed, Thomas had died.

11 *The Age of Innocence* (*c.* 1788) by Joshua
Reynolds. Reynolds's portrait of his great-niece,
Offy, is typical of romantic paintings of children
in the late eighteenth century. Seated in the
countryside, Offy is spotlit, the dark background
hinting that the age of innocence, as the painting
became known in the 1790s, will not last.
Much reproduced, it deeply influenced how
children were portrayed in the nineteenth and
twentieth centuries.

12 *The Wood Children* (*c.* 1789) by Joseph
Wright. Hugh and Sarah Wood of Swanwick,
Derbyshire, commissioned this painting of
their three children. Mary is playing bat and
ball with her brothers, John (left) and Robert,
who looks a little condescending, the weight of
being the heir on his shoulders. Their clothing
is light and not likely to restrict movement.

13 'Infant Joy', plate 25 from *Songs of Innocence and of Experience* (*c.* 1815–26) by William Blake. The luxuriant plant, its vast petal holding mother, baby and an angel, envelops the words of Blake's poem, a celebration of life at its outset and of mother's love. 'I happy am/ Joy is my name,' says the baby. 'Sweet joy I call thee,' replies the mother. 'Thou dost smile/ I sing the while/Sweet joy befall thee.' These lines are from *Songs of Innocence*, first published in 1789. The darker side of life was portrayed in *Songs of Experience* (1794).

14 The earliest surviving sampler dates back to 1598. Originally the work of adults, from the mid-eighteenth century girls learnt to embroider on printed pattern books. In the nineteenth century samplers were often framed and hung. In this example from 1789, nine-year-old Mary Ann Body imagines a world where 'all Mankind would live in mutual love'.

THE MOTHERS HOPE

ABOVE

15 *A matron old, whom we school-mistress name*
(1791) in a tableau by Frances Wheatley inspired
by 'The School-Mistress', a poem by William
Shenstone. Dame schools were where many
children learnt to read. Later heavily criticized,
here there is a sympathetic, almost sentimental,
rendering, in line with the poet's wish to show
'how modest worth neglected lies'. The setting,
in the old matron's home, is informal and
domestic, the cat as prominent as the children
queuing up to spell out their alphabets.

LEFT

16 *The Mothers Hope* (1808) by T. Rowlandson.
Rowlandson's spoiled child, throwing toys on
the ground, and announcing that 'I won't go to
school. I will stay at home. I will have my own
way in everything!!' is a useful reminder that
not all children in the late eighteenth and early
nineteenth century were as angelic as Reynolds's
great-niece (plate 11). The carer, half-admiring,
thinks that the child may turn out to be 'a
second Buonaparte'.

National initiatives had been paralleled and sometimes prompted by local ones. In London, in the mid-sixteenth century, Christ's Hospital was converted from medieval monastic use 'to take oute of the streates all the fatherless children and other poor men's children, that were not able to kepe them'. Initially clad in a livery of russet cotton and lining the route taken by the lord mayor to St Paul's, they were by Easter 1553 clothed in the blue that has ever since been associated with Christ's Hospital. Closely connected with it was Bridewell, which aimed 'to train up the beggar's child in virtuous exercise, that of him should spring no more beggars'.[82] Samuel Pepys in 1664 was there on business and 'did with great pleasure see the many pretty works and the little children imployed, everyone to do something; which was a very fine sight and worthy incouragement. I cast away a Crowne among them.'[83] In Norwich, modelling itself on Christ's Hospital, Thomas Anguish's pleas led to the opening of a Children's Hospital in 1621, not primarily a medical institution, though it had that role, but a place of sanctuary and training for children aged between five and 12. Norwich was famous for its provisions for poor children. Public money went to the support of sick children. Parents could ask the city to chastise children whom they couldn't control. A mother who beat a child too hard had it removed from her custody. Above all, there was extensive input into the apprenticeship of poor children, with a recognition that some children had a better case than others, especially those who had lost their fathers. During the apprenticeship, masters, the city insisted, had responsibility for the health of their apprentices.[84]

How far all these measures helped to resolve the problem of child poverty is uncertain. When contemporaries, as they did, tried to count the numbers of the poor, children always loomed large. A survey of poverty in London in 1552, found 350 'poor men overburdened with their children'. In Harlow, Essex, towards the end of the sixteenth century some employed men needed relief because they were 'greatly charged with young children'.[85] We, in the twenty-first century, are not the first to find that children are expensive. It is often thought that in pre-industrial economies children are an asset, and indeed they can be, but there are times in the life cycle when families with children are likely to be in great difficulty. The eldest child in a family might begin to earn something when it reached about seven – certainly in the Norwich textile industry they were thought able to earn by that age – but by then younger siblings would be putting a strain on the family budget. It has been estimated that it was only in the eighteenth year of a marriage that a family would be in net profit from its children[86] – a very long-term investment even if we think, and we would almost certainly be wrong to do so, that parents thought economically when conceiving their offspring.

The ambitious hopes that institutions like Bridewell could gain economic viability through the labour of their children nearly all foundered. In Bristol where children were put to work in a workhouse, 'our Children could not get half so much as we expended in their Provisions'. Begging, it began to be realized, was the outcome of 'the low Wages of Labour' not of idleness. 'Our Boys and Girls are educated to Sobriety, and brought up to delight in Labour,' trumpeted the Bristol report, but we may perhaps doubt whether the boys and girls felt quite as much delight as was imputed to them.[87]

In desperation the authorities turned to other remedies. For the first time in our story, but not the last, the empire seemed as though it might provide a solution. In 1617 the Lord Mayor of London instituted a charitable collection to raise money to send 100 poor children to the colonies. James I added his support, writing to Sir John Smith, who was about to become governor of Virginia, how London

> hath been troubled with divers idle young people whoe although they have been twise punished still continewe to followe the same haoeing noe ymploymente. Wee haveinge noeother course to cleere our court from them have thought fitt to send them unto you, desireing you att the next oportunitie to send them away to Virginia and to take such order that they may be sett to worke there, wherein you shall onlie doe us good service, but also doe a deed of charitie by ymploying them whoe otherwise will never be reclaimed from the idle life of vagabonds.

In 1627 it was reported that 'There are many ships now going to Virginia, and with them, some 1400 or 1500 children, which they have gathered up in diverse places.' Some parents and children protested at this fate, but the children were sent nevertheless, the Privy Council giving power to 'such as shall have the charge of this service to imprison, punish, and dispose any of those children, upon any disorder by them committed, as cause shall require, and so to shipp them out for Virginia with as much expedition as may stand with convenience'. Many of the children died *en route*; few survived to adulthood.

As one contemporary put it, 'It is to be feared that nearly all of them were persons on whom charity descended as a heavy penalty rather than a gentle mercy.'[88]

By the end of the seventeenth century about 5 per cent of the total population of England and Wales could be supported by the poor rates and others by charity.[89] Children almost certainly received a more than proportionate use of this. It is perhaps a fair guess that about one in ten children would at any one point in time be receiving some help from the Poor Law or charity. Some of them must have wondered what was happening to them. In 1700 it was reported that George, Mary and Eve Smith, three poor children, the eldest not more than six, had been moved from Southampton to Canterbury and back again eight times as each city denied its responsibility for their upkeep. This was the Poor Law at its bureaucratic worst. But consider more positively the resident population of the Kent parish of Headcorn in that same year, 1700. Relief was given for John Kemp's two boys, Henry, aged six, and William, aged three, who were put out to keep by the parish. Perhaps they were orphans, or John a widower, not able to bring up his children. John Elger, aged 70, perhaps beyond the age when he could expect to earn much, and his wife, aged 38, received help for their children, Mary, a lame girl aged 13, James, eight, Thomas, seven, and Sarah, three. Richard Baker and his wife had five children and were at the critical point in the life cycle, the eldest, Mary, aged 11, the youngest Susannah, only one. Mary Wood, a 33-year-old widow, received help for her three children aged between nine and six.[90] This was a society where everyone knew everyone, and where the poor could expect some assistance when age, disability, the death of a wage earner or simply too many young children made life difficult.

Chapter Three

The Eighteenth Century

THE EIGHTEENTH CENTURY is often taken to begin with the 'Glorious Revolution' of 1688–9. It put an end to the danger that the Stuarts might try to impose Catholicism. It also ushered in new approaches to childhood, the most telling sign being the publication in 1693 of the philosopher John Locke's *Some Thoughts Concerning Education*. There were threats, in 1715 and 1745, to the Protestant constitutional monarchy established in 1689, but over the course of the eighteenth century the inhabitants of the British Isles gained in confidence and pride in their country. Moreover, with the union of England and Scotland in 1707, they could for the first time in our history begin to think of themselves as 'Britons'. The incentive to do so was heightened by the frequency of war with France, a kind of second Hundred Years War that Britain won decisively at Trafalgar in 1805 and Waterloo in 1815. The eighteenth century is the century in which Britain rose to global dominance, a position with multiple consequences for children and how they were regarded. For a start, if some kind of Protestant providence had raised Britain to this position, it was incumbent on Britons to live up to the ideals that had made God favour them. Above all, this meant a public display of British charity for children in need.

Charity and children

Tom Grenville was a foundling. He was also blind. His early years were spent in the care of the Foundling Hospital in London. Like other foundlings, children whose parents had abandoned them, he would first have lived in the country with a foster family before returning to the imposing Foundling Hospital when he was somewhere between three and five. The hospital aimed to train children in its care for some useful occupation. What future awaited a blind boy? When Tom was seven in 1753 the governors of the hospital agreed that he should be taught a harpsichord that had been given to the hospital so that he might become 'a performer of Musick in the Chapel'. It was an inspired decision. Tom learnt so well that in 1758 the governors authorized payment of two guineas a quarter so that Tom could be taught to play the organ. In 1767, when he was 21, Tom left the hospital to become organist for the parish of Ross in Herefordshire. In 1773 he came back as the hospital organist and was paid £40 a year, raised to £50 in 1796. He married and had one son and two daughters. When he resigned to become organist for a parish church, the governors found it very difficult to replace him. In his later years, when he fell on hard times, the governors granted him a pension of £10 a year, later increased to £20, until his death in 1827.[1]

Tom Grenville is a fine example of how a charity could help a poor child. In the seventeenth century the story of children in poverty is dominated by the introduction and spread of the Poor Law. In the eighteenth century the focus of attention switched to what contemporaries called 'associated philanthropy'. Rather than an individual founding a school or supporting scholars, more could be achieved, it came to be thought, by a group of people coming together to form a society with a specific object in mind. It was not that the Poor Law was any less important in the lives of the poor, nor that the way it was implemented faded from public discussion. Rather, added on to it, and rather more glamorous, were the new organizations of 'associated philanthropy'.

The Foundling Hospital in London, opened in 1741, was not the first example of associated philanthropy in Britain, but for many years it was the most famous. In Catholic Europe, in Italy, France and Spain, there were many foundling hospitals, some dating back to the fourteenth century. Yet Britain had never had one. Christ's Hospital, as we saw, took foundlings when it opened in 1552, but none had been admitted since 1676. Supporters of foundling hospitals said that they allowed a woman who had an illegitimate baby to preserve her honour by abandoning her baby, anonymously, to the hospital; that they helped to prevent what might all too likely have been the alternative, infanticide. Critics said that they encouraged immorality; only the ever present threat of ruin would stop an avalanche of bastards. And yet no-one could pretend that there was not a problem in Britain. In 1715 there was a House of Commons report on the parish of St Martin-in-the-Fields in London where more than three-quarters of the infants in care under the Poor Law died every year: 'a great many poor Infants, and exposed Bastard Children, are inhumanly suffered to die by the Barbarity of Nurses, especially Parish Nurses, who are a sort of People void of Commiseration, or Religion; hired by the Churchwardens to take off a Burthen from the Parish at the cheapest and easiest Rates they can; and these know the Manner of doing it effectually, as by the Burial Books may evidently appear.'[2] The infants, to put it at its kindest, seemed to be being allowed to die to save on the rates.

In 1722, Thomas Coram decided to do something about the babies he saw abandoned in the streets. Born in 1668 in Lyme Regis, Coram had been sent to sea when he was 11 and then, when he was 16, became apprenticed to a shipwright in London. After a career of ups and downs, much of it spent in America, by the 1720s Coram was settled in London, where he began a campaign for a foundling hospital. It was nearly 20 years later that his efforts bore fruit. In 1741, the lease of a house in Hatton Garden having been secured, a public notice went up: 'The governors give notice, that on Wednesday, the 25th March, at 8 o'clock at night, and from that time till the House should be full, their House will be opened for the reception of Children ... no questions whatsoever shall be asked of any person bringing a child.'

By about midnight, the house was full (it had a capacity for 30 infants), and some disappointed mothers with their children, still waiting out in the street, had to be turned away. As the Minutes of the Hospital put it, 'the Expressions of Grief of the Women whose Children could not be admitted were Scarcely more observable than those of some of the Women who parted with their Children, so that a more moving Scene can't well be imagined.'[3] The infants, if they seemed to be healthy, were sent off to nurses in Yorkshire, Staines and Egham, and then returned to London or to one of the six branch hospitals, as far away as Ackworth in Yorkshire or Shrewsbury. There, from the age of three upwards, they would be educated and trained, the boys mostly for service at sea, the girls for household service.[4]

In the 1740s and 1750s foundlings were fashionable. There was a famous one in fiction, Henry Fielding's *The History of Tom Jones, A Foundling* coming out in 1749. And the Foundling Hospital itself attracted much attention. Built on open land in north London, it became a magnet for the fashionable, who came to make donations, to gaze at the children, to hear the music of Handel and to see the paintings of Hogarth. What the children made of all this we cannot know. But they were not encouraged to have high expectations of what might become of them. It was the governors' intention that children should learn to accept 'with Contentment the most Servile and laborious Offices; for notwithstanding the innocence of the Children, yet as they are exposed and abandoned by their Parents, they ought to submit to the lowest stations, and should not be educated in such a manner as may put them upon a level with the Children of Parents who have the humanity and Virtue to preserve them, and the Industry to Support them.'[5]

Later, and Tom Grenville was a beneficiary of this, the governors became more relaxed about the kind of education children could receive. And even if the jobs the foundlings got might be lowly ones, the hospital continued to keep a watching eye over its charges after they had left to become apprenticed – but sometimes their intervention came only after the apprentice had suffered. Sarah Drew reported that her master, Job Wyatt, a wood-screw maker of Tatenhill 'had attempted to debauch her at Eleven Years of Age and completed it afterwards and continued the same ill Usage till Xmas last & beat her if she refus'd to submit to his Will. That she likewise was inform'd her Master had also debauch'd several other Apprentices amongst whom were Mary Johnson, Mary Rise and Ann Beauchamp who often talk'd of it to her.' The governors immediately applied to the local magistrates for the discharge of their apprentices bound to Wyatt.[6]

There were always more children being brought for admission to the Foundling Hospital than could be accepted. Admission was by lottery, and on each receiving day there was, though within doors now, a repetition of the scene on the opening night. On 15 November 1745, for example, 57 children were brought but only 18 admitted. Most of these children were illegitimate, but as many as one in three were legitimate, the parents presumably driven by poverty to abandon their child. Many left tokens on the child, intending to reclaim it when circumstances allowed, and a small number, three or four a year, were returned to their parents.[7]

In 1756 the governors persuaded parliament, perhaps worried about fears of a declining population, to give a grant to the hospital, and for the next five years there was an open-door policy. The results were not encouraging. Mortality rates escalated; eight out of every ten babies admitted died.[8] In 1760 the parliamentary grant came to an end, and a restricted entry policy was re-introduced. But the gloss that had surrounded the Foundling Hospital in its early days now faded, and it came under attack.

The Foundling Hospital had been preceded by an example of 'associated philanthropy' that outlasted it in public esteem. The Society for the Propagation of Christian Knowledge was founded in 1699 by Anglican laymen to set up 'charity schools' for the children of the poor, teaching them religion, reading and writing. They were an immediate success, and by 1729 there were 1419 such schools with over 22,000 pupils. The driving force behind the charity schools was less a concern for the individual children than a fear of Catholicism. Every charity school, it was hoped, would become 'a Fortress and a Frontier Garrison against Popery'. The schools were also seen as an answer to a problem that had been endemic and much commented on, since Tudor times: the idleness of children and the lack of jobs for them. Children on the streets had long been seen as a threat, particularly in towns. In London, in the seventeenth century, it was said, there were children who 'lie all day in the streets, playing, cursing [and] swearing'. The archdeacon of Huntingdon, preaching to the children themselves in 1706, declared that 'The greatest Disorders in any Neighbourhood do most commonly proceed from the Folly of Children'. In the eighteenth century the poet William Cowper, in the small town of Olney in Buckinghamshire, lamented that 'children of seven years of age infest the streets every evening with curses and with songs'. There were numerous attempts in the eighteenth century to impose some controls, to get the street children into some structured work or schooling: charity schools were the first attempt at national level to do something about the problem.

By the 1720s the early emphasis on teaching Christianity had begun to be overtaken by another: the need to put the children to work. In 1722 the society's secretary, Henry Newman, claimed that 'twenty four years of experience had shewn that a working school is in all respects preferable to one without labour and more in keeping with the present trend of public opinion'. And no more than the Foundling Hospital did the charity schools aim to encourage social mobility. In 1733 supporters were assured that: 'The utmost care [is taken] not only to instruct the children in the knowledge of the Christian religion, but also to breed them up in such a manner that as they are descended from the laborious part of mankind, they may be bred up and inured to the meanest services.'[9]

And yet, despite or perhaps because of this outlook, the charity schools, like the Foundling Hospital, became the focus for much self-congratulatory celebration. There was nothing that so moved an eighteenth-century fashionable assembly as the sight of charity children, in their neat uniforms, on parade to be viewed by their social superiors. Every year, from 1704, and on special occasions, such as the public thanksgiving for the passing of the Treaty of Utrecht in 1713, the charity children paraded through London to a church service. Here is how *The Times* anticipated it in 1788: 'This day will again bring to the sight of Englishmen one of the most glorious objects of their pride; six thousand children seated like an angelic choir round the dome of St. Paul's, with one voice, proclaiming their gratitude to their God and Nation, not merely for the clothing of their bodies, but for that which passeth shew, the education and culture of their minds.' This would be a sight that 'foreigners must behold with wonder, but which Englishmen must feel with pride, when they reflect that no nation upon the face of the earth can produce its parallel'.

The charity children were being commandeered to the service of the nation. What did they themselves think about it? Their voices could be heard in song, but what they actually felt, we don't know. What we do know is that the annual festival required considerable organization. There were strict regulations that 'the Children have nothing improper to eat, and that they do not take any thing in their pockets to the Cathedral on that morning'. Perhaps even more important, it was essential 'to prevent the Parents or Relations of the Charity Children appearing in public with the Children on that day'. Charity demanded that the children be seen as orphans, not, as the vast majority of them were, the children of impoverished parents.[10] William Blake, like everyone else, was moved by the spectacle, but saw more in it than his contemporaries. Here, in his *Songs of Innocence*, he describes what he saw:

'Twas on a Holy Thursday, their innocent faces clean,
The children walking two & two, in red & blue & green,
Grey-headed beadles walk'd before, with wands as white as snow,
Till into the high dome of Paul's they like Thames' waters flow.

O what a multitude they seem'd, these flowers of London town!
Seated in companies they sit with radiance all their own.
The hum of multitudes was there, but multitudes of lambs,
Thousands of little boys & girls raising their innocent hands.

Now like a mighty wind they raise to heaven the voice of song,
Or like harmonious thunderings the seats of heaven among.
Beneath them sit the aged men, wise guardians of the poor;
Then cherish pity, lest you drive an angel from your door.

This, but for the last line, seems to reinforce the self-congratulatory mood. But read it alongside its partner in *Songs of Experience*, and a very different picture comes through. There the emphasis is on the poverty, misery and lack of sunshine in the lives of the children of the poor:

Is this a holy thing to see
In a rich and fruitful land,
Babes reduc'd to misery,
Fed with cold and usurous hand?

Is that trembling cry a song?
Can it be a song of joy?
And so many children poor?
It is a land of poverty!

And their sun does never shine,
And their fields are black & bare,
And their ways are fill'd with thorns;
It is eternal winter there.[11]

Most people, unlike Blake but like *The Times*, took comfort from Holy Thursday, rejoicing in patriotic pride. But alongside the annual celebration in prose and verse there remained the old worry about the idleness and misbehaviour of children. A favoured solution in the late eighteenth century was the accurately named schools of industry. In these, work was found for young children. An official committee in 1775 argued 'That the employing of the infant and able Poor in such Works as may be suited to their Strength and Capacity will be very beneficial to this Kingdom. [From the age of four, these infants] shall be sent to the House to which such Parish or Place shall belong, to be instructed in all necessary Duties, and employed in such Manner as shall be most suitable to their Age and Capacities.'[12]

All suggestions of this kind, including Prime Minister William Pitt's belief in 1796 that 'Experience had already shown how much could be done by the industry of children', carried the authority of a major figure in European thought: John Locke.[13] As late as 1817 a select committee on the Poor Laws reprinted – because of its 'high authority' – Locke's recommendations to the Board of Trade 120 years earlier, in 1697: 'The children of the labouring people are an ordinary burthen to the parish, and are usually maintained in idleness, so that their labour also is generally lost to the public, till they are twelve or fourteen years old.' His idea was to establish working schools in each parish for all children 'above three and under fourteen years of age' while they lived at home with their parents and were not otherwise earning a wage. This way the children would be kept on the straight and narrow, be better provided for and 'from their infancy be inured to work, which is of no small consequence to the making them sober and industrious all their lives after. [They should be fed] their bellyful of bread daily at school with, in cold weather, if it be needful, a little warm water-gruel.'[14]

Locke's recommendations remained a benchmark. Associated philanthropy might help rescue some children, particularly foundlings, but it could not cope with the nation-wide poverty of children. For them, the Poor Law remained crucial for survival; increasingly the price to be paid was the labour of the children. The John Locke of these recommendations to the Board of Trade was the same man who gained an even wider reputation for his liberal advice on child rearing.

Mr Locke and Monsieur Rousseau

One day in the late 1760s, the philanthropist and author Thomas Day and his friend John Bicknell turned up at the Shrewsbury orphanage. Day had been deeply influenced by Jean-Jacques Rousseau's *Émile* published in 1762, and he wanted to see if he could put its principles into practice. For this he needed a child, one who could be brought up like Sophie in *Émile*, and in due course become his wife. Day chose an attractive 11-year-old from the orphanage and renamed her Sabrina Sidney, Sabrina in honour of the River Severn, Sidney for the seventeenth-century republican martyr. To keep within the law he bound her apprentice to another friend, Richard Edgeworth, though without seeking his prior permission. Day then went to the Foundling Hospital in London, where, as a kind of insurance, he acquired a second girl, Lucretia, as he named her. Day and the two girls then took off to France, to Avignon, where a course of education was put in train. Sabrina, in a dictated letter, her writing skills not yet very advanced, told Edgeworth how 'I know how to make a circle and an equilateral triangle – I know the cause of night and day, winter and summer. I love Mr Day best in the world, Mr Bicknell next, and you next.'

But soon things began to go wrong. The girls constantly quarrelled with one another, and they caught smallpox. Day returned to England with them in the spring of 1770 and, disappointed with Lucretia, apprenticed her to a London milliner. Sabrina was then put through a series of tests to see if she had acquired a Rousseauian standard of hardiness: hot sealing wax was dropped on to her bare arms, pistols fired at her petticoats. Sabrina sensibly failed these tests, was found to be taking a depraved interest in millinery and was packed off to a boarding school in Sutton Coldfield. Eight years later, John Bicknell married her, and when he died three years later she went to work as a housekeeper for novelist and diarist Fanny Burney's brother, Charles, and was much loved.[15]

If this story had been fiction it might have been thought too far-fetched to have any credibility. It is an indication of the influence that a book can exercise over child rearing. And *Émile* was not the first book to have such an influence. It was written in some ways as a response to another equally famous book, also written by an eminent philosopher: John Locke's *Some Thoughts Concerning Education*. Locke's book began as a series of private letters to a friend, Edward Clarke, on how he should rear his son. A middle-aged bachelor, Locke had taught at Oxford University and had then entered the household of Anthony Ashley Cooper, Earl of Shaftesbury, where, qualified in medicine, he helped to rear and tutor the earl's sickly child, and in due course his grandchildren. His reputation spread, and other fathers entrusted their sons to his care. So it was no surprise that Edward Clarke, a landed gentleman from Somerset, and a distant relative by marriage, should, in 1684, turn to Locke for advice. The letters Locke wrote began to circulate outside the Clarke family, and eventually, in 1693, Locke was persuaded to publish them. In this way a series of letters to a friend became, in the eighteenth century, one of the most famous and influential books on how to rear a child. In a fifth edition by 1705, shortly after Locke's death, by 1777 it was in its fifteenth edition. It was translated into French and Dutch before the end of the seventeenth century, and into German, Italian and Swedish in the course of the eighteenth century.[16]

If we read Locke now, we are drawn both backwards and forwards in time. Backwards to the courtesy literature that flourished in the late Middle Ages. This aimed to teach the young how to behave properly at table or in the presence of elders and superiors. It was rejuvenated by the humanists in the Renaissance, Erasmus, for example, writing a famous tract of this kind that remained popular into the nineteenth century. Erasmus also addressed parents, reflecting, in a very similar way to Locke two centuries later, on the necessity of starting education early in life and on the ways in which an educator can influence a child who is, like wax, easily moulded. Anselm, archbishop of Canterbury at the turn of the eleventh and twelfth centuries, had also used the wax image, but he had thought it was in adolescence rather than in infancy that someone was like wax. Erasmus said you couldn't start too early: 'The child that nature has given you is nothing but a shapeless lump, but the material is still pliable, capable of assuming any form, and you must so mould it that it takes on the best possible character. If you are negligent, you will rear an animal; but if you apply yourself, you will fashion, if I may use such a bold term, a godlike creature.'[17]

So, many of Locke's ideas have little claim to originality. And if we look forwards in time, to the twenty-first century, we will find in some of the advice literature distinct echoes of Locke. For what Locke insisted on was the desirability of inculcating good habits, and that could only be achieved by insisting on the authority of the parents as 'Absolute Governors':

> It seems plain to me, that the Principle of all Vertue and Excellency lies
> in a power of denying our selves the satisfaction of our own Desires,
> where Reason does not authorize them. This Power is to be got and
> improved by Custom, made easy and familiar by an *early* Practice.
> If therefore I might be heard, I would advise, that, contrary to the ordinary
> way, Children should be used to submit their Desires, and go without
> their Longings, even *from their Cradles*. The first thing they should learn
> to know should be, that they were not to have any thing, because it
> pleased them, but because it was thought fit for them. If things suitable
> to their Wants were supplied to them, so that they were never suffered to
> have what they once cried for, they would learn to be content without it;
> would never with Bawling and Peevishness contend for Mastery; nor be
> half so uneasy to themselves and others as they are, because *from the first*
> Beginning they are not thus handled. If they were never suffered to obtain
> their Desire by the Impatience they expressed for it, they would no more
> cry for other Things, than they do for the Moon.[18]

Aware that an insistence on parents being 'Absolute Governors' of their children might sound a little harsh, Locke quickly goes on to soften the message: children must 'be tenderly used ... must play, and have Play-things'. And there should be careful observation to find out a child's natural disposition, its 'natural Genius and Constitution'. Above all, there should be an almost total ban on corporal punishment.[19] What is needed is the inculcation of a habit that leads to the constant deferment of gratification. The goal in child rearing is to produce a good and rational adult, capable of fulfilling her or his role in the niche marked out by social rank; in the case of Clarke's son, Locke was aiming to produce an English gentleman.

Within this overall schema, Locke's recommendations range from the eccentric to what we are likely to think of as thoroughly sensible. Few modern parents are likely to follow Locke's advice that a child's feet be washed every day in cold water, and that his shoes should be so thin that they leak and let in water whenever he comes near it. All this was designed to toughen the body. There is rather more resonance in his comments on children's clothes:

> The Coverings of our Bodies, which are for Modesty, Warmth, and Defence; are, by the Folly or Vice of Parents, recommended to their Children for other Uses. They are made Matter of Vanity and Emulation. A Child is set a longing after a new Suit, for the Finery of it: And when the little Girl is tricked up in her new Gown and Commode [a tall head-dress], how can her Mother do less than teach her to Admire her self, by calling her, *her little Queen* and *her Princess*? Thus the little ones are taught to be *Proud* of their Clothes, before they can put them on. And why should they not continue to value themselves for this out-side Fashionableness of the Taylor or Tire-woman's [dressmaker] making, when their Parents have so early instructed them to do so?[20]

Most of Locke's work is on how children learn. 'I have always had a Fancy', he wrote, 'that *Learning* might be made a Play and Recreation to Children.' Get an ivory ball with 25 sides to it and paste on the letters, and make it a game to see who can roll an A, a B or a C and so on. Then replace the letters with syllables, and soon the child will learn to read. But what was a child then to read? Locke recommended *Aesop's Fables* with pictures and *Reynard the Fox*, the latter originating as a satire on German feudal society and published in an English translation by William Caxton in 1481, two centuries before Locke gave it his imprimatur.[21]

Locke writes with an underlying passion. He had seen so many parents making mistakes and setting a child's life off in the wrong direction. All too often, he felt, the fault lay with servants who spoilt their charges or would tell them about goblins in the dark, frightening them in a harmful way. Mothers, with their 'Cockering and Tenderness', were not much better. And child rearing was so important: 'Nine Parts of Ten, are what they are, Good or Evil, useful or not, by their Education,' the kind of sentence to resonate among anxious or ambitious parents.[22]

It is easy to see why Locke's book had such an impact. It provided useful day-to-day advice within an overarching vision of how a child developed. And it carried on its cover the enormous authority of the name of John Locke. One sign of that authority was that in the 1740s in Samuel Richardson's *Pamela*, one of the first English novels, the heroine gives her views on Locke's educational ideas at inordinate length. The narrative drive, such as it is, is suspended for some 70 pages.[23]

If Locke, as a bachelor, might seem under-qualified to pronounce on children's upbringing, what can be said for Rousseau, who had abandoned all of his children to a foundling hospital? Rousseau, who loved paradox, would have accepted the irony that he became known as an expert on child rearing. His book is a scarcely veiled attack on all that Locke stood for. 'The wisest writers', he wrote, 'devote themselves to what a man ought to know, without asking what a child is capable of learning. They are always looking for the man in the child, without considering what he is before he becomes a man.'[24]

'We know nothing of childhood,' says Rousseau. But of course Rousseau thought he did. In child rearing, 'reverse the usual practice and you will almost always do right'. Don't follow Locke's advice, 'in the height of fashion at present', to reason with a child. Let a child grow up in accordance with the dictates of nature, not being told things, but learning that fire burns or that stones are hard. Don't get caught up in conversations like this one:

> *Master.* You must not do that.
> *Child.* Why not?
> *Master.* Because it is wrong.
> *Child.* Wrong! What is wrong?
> *Master.* What is forbidden you.
> *Child.* Why is it wrong to do what is forbidden?
> *Master.* You will be punished for disobedience.

> *Child.* I will do it when no one is looking.
> *Master.* We shall watch you.
> *Child.* I will hide.
> *Master.* We shall ask you what you were doing.
> *Child.* I shall tell a lie.
> *Master.* You must not tell lies.
> *Child.* Why must not I tell lies?
> *Master.* Because it is wrong.

If we are going to try to reason with a child, this, says Rousseau, is 'the inevitable circle'. How to avoid it 'would have puzzled Locke himself'. Rousseau of course has the shocking answer: 'It is no part of a child's business to know right and wrong.'[25]

Read on in Rousseau and there are more shocks to come. Mothers' blind love and indulgence of their children is much less harmful than 'the mistaken foresight of fathers'; 'Reading is the curse of childhood.'[26] We should do nothing to stimulate the imagination, which only conjures up desires that are beyond our capacity to achieve them and leads to unhappiness. Childhood is the one time of life in which we can be happy and should be treasured as such: 'Love childhood, indulge its sports, its pleasures, its delightful instincts. Who has not sometimes regretted that age when laughter was ever on the lips, and when the heart was ever at peace? Why rob these innocents of the joys which pass so quickly, of that precious gift which they cannot abuse? Why fill with bitterness the fleeting days of early childhood, days which will no more return for them than for you.'[27]

Locke and Rousseau are sometimes seen as stepping-stones on the road to modern ideas about children. In fact they offer two opposing views of how children should be reared, and the debate between them has never been resolved. Do you as a parent or teacher concentrate most on the adult in the making, or do you cherish childhood for its own sake, letting adulthood take care of itself?

Locke wrote about his friend's son. Émile was a boy. Locke occasionally acknowledges the existence of girls, but doesn't think his schema will need to be altered much to meet their needs. With the major exception, of course, that the boy's sister will be brought up to be an English lady not an English gentleman. As for Rousseau's Émile, in due course he needs a female partner, and we are introduced to Sophie. And if Sophie too learns from things, she somehow learns very different things from Émile. Rousseau, so radical in many things, was here entirely conventional: 'The man should be strong and active; the woman should be weak and passive.'[28]

Many people tried to bring up their children on the principles enshrined in Locke and Rousseau. Most of them were much more discriminating than Thomas Day. They were not slavish adherents. Richardson's Pamela, for example, had many perceptive criticisms of Locke – and would have nothing to do with the leaking shoes argument. Caroline Fox reported of her seven-year-old son: 'Dear little Harry is a pleasant child ... he really works very hard all day out of doors, which is very wholesome and quite according to Monsr. Rousseau's system. He eats quantities of fish and is so happy and pleased all day. At night we depart a little from Monsr. Rousseau's plan, for he reads fairy-tales and learns geography on the Beaumont wooden maps; he is vastly quick at learning that or anything else.'[29]

So Locke and Rousseau certainly had an influence. But we know that today parents do not always follow the prescriptions of the advice books. How far was there in the eighteenth century a change in parenting practice to match the advice being given?

'Papa', 'dear Mama'
In 1779, the biographer, diarist and travel writer James Boswell recorded a conversation he had with his six-year-old daughter, Veronica.

> At night, after we were in bed, Veronica spoke out from her little bed and said 'I do not believe there is a God.' 'Preserve me', said I, 'my dear, what do you mean?' She answered, 'I have *thinket* it many a time, but did not like to speak of it.' I was confounded and uneasy, and tried her with the simple arguments that without God there would not be all the things we see. It is He who makes the sun shine. Said she, 'It shines only on good days.' Said I: 'God made you.' Said she: 'My Mother bore me.' It was a strange and alarming thing to her Mother and me to hear our little angel talk thus. But I thought it better just to let the subject drop insensibly tonight. I asked her if she had said her prayers tonight. She said yes, and asked me to put her in mind to say them in the morning. I prayed to God to prevent such thoughts from entering into her mind.

The next morning, by talking calmly with Veronica, I discovered what had made her think there was not a God. She told me, 'she did not like to die.' I suppose as she has been told that God takes us to himself when we die, she had fancied that if there were no God, there would be no death ... I impressed upon her that we must die at any rate; and how terrible it would be if we had not a Father in Heaven to take care of us. I looked into Cambray's *Education of a Daughter*, hoping to have found some simple argument for the being of God in that piece of instruction. But it is taken for granted.[30]

It is difficult to imagine a conversation of this kind between father and daughter taking place a hundred or even fifty years earlier. It was still shocking for a child to express such doubts as Veronica had, and both she and her father were aware of that. As Veronica's answers show, she had thought deeply about the matter, and Boswell's confidence the next morning that he had found out why she thought there was not a God may have convinced him, but it is unlikely to convince us or, probably, Veronica at the time. And then Boswell, like any modern parent, turns to his advice book to see what he should say to her – in his case a book written nearly a century earlier by the archbishop of Cambray and translated into English in 1707 as *Instructions for the Education of a Daughter*.

There are other incidents in the second half of the eighteenth century that suggest that parenting practice was changing, with consequent effects on children's behaviour. The most advanced thinking and practice were to be found in the circle of aristocrats who were to be instrumental in the founding of the Whig party. The young Charles James Fox, a future leader of the party, born in 1749, was brought up on 'a system of the most unlimited indulgence of every passion, whim or caprice'. Lord Holland, his father, held a great dinner at Holland House for foreign ministers. The children came in at dessert, and the young Charles, seeing a large bowl of cream in the middle of the table, wanted to get into it. His mother protested, but the indulgent father had the bowl placed on the floor, and Charles jumped about and splashed in it to his heart's content.[31]

This, of course, was quite exceptional. And, just like today, there would be many different ways of bringing up a child in place at any one time, even within a restricted group like the aristocracy. If we want to find unindulgent or even harsh upbringings, we can find them. Consider the famous letter, in Latin, that Lord Chesterfield wrote to his eight-year-old son Philip, in 1741:

'This is the last letter I shall write to you as a little boy, for tomorrow, if I am not mistaken you will attain your ninth year; so that, for the future, I shall treat you as a *youth*. You must now commence a different course of studies. No more levity: childish toys and playthings must be thrown aside, and your mind directed to serious objects. What was not unbecoming to a child, would be disgraceful to a youth.'[32]

Or turn to the experiences of Elizabeth Grant, born in 1797, the daughter of a Scottish laird and lawyer. Scottish upbringings perhaps had a tendency to be harder than English, and there is absolutely no sign of the influence of new ways of parenting in what she records. First, there were battles over food, in this instance a milk rebellion that was crushed with some ferocity: 'in his dressing-gown, with his whip in his hand, he [father] attended our breakfast ... that disgusting milk! He began with me; my beseeching look was answered by a sharp cut, followed by as many more as were necessary to empty the basin; Jane obeyed at once, and William after one good hint. They suffered less than I did; William cared less, he did not enjoy his breakfast, but he could take it; Jane always got rid of it [by vomiting].'

And then there were cold baths downstairs in the kitchen quarters, in a huge tub: 'the ice on the top ... had often to be broken before our horrid plunge into it; we were brought down from the very top of the house, four pairs of stairs, with only a cotton cloak over our night-gowns, just to chill us completely before the dreadful shock. How I screamed, begged, prayed, entreated to be saved, half the tender-hearted maids in tears besides me: all to no use, Millar [her nurse] had her orders.'

If her father were the disciplinarian, 'My mother never had such an idea as that of entering her nursery, when she wanted her children or her maids she rang for them.' The only positive side to this upbringing – and it may have been a considerable one – was that the children were often left alone to amuse themselves.[33]

There could be no more different upbringings than those of Charles James Fox in London in the middle of the century and Elizabeth Grant in Scotland at its close. Neither was typical; perhaps no childhood was typical. But there is good evidence of a change affecting a significant number of aris- tocratic and upper-middle-class families in the second half of the eighteenth century. There are, as one might expect, early signs of what was to come a little later. Here is John Verney, aged 12 and at school, writing to his father in 1723:

'Dear papa, George brought me some gingerbread which you was so kind as to send me, as also a couple of handkerchiefs, but we have found the other again in one of my coat pockets. I beg the favour of you, if it will not be troublesome, that you will desire my dear Mama to send me a little tea and sugar, as also a pair of battledores and shuttlecocks.'[34]

'Papa', 'dear Mama'; these are new terms in addressing your parents.[35] Locke had said that if you brought up your child in his approved manner, the relationship would gradually ease from one of rule and subordination to one of friendship. John Verney seems to be enjoying that shift.

Forty years later, in 1765, there is a confident familiarity in the poem that Frances and Jane Grimston, aged about ten and nine, wrote for their father while they were on holiday by the seaside:

> Thanks to papa for his kind card
> A pleasing token of regard
> The partridges and hare were good,
> None tasted better since the flood.
> So plentiful was your supply
> As to enable us thereby,
> Other friends to gratifye.
>
> Our health is good, our spirits cheerfull,
> Bathing we like ... scorn to be fearfull.
> We ride, we walk, we pick up shells
> To day we guns have heard and bells
> In honour of great George our King
> You will suppose the bells did ring
> That was indeed the very thing.
>
> And now Papa, we pray excuse,
> These infant babblings of our Muse,
> The attempt is new, our time is short,
> If it contributes to your sport,
> Our end is answer'd; so shall We,
> Ever remain most cordially
> Your duteous daughters.[36]

If the poem itself is revealing, it is more so that the proud father, a Yorkshire squire, kept it.

These affectionate relationships between parents and children may have had one source in a change in who looked after infants. In the 25 years from 1750 the death rate of aristocratic children under the age of five dropped by 30 per cent. The reason for this, it has been argued, is not because the children were less likely to catch diseases or be better fed: it was because they spent more time with their mothers.[37] Emily Kildare, Duchess of Leinster, here writes about her children, George, two, and William, one. 'George [is] the most entertaining, comical, arch little rogue that ever was, chatters incessantly, is immensely fond of me and coaxes me not a little, for he is cunning enough, very sweet-tempered and easily governed by gentle means; in short, if I was to set down and wish for a child, it would be just such a sort of boy as he is now.' She goes on to praise her other son, William, describing him as a sweet boy but not as lively as George. He has begun to talk and walk alone, she says, and: 'He is the best-natured little creature that can be and excessively passionate already, but puts up his little mouth to kiss and be friends the very next minute.' However, in contrast to George he is very fond of his nurse and does not care 'twopence for me; so, as you may imagine, I cannot for my life be as fond of him (though in reality I love him as well).'[38] Emily Kildare was no remote mother-figure summoning her children by bell. She is observant both of her children and of her own responses. Other mothers in previous centuries may well have felt like she did, but they haven't left a record like this.

There were an increasing number of guides to child rearing, nearly all of them echoing Locke and Rousseau in arguing that, particularly with young babies, mothers should follow the dictates of nature. This meant, first of all, breast-feeding. Experts before the eighteenth century had argued the same case, but only in the late 1760s do their arguments seem to have broken through to affect a whole class of mothers rather than individuals. By 1780 a knowledgeable physician estimated that most aristocratic women were now breast-feeding, itself a major contributory cause of the decline in infant mortality.[39]

Swaddling, another relic from the past, disappeared more completely but on much the same time-scale as the wet-nurse. There had been many apparently rational arguments for it: it helped straighten the baby's bones; it kept the baby warm and so on. Two very influential doctors, Dr William Cadogan in 1748 and Dr William Buchan in 1769, came out strongly against it. Buchan was horrified that 'the poor child, as soon as it came into the world, had as many rollers and wrappers applied to its body as if every bone had been fractured in the birth. [True], in several parts of Britain the practice of rolling children with so many bandages is now in some measure laid aside.'

There is other testimony to the same effect. Probably the move had started in the early eighteenth century when the swaddling bands began to be removed after three months. By the late eighteenth century swaddling seems to have become by and large a thing of the past. In 1785 the *Lady's Magazine* thought that most of its readers wouldn't know how to swaddle, and a German visitor at about the same time was surprised to find that 'the children are not swaddled ... they are covered with light clothing, which leaves all their movements free'.[40]

A belief in the beneficence of nature also helped liberate slightly older children from restraining clothing. [Fig. 12] Locke was outspoken on the issue: 'Let nature have Scope to fashion the Body as she thinks best ... I have seen so many Instances of Children receiving great Harm from *strait-lacing* ... Narrow breasts, short and stinking Breath, ill Lungs, and Crookedness, are the Natural and almost constant Effects of *hard Bodice*, and *Cloths that pinch*.'[41]

Children of both sexes were dressed in long petticoats, or 'coats, until they reached an age somewhere between three and seven – the age for the change seems to have gone down over time. For boys there was then the ceremony of breeching when they were clothed in doublet, jerkin and hose like their fathers. This was an important step in the acquisition of a masculine identity. In 1747, Frances Boscawen wrote to her husband, a distinguished admiral, about their son, Edward, aged almost three. Edward's friend Charles Masham, aged three, had been to visit. Charles was already in breeches, 'looking much better than I could have imagined ... My Lord [Edward] scolds me vastly for keeping him in petticoats.' Girls at this age began to wear clothes resembling those of adult women.[42]

We can see some of these changes in paintings of children, and these also suggest new parental attitudes, though they are rarely easy to decode. Take William Hogarth's famous painting of the Graham children in 1742. [Fig. 10] Daniel Graham, their father, was a successful apothecary. We see four children, Richard, aged seven, a cheerful-looking boy to the right playing a bird-organ, an instrument that reproduced the sound of birds singing. Anna-Maria, aged about five, is immediately next to him, holding up her skirts and about to dance to the music. Then comes Henrietta, aged nine, holding two cherries, the symbolic 'fruit of Paradise' and childhood. She looks directly out from the canvas, Hogarth telling us, and Henrietta knowing, that she is nearing the end of childhood – though she couldn't have known then that she would become the mother of the famous economist Thomas Robert Malthus. Finally, on the left, holding the hand of his elder sister, is Thomas, wearing the unisex petticoats of the very young, seated in a go-cart. Above his head is a clock, and on top of it a winged cherub with an hour-glass and a scythe. Thomas, we are being told, died before the painting was complete. The painting is full of symbols. But that said, there is an informality about the children rarely seen in the seventeenth century. One can only imagine the pride the parents would have taken in this depiction of their children.[43]

There is then much evidence that parenting practices changed quite substantially in the eighteenth century and especially in the second half of it. Possibly it had some connection with political change. The British celebration of themselves as above all a nation of the free may have rubbed off on parenting: babies and children should no longer be kept in the state of subjection that had for so long been recommended (though by no means always acted on).

We need always to remember, however, that even in the classes where new ideas most easily took root, the aristocracy and upper-middle classes, old ideas still had a hold. James Boswell, a year after he had discussed the existence of God with his daughter, made an entry in his journal about his three-year-old son, Sandie: 'I this morning beat Sandie for telling a lie. I must beat him very severely if I catch him again in falsehood. I do not recollect having had any other valuable principle impressed upon me by my father except a strict regard to truth, which he impressed upon my mind by a hearty beating at an early age, when I lied, and then talking of the *dishonour* of lying.'[44] So much for Locke's strictures against corporal punishment.

The battle for children's minds

Francis Place was born in London in 1771. His playmates were mostly the sons of tradesmen, a little way up the social ladder. He described how, when he was about 12, a bit of old iron he found and sold

> enabled me to purchase the materials for a paper kite, it was a large one taller than myself and had upon it a multitude of stars and turkscaps

[reddish or purplish lilies] in gaudy colours a pair of glass eyes and fine fringed tassels. The great difficulty was, how to procure the necessary quantity of twine to send it up to a great height which in regard to the kite was the height of my ambition. I chopped wood after school hours, and on Thursday and Saturday afternoons for a man who kept a Chandlers shop and as I was dextrous he gave me three halfpence an hour, thus I amassed half a crown the largest sum I had ever possessed with this I bought twine, sent up the kite in the long fields and sold it on the spot twine and all for half a guinea. From this time I never wanted money. I made models of boats and rigged them Moulds for Cocks and Dumps and sold them. I excelled in all boyish games, won from the boys all their marbles, cocks and dumps and every thing else they had to lose until no one would play with me.[45]

Cocks were lead models cast in moulds; dumps were lead counters, a kind of currency. Playing at cocks involved shying at them to see who first knocked them over. Other games, which Place describes in detail, were pitch in the hole and tossing up. Swimming was the only sport he couldn't immediately master. He says that 'Almost every boy who was eleven years of age and some who were younger could swim,' he himself eventually learning after being pushed into the Thames near Millbank. Soon he could swim across the river. These activities were interspersed with numerous fights with boys in his school or as part of a gang against other boys.'[46]

Francis Place describes a largely self-contained world of childhood. It stands in contrast to another world fast developing in the eighteenth century, one where children lived out their childhoods at home or in carefully supervised sorties outside it, a world where there were toys and books to be bought, and adults were buying them. It was class that divided Francis Place's world from this more cosseted one to be found among those whom contemporaries called 'the middling sort'.

Books were central to both these cultures. Child readers often read indiscriminately whatever print they could lay their hands on. Samuel Bamford, brought up in a weaving family in Middleton, near Manchester, at the end of the eighteenth century, was captivated first of all by Bunyan's *The Pilgrim's Progress*, but he remembered also the fascination of Swindell's bookshop. 'In the spacious windows of this shop ... were exhibited numerous songs, ballads, tales, and other publications with horrid and awful-looking woodcuts at the head; which publications with their cuts, had a strong command on my attention.' Every farthing he could scrape together was spent on books, including 'Histories of Jack the Giant Killer, Saint George and the Dragon, Tom Hickathrift, Jack and the Bean Stalk, History of the Seven Champions, tale of Fair Rosamund, History of Friar Bacon, Account of the Lancashire Witches, The Witches of the Woodlands and such like romances'.[47]

Sometimes a modern book in abridged and truncated form joined these classics, the most popular being Daniel Defoe's *Robinson Crusoe*. Samuel Bamford read it to his friend Sam, and then, when they went to play on an island in a reservoir, they became Robinson Crusoe and his Man Friday: 'The cock-clod was our "desert island"; the brushwood was our means of concealment ... we had "savages" also, whose "foot-prints" made us pause and look around; those savages being the men from the brewery ... Nor were we without our perils and "shipwrecks"; for getting some old planks and a split board or two, we made a raft, on which whenever we found it necessary to "go on a voyage", we paddled the length and breadth of this our "ocean".' They often returned to shore only when the raft timbers were about to split.[48]

Another boy inspired by *Robinson Crusoe*, this time in Northumberland, was the future wood-engraver, Thomas Bewick, born in 1753, who recalled how 'in imitation of the Savages described in "Robinson Crusoe" or some other Savages, I often, in a morning, set off *stark naked* across the Fell where I was joined by some associates, who in like manner, ran about like mad things'.[49]

Both in what was read, and in the activities that followed from it, this seems to be a culture of boys. We hear much less about what girls were reading or doing. They weren't totally excluded. Place wrote how:

I remember the time when 'drop handkerchief' was common at all merry makings round London and have joined in the game many times on a Sunday afternoon. Any one who pleased was admitted into the ring, which consisted of a male and female alternately holding hands round, when the girl dropped the handkerchief she started off in the direction she thought most likely to enable her to avoid being caught unless she wished it, and few wished it at the first run as by avoiding being caught, the girl was sure to be again selected by the next boy, since not to have a run after the girl who had beaten the first boy would have been a want of pluck, when the handkerchief was dropped, the lad at whose back it fell was usual held by the girls on each side of him as long as they could hold him, this checked him for a moment or two and another or two were lost in picking up the handkerchief so that the girl had fairly the start of him and by running round some trees or groups of people not unfrequently regained the ring without being caught ... the girl went round the ring again, and was almost sure to be caught the second time as she never had time enough to recover from the exertions she had made ... The matter ended by the lad kissing the girl in the centre of the ring.

Parents, to the astonishment of the adult Place, would allow their daughters to take part in these games and complacently watch them.[50]

Higher up the social scale, parents would certainly not have allowed their daughters such liberties. Here childhood was becoming carefully controlled and monitored, and at the same time some children were beginning to be spoilt. [Fig. 16] We can see these two tendencies most clearly in the toy market. The market for toys dates back to the Middle Ages.[51] By the end of the seventeenth century it had developed to the point where there were many toys that parents could buy for children. Locke complained forcefully about too many toys being given to children:

> By it they are taught Pride, Vanity, and Covetousness, almost before they can speak: And I have known a young Child so distracted with the number, and Variety of his Play-games, that he tired his Maid every day to look them over; and was so accustomed to abundance, that he never thought he had enough, but was always asking, What more? what more? what new Thing shall I have? A good Introduction to Moderate Desires, and the ready way to make a contented happy Man! [Children should play with] a smooth Pebble, a piece of Paper, the Mother's Bunch of Keys, or any thing they cannot hurt themselves with. [This] serves as much to divert little Children, as those more chargeable and curious Toys from the Shops, which are presently put out of order, and broken . Play-things I think Children should have, and of diverse sorts; but still to be in the Custody of their Tutors, or some body else, whereof the Child should have in his Power but one at once, and should not be suffered to have another, but when he restor'd that.[52]

This was Locke in 1693, advocating control and moderation – and perhaps providing us with the first documented case of pester power. Ironically, his comments seem to have inspired some of the enormous expansion of the toy market in the eighteenth century. Post-Locke, toys were designed to encourage and facilitate learning and the acquisition of knowledge. Playing-cards were perhaps the first to do this. The *Ipswich Journal* in 1746 advertised 'a set of 56 square, with cuts upon a plan of Mr Locke'. A York newspaper in 1774 carried an advertisement for a set of Riley's Royal Spelling Cards, beautifully coloured in a new and handsome edition and priced at a shilling. They were, the advertisement claimed: 'Adorned with Cuts, and Verses under each, with their emphasis properly marked, and the words divided so as to prevent false pronunciation. On the top of the cards is the Alphabet, displayed in large and small Letters, so contrived as to cut off at Pleasure, without injuring the Beauty of the Devices; by which Infants may very soon be taught to compose their Names, Words, Dates, etc.'[53] Here was a purchase that could help parents to pursue a course of early learning for their children, and at home.

The jigsaw puzzle, aimed at older children, was seemingly invented in 1762 by John Spilsbury, a 23-year-old printer–bookseller. The initial aim was to use it to teach geography, but it was adaptable to teach history, classics or morals. Dice could also be used to aid learning. John Jeffreys's 'A Journey through Europe or the Play of Geography', in which the players moved along a marked route according to the throw of a dice, dates from 1759 and was quickly imitated.

Some toys were rather less overtly educational. There were models of mechanical apparatus that could be assembled, toy theatres with moving scenes and actors, Noah's Arks, toy soldiers, and dolls and doll's houses. One London retailer in the 1780s sold cattle, milkmaids, armies in boxes and 'babies, dressed or undressed, jointed, wax or common'. In London by 1800 there were at least two shops specializing in making rocking horses.[54] [Fig. 21]

The toy culture that grew up in the eighteenth century was a culture controlled by adults and designed fundamentally to manipulate the child into learning by pretending it was play. A century after Locke had expressed his reservations about the proliferation of toys, his critique was repeated by author and educationalist Maria Edgeworth. Dolls and doll's houses, rocking-horses, baa lambs, squeaky pigs and cuckoos, and simple action toys, all met with her disapproval.[55]

If there were a debate about toys, it was nothing to the debate about books. For whereas Francis Place and Samuel Bamford made their own playthings, they saved up to buy the books that attracted them. And the chapbooks – cheap books, often sold by chapmen or itinerant dealers – that attracted them were anathema to most middle-class parents and to a multitude of commentators who helped form their opinions. Isaac Watts's *Divine Songs, Attempted in Easy Language for the Use of Children*, first published in 1715, and reprinted over 200 times in the next hundred years, was a publication of which they approved. Not that *Divine Songs* was only for the middle classes. William Lovett was born in Newlyn, Cornwall, in 1800 and endured much poverty in childhood. While staying with his great-grandmother who was teaching him to read, he was one day brought Watts's *Divine Songs* by his mother, with a promise that when he had learnt them he would get a Bible. Within a fortnight he had them by heart.[56]

Isaac Watts was in no doubt that children needed to be protected from the chapbook tradition: 'Let not Nurses or Servants be suffered to fill their Minds with *silly Tales and with senseless Rhimes* ... LET not any Persons that are near them terrify their tender Minds with dismal *Stories of Witches and Ghosts, of Devils and evil Spirits, of Fairies and Bugbears in the Dark*. This hath had a most mischievous Effect on some Children.'[57] The modern reader is likely to think that Watts simply exchanged one set of terrors with another. Consider the fate of the disobedient child: 'What heavy Guilt upon him lies! / How cursed is his Name! / The Ravens shall pick out his Eyes, / And Eagles eat the same.'

Tell a lie, and your fate is spelt out:

> The Lord delights in them that speak
> The Words of Truth; but every Lyar
> Must have his Portion in the Lake
> That burns with Brimstone and with Fire ...
>
> Then let me always watch my Lips,
> Lest I be struck to Death and Hell,
> Since God a Book of Reckoning keeps
> For every Lye that Children tell.[58]

Some children might have access both to the chapbook tradition and to Isaac Watts. And soon there was to be another kind of book for them. In 1744, John Newbery placed an advertisement for:

A Little Pretty Pocket-Book, intended for the Instruction and Amusement of Little Master Tommy and Pretty Miss Polly, with an agreeable Letter to read from Jack the Giant Killer, as also a Ball and Pincushion, the use of which will infallibly make Tommy a good Boy, and Polly a Good Girl. To the whole is prefixed a letter on education humbly addressed to all Parents, Guardians, Governesses, etc, wherein rules are laid down for making their children strong, healthy, virtuous, wise, and happy...[59]

Newbery here seems uncertain whom he is addressing: children, parents, governesses? At a price of 6d, or 8d if you opted for either the ball or the pin-cushion, Newbery was aiming at the middle classes. A supremely good publicist, he has gained an undeserved reputation as the first producer of children's books. He was not. Even at the time he had competitors in the market-place. Newbery, most of whose fortune came from the sale of patent medicines, had seen a niche and was determined to fill it.

Read the *Pretty Little Pocket-Book* now and we are likely to think that it didn't need much to do that. There is a dose of watered-down Locke and a pervasive insistence on the qualities that will lead to success and esteem in adult life. Part of the book is given over to woodcuts describing various games, each with a moral attached. Here is Chuck-Farthing: 'As you value your Pence, / At the Hole take your Aim; / Chuck all safely in, /And you'll win the Game.' The moral followed, also in verse: 'Chuck-Farthing, like Trade, / Requires great Care; / The more you observe, / The better you'll fare.'[60]

It is difficult to see how any child could get much pleasure from banalities of this kind. Parents seemed to have liked them. Mrs Hester Thrale, well known for her salons where authors, poets and writers congregated, reported the acerbic views of the acclaimed lexicographer, critic and poet Samuel Johnson: 'He used to condemn me for putting Newbery's books into [her children's] hands as too trifling to engage their attention ... Babies do not want to hear about babies; they like to be told of giants and castles, and of somewhat which can stretch and stimulate their little minds ... Remember always that the parents *buy* the books, and that the children never read them.'[61]

In the seventeenth century, there was a rift in children's culture. On the one side stood Puritanism and on the other the chapbook tradition. In the eighteenth century that rift continued, but superimposed on it was another, a secular division this time, and one where class dominated. The children of the middling sorts were being told to keep themselves clear of the chapbooks. Increasingly they were under supervision, and their entertainment was family entertainment. Sir Ashton Lever's Museum of Natural History at Leicester House, London, in the 1770s and 1780s advertised annual family tickets, to include tutor and governess. Zoos, museums, circuses, puppet shows, all aimed to attract families. So also did public assemblies at spas and other places of fashionable resort. For it was thought desirable to introduce children as early as possible to the social world in which, eventually, as daughters, they would find husbands and, as sons, make the connections and learn the manners that would lead to success.[62]

Francis Place as a boy had managed to borrow and read *Aristotle's Master Piece*, a combination of sex guide and obstetrical manual with lurid illustrations. He remembered how you could go into print-shops selling playbooks and school-books, and how, in one, a Mrs Roach would open up to any boy who made a purchase a portfolio of obscene prints and encourage them to look at them.[63] This was the world against which the children of the respectable, middling sort were to be insulated. But theirs was a world where the emphasis on getting on could seem like a repudiation of everything for which Rousseau stood and a bastardization of John Locke.

'The Child is father of the Man'

In 1789, when she was nine years old, Mary Ann Body sewed a sampler that she gave to her mother. [Fig. 14] In the top half of it, Mary's sewing reads:

> Dear mother I am young and cannot show
> Such work as I unto your goodness owe.
> Be pleased to smile on this my small endeavour
> I'll strive to learn and be obedient ever.

There is then an idyllic scene of birds, trees, flowers and deer, and underneath it some more lines: 'If all Mankind would live in mutual love / This world would much resemble that above.'[64]

Mary Body was doubtless supervised in her sewing and may simply have been copying, but the two sets of verse seem appropriate to the year in which they were written: 1789. For if the first set were conventional in its obeisance to mother, the second, with its vision of a better world, one like heaven, seems to breathe the atmosphere of the French Revolution. We are reminded of Wordsworth, for whom in that year it was 'Bliss ... to be alive / But to be young was very Heaven!'

Events in France, and the long wars with Britain, almost uninterrupted from 1793 to 1815, had their impact on childhood and on children in Britain. Initially, the revolution gave encouragement to British reformers who wanted much wider participation in politics. It was also a time when people's minds opened to all kinds of new possibilities – of new roles for women, for example, and of new ways of thinking about children. Prominent among such people was William Blake. He, too, was writing verses, his *Songs of Innocence*, in 1789, and in them, very simply, he gives a voice to a baby, talking with its mother [Fig. 13]:

'I have no name;
I am but two days old.' –
What shall I call thee?
'I happy am,
Joy is my name.'
Sweet joy befall thee!⁶⁵

If there are moments in our long story that mark a change of direction, Blake's lines of 1789 have a claim to that status. True, hardly anyone bought or read his poems in his lifetime. But what we are hearing and seeing here is an almost revolutionary perception that a child is not a piece of paper or wax that adults can write on or mould at will, nor scarred by original sin. There is, at birth, an individuality, a voice, which we can hear. The poem was accompanied by an etching of a luxuriant flower, its petals, like a womb, enveloping the mother with her child on her knee and a winged figure in attendance. It is a kind of annunciation, perhaps telling us that, even from conception, a child, like a seed, is growing.

What were seen as the excesses of the revolution soon encouraged conservatives to stamp down on new ideas and the organizations that had sprung up to give voice to them. Evangelicals, in many ways the successors of the

Puritans, who had been preaching against the laxity of British society before 1789, now gained more strength. The end of the eighteenth and the early years of the nineteenth century witness a battle between evangelicals and romantics, with, lying between them, the Lockeian rationalists whose books held sway on the shelves of concerned parents. Out of this battle came a perception of childhood that shapes much of how we still think about children in the twenty-first century.

William Wilberforce, best known now for his opposition to the slave trade but also a prominent evangelical, spelt out the view that a human being is 'degraded in his nature, and depraved in his faculties: indisposed to good, and disposed to evil; prone to vice – it is natural and easy to him; disinclined to virtue – it is difficult and laborious; he is tainted with sin, not slightly and superficially, but radically and to the very core'.[66]

Parents, advised the *Evangelical Magazine* in 1799, should teach their children that 'they are sinful and polluted creatures'.[67] In practice, this came to mean a lasting concern about the influences that might play on children, particularly books. In the beginning of the eighteenth century at the school set up by the Wesleys at Kingswood, children were taken to see a gibbet with the body of a criminal swinging on it to impress on them the importance of being good. In the early nineteenth century, in children's writer Mrs Sherwood's *The History of the Fairchild Family*, the visit to the gibbet was kept to the pages of a book, but its impact perhaps none the less powerful for that. The evangelicals themselves produced much literature of the kind of which they approved, and they also waged a campaign against literature of which they disapproved.

The evangelicals were also deeply concerned about the way people were spending Sunday, fearing that the judgement of God would fall upon a land that seemed to be enjoying itself in all kinds of secular activity. It was this that was one prime motive behind the foundation of Sunday schools; another being the sense that on Sundays children were most out of control and most likely to be a danger to society. The poet Anna Sawyer, at the end of the century, put into verse the change that Sunday schools could bring about:

> Oft have I seen, with pensive eye,
> > Children in groups our streets disgrace,
> Exposed to infamy and vice,
> > With shameless, yet with ruddy face.

Along the fields, along the lanes,
    Rambled the giddy, giggling throng,
Eager to strip the flowering thorn,
    Or rob the poor bird of its young.

No fears had they of God above,
    No reverence for the Sabbath Day;
But thought those hallowed hours were meant
    For naught but frolic – naught but play.

Celestial Charity advanced,
    Instant their idle clamour ceased;
Smiling, she seized each vagrant's hand,
    And led them to the 'paths of peace'.

How changed the scene! In decent garb,
    With sober step and serious air,
Obsequious to their tutor's voice,
    To church the cherub-train repair.[68]

The Sunday schools met another need. They were consistent with the requirement that children work on the other six days of the week. Robert Raikes, one of the founders of the schools in the 1780s, lived in Gloucester, where there was employment for children in the pin industry. 'The machine', said Raikes, 'could not spare the children on week-days.'[69]

As with all the other major charitable endeavours on behalf of children, it is easier to hear the voice of the organizers than of the children. For many children Sunday schools offered a means of picking up key skills, reading above all. There was fierce debate as to whether teaching writing on a Sunday was consistent with keeping the day holy, but eventually, perhaps succumbing to consumer demand, many of the schools began to offer a basic education to those who were at work on other days of the week. They became incredibly popular, often fondly remembered, 'an oasis in the desert to me', wrote Charles Shaw, in his memoir of his impoverished childhood in the Potteries in the 1830s. By the 1820s most working-class children would have been attending at some point in their childhood. We may doubt whether they were all as sanctimonious as Anna Sawyer imagined in her poem or as they are made to speak in this dialogue in Manchester, in 1789, before the school visitors:

> First.　　O! happy day, appointed for reproof
> 　　　　　Which brings our feet beneath this welcome roof,
> 　　　　　Where we may learn to read, to hear, and speak
> 　　　　　The paths of Virtue, which we ought to take:
> 　　　　　Where we can find instruction, and delight
> 　　　　　To pass in cheerful songs the sabbath night.
>
> Second.　　I too with joy this blessed day receive,
> 　　　　　And hope we shall assemble here at eve;
> 　　　　　Yea, gladly welcome ev'ry sabbath day –
> 　　　　　For we shou'd love the school more than our play.
>
> First.　　It gives me pleasure much to find that we
> 　　　　　In these respects so happily agree;
> 　　　　　And children yonder playing in the street
> 　　　　　Had better here some useful task repeat.
>
> Second.　　I think so too; for though I love right well
> 　　　　　To play, I love to sing, and read, and spell:
> 　　　　　But play in school time we ought not indeed,
> 　　　　　For if we do, how shall we learn to read?[70]

Neat and tidy, obedient, even obsequious, 'tractable', a favourite evangelical word, that was how those running the Sunday schools liked to picture their charges. How different from the vision of Blake and the romantic poets. It was perhaps best expressed in Blake's 'The Ecchoing Green'.

> The Sun does arise,
> And make happy the skies;
> The merry bells ring,
> To welcome the Spring;
> The sky-lark and thrush,
> The birds of the bush,

Sing louder around
To the bells' cheerful sound,
While our sports shall be seen
On the Ecchoing Green.

Old John, with white hair,
Does laugh away care,
Sitting under the oak,
Among the old folk.
They laugh at our play,
And soon they all say:
'Such, such were the joys,
When we all, girls & boys,
In our youth time were seen,
On the Ecchoing Green.'[71]

Here the children's play, 'our play' – for we are again seeing life through the eyes of a child – is in harmony with nature and brings together the old and the young. In the etching, the children play with bat, ball and kite while old John and three motherly women sit on a bench round an old oak tree, the symbol of strength and security.

Blake's vision is of what might be, not a description of the world as he knew it. But when Wordsworth began to look back into his childhood, he found memories of that harmony with nature that was at the root of the romantic view of the world. For Wordsworth, childhood was 'the seed-time' of the 'soul', and the main influences on it were from nature:[72]

There was a time when meadow, grove, and stream,
The earth, and every common sight,
To me did seem
Apparel'd in celestial light,
The glory and the freshness of a dream.

Growing up, growing old, one loses this sense of intimacy with nature. But the remembrance of childhood can keep the spark alive.

O joy! That in our embers
        Is something that doth live,
That nature yet remembers
        What was so fugitive!
The thought of our past years in me doth breed
Perpetual benediction.

Such thoughts could and for many did become nostalgia. But, more positively, they pointed to a radically new vision of what a child was. Children had access to levels of understanding greater than those available to adults. In Wordsworth's famous lines:

Not in entire forgetfulness,
        And not in utter nakedness,
But trailing clouds of glory do we come
        From God, who is our home:
Heaven lies about us in our infancy![73]

Wordsworth's impact on thinking about childhood was deep and pervasive. He was as important for the nineteenth century as Freud was for the twentieth. By the middle of the nineteenth century, many Christians had come to believe that children came direct from heaven, bearing messages from God, 'trailing clouds of glory'.[74] What Wordsworth had done was to break decisively with all previous thinking about children. Childhood now became a repository of sensitivity and wisdom. And if that were so, it became almost a duty to stay in touch with childhood, to remember as an adult what it felt like to be a child.

Wordsworth would not have made the impact he did if his thinking hadn't been in tune with that of his contemporaries. It is from the late eighteenth century that we begin to see romanticized paintings of children, either on their own or with their mothers. The most famous of them was Joshua Reynolds's portrait of his great-niece Offy, about six years old and sitting in the countryside; it was aptly entitled *The Age of Innocence* [Fig. 11]. It is from the 1780s that there emerges a new kind of writing, the autobiography, the word itself dating from these years. People had written the story of their lives before this, but they had rarely given much attention to childhood. In the lives of saints that we encountered in the Middle Ages, childhood was registered simply to show the signs of the saintliness that lay in the future. In the stories of their lives that Puritans wrote, childhood was important as a time before conversion: the more sinful you could show yourself to have been, the more dramatic the change after you had seen the light. But from the late eighteenth century people use the autobiography as a means of understanding themselves, searching into their childhoods to find the self.[75] Psychoanalysis lay a century ahead, but the autobiographers of the late eighteenth century and early nineteenth were fully conversant with its assumption that the key to the adult life lay in childhood, that, in Wordsworth's famous formulation, one of those phrases that passes into popular speech: 'The Child is father of the Man.'

But how should we keep this precious childhood alive? For all too soon, as Wordsworth recalled, 'Shades of the prison-house begin to close / Upon the growing Boy.'[76] The prison-house was the system of education and learning that was dominant. Here Wordsworth probably had in mind not the evangelicals, but rather the rationalist type of learning that stemmed ultimately from Locke. Its best-known exponent in the late eighteenth century was Anna Barbauld, who in the 1790s, with her brother John Aikin, wrote six volumes of *Evenings at Home*. They are full of useful information. Here is a typical exchange:

George: Harry, can you blow off all these dandelion feathers at a blast?
Harry: I will try.
George: See, you have left almost half of them ...
Tutor: A pretty child's play you have got there. Bring me one of the dandelion's heads, and let us see if we can make no other use of it.

There ensues a lesson on 'the compound-flowered plants, a difficult class to make out botanically ... You must get acquainted with them.'[77]

The romantics hated these desiccated works. Wordsworth ridiculed them in *The Prelude*. Charles Lamb, in a letter to Coleridge in 1802, wrote: 'Think what you would have been now, if instead of being fed with Tales and old wives' fables in childhood, you had been crammed with Geography and Natural History? *Damn them*. I mean the cursed Barbauld Crew, those *Blights & Blasts* of all that is *Human* in man & child.'[78]

Coleridge concurred, recurring frequently to the theme, here in a lecture in 1811: 'Give me the works which delighted my youth. Give me the History of

St George and the Seven Champions of Christendom, which at every leisure moment I used to hide myself in a corner to read. Give me the Arabian Nights' Entertainments, which I used to watch till the sun shining on the bookcase approached it, and glowing full upon it gave me courage to take it from the shelf.'[79]

The imagination is here set against reason. From here we can trace a line that leads to the emergence of the fairy tale for children in the 1840s and to the stimulation to the imagination that writers for children have so often sought. But we can also trace a line that leads to Dickens's Mr Gradgrind in *Hard Times* with his devotion to facts.

The debates about childhood during the years of revolution and war were mainly conducted out of the hearing of children. If children's lives were changed, it was, initially at any rate, more through the foundation of Sunday schools than anything written by Blake or Wordsworth. As to the war, children overheard adults talking and responded in their own way. Samuel Bamford remembered how he and his playmates heard the rumours of impending war; a war that was coming from afar, brought by the French. A war that 'would come to Middleton, and kill all the fathers, and mothers, and children, that it could find ... I hit on a scheme which I thought would avert the danger. This was that I and all our family, at least, should hide in the wooden coal-shed at the Free Grammar School, and there I was quite certain "the war" could never find us.'[80]

Luckily the war never did find Bamford or his friends, but the conflict between the romantics and their opponents that coincided with it was to shape childhood from that moment onwards.

CHAPTER FOUR
The Victorians

THINK OF VICTORIAN CHILDREN and certain phrases and images are likely to flash through our minds: little children who should be seen and not heard, under-tens slaving away in cotton factories and coal mines, Oliver Twist asking for more or the velveteen Little Lord Fauntleroy. We see children on the one hand protected by a formidable array of nannies and governesses, and on the other exploited to an extent previously unknown. It is, in short, a world of contrasts. The extremes were quite as apparent to contemporaries as they are to us, and they led a substantial body of reformers to try to provide the children of the poor with some of the ingredients of the childhoods of the well-to-do. The outcome was that in the adult imagination childhood as an ideal became more separated from adulthood than it had ever been before. Children were valued, rather than chided, for their childishness. Precocity, much esteemed in previous centuries, was now to be avoided. Some adults even began to think that childhood was the best time of life, something unknown before the romantics had sown the seed of that idea.

The contrasts between the childhoods of the poor and the better off were the outcome of the unprecedented speed of the economic and social changes in Britain consequent on the Industrial Revolution of the late eighteenth century and early nineteenth. Victorian Britain was a society unlike any previously known, half its population urban dwellers by mid-century, agriculture of diminishing importance and the population of some rural areas in decline in the second half of the century – and this at a time when the overall population rose from under 11 million in 1801 to over 37 million a century later. The cities and towns grew at an exponential rate, creating enormous social problems, not least for children.

The upper and middle classes, about a quarter of the total population, managed to retain power and influence, their ideas and practices setting the tone for society as a whole. They faced challenges, from Chartists in mid-century, from socialists later, and they themselves were by no means united in their beliefs or ideas. There was a huge difference between the lifestyle of a wealthy aristocrat and that of a lower-middle-class family struggling along on a clerk's salary. But the crucial divide was between the middle and upper classes, and the three-quarters of the population in the working classes, dependent for their survival on manual labour.

The working classes were, however, being absorbed within the political nation. Britain edged slowly towards democracy via a succession of Reform

Acts in 1832, 1867 and 1884, each extending the right to vote to include most men but no women. After the second of these it famously became necessary 'to educate our masters', to make provision, in an Act in 1870 in England and Wales, for more government-funded schooling for working-class children. For these children would grow up to be voters, and there was much concern that they might not cast their votes in a responsible way. If these working-class voters were now the 'masters', they held in their hands the destiny not only of Britain but also of the vast empire that was being accumulated across the globe. All this impacted upon the lives of children in Victorian Britain.

'How I wish I were a boy!'

Molly Hughes grew up in London in the 1870s, her father a less than successful stockbroker. Molly had four elder brothers:

> 'How I wish I were a boy!' Mother caught me saying this aloud one day, and promptly told me that this was a wicked thought. She did not go on to give a reason, but merely insisted that it was splendid to be a girl, and with such exuberant enthusiasm that I was quite convinced. My father's slogan was that boys should go everywhere and know everything, and that a girl should stay at home and know nothing ... The boys used to go to the theatre and music-halls. The latter sounded rather dull, but mother explained that they were not dull, only not very nice. However, it made no difference to me what they were like, since I was never allowed to go even to a theatre.[1]

Was this emphasis on the proper differences in bringing up boys and girls in the middle and upper classes simply a residue of old divisions? Or did it have new sources in Victorian Britain? What kind of impact did it have on society as a whole?

There was a brief moment in the early nineteenth century when progressive parents tried to play down differences of gender in rearing their children. In the 1830s knee-length dresses and long white trousers, with hair cut short, were recommended for both boys and girls, the aim being explicitly to blur gender distinctions. Advice books of the same period stressed that both boys and girls should avoid anger. But thereafter, anger for boys, properly directed and properly controlled, was acceptable.[2] Once the public schools had reformed themselves in the 1830s and 1840s, sharply divergent paths for boys and girls became the norm.

These separate paths had their origin in the feminization of the home. The romantics had placed a premium on the intensity of the bond between mother and child. Despite their many differences, the evangelicals reinforced this. Changes in the world of work conspired to the same end. Increasingly the middle-class home was separated from the workplace, and the wife and mother was left, or was free, to concentrate on domestic duties. The difference between a public male world and a private female one was accentuated. Homes were becoming more and more feminized in layout and in décor. In Edinburgh and Glasgow the dominance of the dining room with its male rites was, by 1840, being overtaken by the place given to the feminine piano.[3] Women as mothers devoted themselves to the care of their children, watching, anxious, reflective. Elizabeth Gaskell, the novelist, kept a diary of her daughter Marianne's development, dedicating it in these words: 'To my dear little Marianne I shall "dedicate" this book, which, if I should not live to give it to her myself, will I trust be reserved for her as a token of her mother's love, and extreme anxiety in the formation of her little daughter's character ... I wish that ... I could give her the slightest idea of the love and the hope that is bound up with her.'[4]

What, then, was the role for fathers? They were no longer required, as they had been in the Puritan household, to direct everything. True, family prayers, an evangelical re-invention of Puritan practice, while they survived, would be conducted by father. But they were in sharp decline by the 1880s. Mothers, at the child's bedside, were coming to be thought better equipped to meet the spiritual needs of the children. In place of this loss of role, fathers were coming to see the home as a place for relaxation from the pressures of work and of the world – a haven in a heartless world. Their children might now amuse them; they themselves might even climb down from their dignity and romp with them on the floor. Of course, there were fathers who came nowhere near to fulfilling this ideal, but that it was an ideal, from about the 1830s to the 1880s, seems undeniable. We can see it most poignantly in the way William Lucas, a Quaker and brewer, in 1847 expressed his sense of his failure to achieve any easy familiarity with his children. 'I feel at times much depressed from not being able to make myself so companionable as I ought to be with my children. I never had the art of winning children or getting free with them ... It is so difficult to put up with their extreme vivacity ... to remember what we once were at their age, and to make due allowance for it.'[5]

The feminization of the home was fine for young boys and for girls. Family life began to centre round them. Their birthdays began to be celebrated, punctuating the year with a repeated ritual. [Fig. 18] Christmas became a family celebration with children centre stage, particularly with the import from the United States of the present-bearing Santa Claus in the 1870s.[6] Until they were about six or seven, as the dress they wore indicated, boys themselves were thought to be essentially female. [Fig. 22] But for boys over seven the home was thought all too likely to result in effeminacy. Female influence had to be reduced. Hence one reason for the growth of the public school and the expectation that all boys whose parents could afford it would send their boys to one. For boys had to learn how to become men. One (male) writer, Trevethan Spicer, saw it this way in 1855: there was, he felt, little difficulty for girls, 'they have their needlework, their Dolls, and are content.' But for boys it was different: 'the boy is the father to the man, and as men have to rough it in the outer world, and fight their way to the post of honour that they may select for their goal, so the sports of boys must of necessity be rough, to prepare them for their future turbulent career.'[7]

The public schools in the late eighteenth century and early nineteenth were unruly places where boys were frequently in rebellion. Reform came in the 1830s, a landmark date being the appointment of Thomas Arnold as headmaster of Rugby in 1828. Arnold sought to make the sixth-form pupils allies with the masters in the maintenance of discipline rather than fomenters of disorder. He had no illusions about the material on which he had to work: 'My object will be, if possible, to form Christian men, for Christian boys I can scarcely hope to make.' Despite this, boys from Rugby soon gained a reputation, as a contemporary saw it, for being 'thoughtful, manly-minded, conscious of duty and obligation'.[8] This reputation was sealed in the 1850s with the publication of Thomas Hughes's *Tom Brown's School Days*, an affectionate remembrance of the school under Arnold that Hughes had attended. Tom is here in conversation with Arthur, a religious boy, who asks him:

> 'What were you sent to Rugby for?'
> 'Well, I don't know exactly – nobody ever told me. I suppose because all boys are sent to a public school in England.'

'But what do you think yourself? What do you want to do here, and to carry away?'

Tom thought a minute. 'I want to be A1 at cricket and football and all the other games, and to make my hands keep my head against any fellow, lout or gentleman. I want to get into the sixth before I leave, and to please the Doctor, and I want to carry away just as much Latin and Greek as will take me through Oxford respectably.'

But the conversation did not end with this paean to masculine sports and anti-intellectualism. This was not the message that Hughes wanted to convey. Arthur probes. He asks Tom whether he will give up using cribs, the simple translations that most boys used to help them to pass tests in Latin and Greek. For Arthur, using a crib was dishonest, tantamount to cheating. Tom squirms as Arthur presses the issue, but silently assents.[9]

By the time *Tom Brown's School Days* was in print there was already an ongoing expansion of the public schools. There were new foundations, such as Marlborough in 1843, Wellington, a memorial to the duke who had died in 1852, Cheltenham and Malvern. The new schools promoted themselves as training boys for a career in a global ruling class, as likely to serve in far-flung empire as in Britain. They would imbue the boys with 'manliness'. When Arnold talked about manliness, he had in mind a Christian gentleman, upright, truthful, sensitive and with a sense of obligation to serve. Hughes reflected this, for Tom is saved from becoming a Flashman, the caddish bully of his school-days, by the gentle influence of the religious Arthur. From the 1850s onwards, however, games-playing became a central component of the curricula of the public schools, and manliness changed with the curricula: the manly boy was the boy who was physically tough, having learnt it on the games field. The effect of all this, and it was an extremely powerful one, was to place an emphasis on the repression of emotion, on reserve. Boys needed to have this ideal instilled into them at an early age, and if this were to happen they needed to be removed from feminine influences. Parallel with the public schools there grew up a network of feeder schools, the prep schools, designed in part to give an early training in the classics but also to remove boys from the enervating influences of home. Translator and businesswoman Charlotte Guest expressed her reservations when ten-year-old Ivor was sent away in 1845: 'When I thought of all the sorrow and temptation my poor boys would have to go through in that place I quite shuddered and prayed that assistance might be granted them from above. It seems a sad prospect, but everybody says it is the only way to bring up boys, and what is to be done? How can I, a poor weak woman, judge against all the world?[10]

Charlotte Guest was all too aware that she was about to lose her son. The public schools exercised an extraordinary influence on those who went to them, implanting in them enduring loyalties, stronger often than those of home. Many 'old boys' kept the memory of their school-days alive through the school songs that became a feature in the second half of the century. Lord Rosebery, briefly Liberal prime minister, arranged that he should die to the strains of the 'Eton Boating Song', Winston Churchill revived flagging spirits with Harrow's songs.[11] Military historian and poet Sir Henry Newbolt, known for his sea songs, found his inspiration in Clifton chapel.

> This is the chapel: here, my son,
>> Your father thought the thoughts of youth,
> And heard the words that one by one
>> The touch of Life has turned to truth.
> Here in a day that is not far,
>> You too may speak with noble ghosts
> Of manhood and the vows of war
>> You made before the Lord of Hosts.
>
> To set the cause above renown,
>> To love the game beyond the prize,
> To honour, while you strike him down,
> The foe that comes with fearless eyes;
> To count the life of battle good,
>> And dear the land that gave you birth,
> And dearer yet the brotherhood
>> That binds the brave of all the earth –
>
> My son, the oath is yours: the end
>> Is His, Who built the world of strife,
> Who gave His children Pain for friend,
>> And Death for surest hope of life.

To-day and here the fight's begun,
Of the great fellowship you're free;
Henceforth the School and you are one,
And what You are, the race shall be.[12]

If they were inspired by thoughts such as these, it was hardly surprising that public-school boys, as they grew up, were remarkably reluctant to reproduce the comfortable and feminized domesticity in which they had spent their early years. Towards the end of the century, if they married, they delayed the event until they were in their thirties, and many settled for bachelordom. Deprived of any obvious role in the home, they perhaps became more distant from their children than an earlier generation of fathers. Emotional, and indeed physical distance, became the norm. The all-male world of the gentleman's club became an attractive alternative to home. If fathers were at home, they sought sanctuary in a masculine domain: billiard rooms, smoking rooms, libraries and studies were all male preserves. But the greatest distance was to be found on the outer shores of empire, where the cloying domesticity of the feminized home could be escaped in its entirety.[13]

In most middle-class homes, girls, as Molly Hughes found out, had second place. It was partly a matter of money. Another young woman, Blanche Dundas, aged 24, wrote a little bitterly to a friend who was at a finishing school, how: 'I wish I had had your chances of improving myself but brothers howsoever charming they may be are expensive creatures and take *all* the money, and the sisters have to grow up ignorant and make their own dresses, neither of which processes is pleasant nor am I enamoured of either.'[14]

What sort of education was available to upper- and middle-class girls in Victorian Britain? We have a snapshot in the 1860s when there was a government inquiry. Among the merchant and professional classes, daughters were commonly taught at home by governesses until they were about ten, often sharing lessons with brothers. Then they might go to a local day school for two or three years before finishing off their education with a boarding school up to about 17. Sometimes there was then a finishing school, but that, it was said, 'is not so much an educational agent as a tribute which the parent pays to his own social position'. This pattern seems to have survived right up to the First World War. In the burgeoning lower-middle classes, girls were again at home until about ten, then passing on to local day schools for four or five years but often missing school to help mother. The purpose of all this, the commissioners of the 1860s inquiry noted, was to prepare girls for marriage: 'Parents who have daughters will always look to their being provided for in marriage, will always believe that the gentler graces and winning qualities of character will be their best passports to marriage, and will always expect their husbands to take on themselves the intellectual toil and the active exertions needed for the support of the family.'[15]

As one of the commissioners noted, boys were educated for the world, girls for the drawing room. The private schools that girls attended – and there may have been as many as 15,000 such schools in England by the end of the century – were generally small, some with as few as six or eight children, and designed to be family-like. If this sounded cosy, the obverse, in the words of an observer of schools in Devon at the end of the century, was 'the unblushing assertion of caste exclusiveness ... The dominant idea about girls' education is that it should be as far as possible claustral, that girls should be kept from any contamination with people who drop their H's or earn their salt. It is thought that careful seclusion is absolutely necessary for the development of that refinement which should characterise a lady.' Such exclusivity went beyond guarding against contact with girls beneath them in the social scale. It included any discussion of politics or reading of newspapers, the latter normally banned, and, if allowed, the permission extending only to carefully chosen cuttings.[16]

There were many new schools for girls founded in the second half of the century that did something to provide more opportunity. There were the ladies' colleges in London and Cheltenham, high schools for girls, many of them organized within the Girls' Public Day School Trust after its foundation in 1872, and, from the 1870s onwards, a handful of schools such as Roedean, modelled on the boys' public schools. Attendance at these schools undoubtedly had the potential to open up a new world for pupils, but, far from being in the vanguard of feminism, they were, in their governance and in their assumptions, thoroughly conservative. Most of them were the initiative of men, and they placed a considerable emphasis on the inculcation of feminine behaviour and attitudes. Consider the announcement of Alice Ottley, headmistress of Worcester High School:

> The Headmistress is anxious that it should be clearly understood that she utterly detests women's cricket. She considers it to be a game admirable for *little* girls and for all boys; exercising some of the best moral qualities

as well as physical powers; but it is one of the things she would have girls lay aside when they leave childhood behind and enter upon maidenhood. She earnestly desires that the 'note' of the Worcester High School should be delicate, womanly refinement, a high-toned courtesy, a gentle manner, a dignified bearing, which shall be as far removed from the loud, romping vulgarity of the hoyden, called 'the girl of the period' as from the mincing affectation of the 'fine lady' of the eighteenth century.[17]

The British public schools in the form they took after the 1830s were a means of educating boys into manliness at a time when the home could no longer be relied on to do that. Tom Brown thought Arthur was a bit effeminate for thinking and talking about home. At the height of their influence in the late nineteenth century and early twentieth, the public schools instilled a gender divide perhaps greater than in any previous period of British history. Some girls tried to match boys in scholastic and sometimes physical prowess, but they did so under the umbrella of assumptions that what was suitable for one sex was unsuited to the other. Feminists and suffragists began to challenge that, but it was a battle that would not easily be won.

This gender divide took place against a background in which Charles Dickens in his novels and many other writers in their books for children were transforming conventional views of the importance of childhood.

'Reinstated divinity'

'Please, sir, I want some more.' Oliver Twist in the workhouse with his empty plate had and has a world-wide resonance. At the time it produced astonishment:

> The board were sitting in solemn conclave, when Mr Bumble rushed into the room in great excitement, and addressing the gentleman in the high chair, said,
>
> 'Mr Limbkins, I beg your pardon, sir! Oliver Twist has asked for more!' There was a general start. Horror was depicted on every countenance.
>
> 'For *more!*' said Mr Limbkins. 'Compose yourself, Bumble, and answer me distinctly. Do I understand that he asked for more, after he had eaten the supper allotted by the dietary?'

'He did, sir,' replied Bumble.

'That boy will be hung,' said the gentleman in the white waistcoat; 'I know that boy will be hung.'[18]

Dickens, quite unlike any novelist before him, created child characters whose names became embedded in the national consciousness: Oliver Twist, Nicholas Nickleby, David Copperfield, Little Nell, Jo the crossing sweeper, Paul Dombey and Louisa Gradgrind. Through children, who like Oliver respond simply to felt needs, he exposed the pomposity and hypocrisy of adults. Scarred by his childhood experience in Warren's blacking factory, where, at the age of 12 he felt himself abandoned, he had reasons in his own life experience to want to try to reproduce what it was like to be a child.

There was very little in the history of fiction to suggest that children and childhood should be centre stage. But Dickens placed them there, and by doing so he not only shaped the attitudes of his contemporaries towards childhood, but also deeply influenced posterity. And of course Dickens was not alone in making children the protagonists and heroes of his fiction. So did Charlotte Brontë in *Jane Eyre* or George Eliot in *The Mill on the Floss* and in *Silas Marner*, where the little girl Eppie rescues the old miser from his misery.

Dickens, like so many of his contemporaries, was an heir of Wordsworth. Children for Dickens became a symbol of all that was good in the world before adult behaviour and adult institutions began to make their impact. Childhood, a proper childhood, not the childhoods suffered by Oliver Twist or Jo, was something you had to keep alive in yourself or else you would, like Scrooge in *A Christmas Carol*, become to all intents and purposes dead. Christmas became so important precisely because it was a celebration of childhood, of birth, a time when children could be centre stage and adults could, from their memories, regain strength for the struggle of life. This requirement that adults feed off their childhood memories had the effect of associating childhood with the past, some timeless past and always rural. If childhood, for adults, could act as an inspiration for the present and future, it could also become a place to which to escape, where one could avoid growing up. Written in the age of the railway, Dickens's novels often seem to be set in the age of the stagecoach. Many of his children, like Paul Dombey, are described as 'old-fashioned', as if the modern world has destroyed a moral world that once existed.

Dickens was writing in the critical period of the Industrial Revolution when urban growth was at its fastest and the social problems at their most acute. Urbanization was accompanied by health and housing problems on such a scale that many, including the prime minister, Sir Robert Peel, wondered whether such a society could survive. It seemed to be unnatural, and if it were so it was emphatically not the place for children. And yet children in swarms seemed to inhabit these cities, ever present in the streets.

One response to these social problems was to try to bring order out of incipient chaos. Order should be imposed. Slums (the word itself new) should be cleared, and a harsh new Poor Law, introduced in 1834, should make relief dependent on a willingness to enter a disciplinary workhouse, where mother and father would have separate wards and the children another one yet. A potentially rebellious working class should be tamed by laws restricting political or trade-union activity and by instilling into its children useful knowledge. Schoolchildren in the 1840s recited a kind of secular catechism, in which they were taught the rules of political economy. Eight and nine year olds were reading how 'Capital is the result of labour and savings. Nothing is more certain than that, taking the working classes in the entire mass, they get a fair share of the proceeds of the national industry.'[19]

It was against this world that Dickens took his stand. His ideological opponent Edwin Chadwick, architect of many of the social reforms of the 1830s and 1840s, spent some time trying to calculate exactly how little time you needed to spend schooling a working-class child so that it acquired a desirable minimum of useful knowledge and could then spend the rest of its time at work.[20] This was the spirit that Dickens opposed. Take, for example, this encounter in *The Old Curiosity Shop*, between Little Nell, reduced to working in a waxwork show, and Miss Monflathers, proprietor of a Boarding and Day Establishment for Young Ladies:

'Don't you feel how naughty it is of you ... to be a wax-work child, when you might have the proud consciousness of assisting, to the extent of your infant powers, the manufactures of your country; of improving your mind by the constant contemplation of the steam-engine; and of earning a comfortable and independent subsistence of from two-and-ninepence to three shillings per week? Don't you know that the harder you are at work, the happier you are?'[21]

Dickens's stories had immediate and deep resonance. They were plagiarized and put on the stage. They appealed to a popular cast of thinking that responded to the melodramatic and that liked to have its heroes and its villains – and no-one was better than Dickens at villains. But he was also good at portraying children who were both heroes and victims. No-one could read or hear them without thinking that there should be a better world for children to grow up in. And for Dickens such a world existed. Against the world of facts he posed a world of fancy.

When George Cruikshank rewrote 'Cinderella' as a temperance tract, Dickens responded with an essay entitled 'Frauds on the Fairies'. Fairy stories, said Dickens, '[were] nurseries of fancy, [from which children could learn] forbearance, courtesy, consideration for the poor and aged, kind treatment of animals, the love of nature, abhorrence of tyranny and brute force ... A nation without fancy, without some romance, never did, never can, never will, hold a great place under the sun.'

By the time Dickens wrote this, in 1853, fancy in children's literature was making a comeback after some decades in which the spirit of useful knowledge had reigned in literature for children. In the 1830s the astute young Emily Shore asked, in her journal, 'Why has our Maker given us imaginations, if they are never to be indulged?' As if in response, Henry Cole in 1841 put forward a prospectus for fairy tales, lamenting the fact that 'The many tales sung or said from time immemorial, which appealed to ... a little child's mind, its fancy, imagination, sympathies, affections, are almost all gone out of memory, and are scarcely to be obtained ... As for the creation of a new fairy tale or touching ballad, such a thing is unheard of.' Five years later Hans Christian Andersen's *Wonderful Stories for Children* was published. Fairy tales were back.[22]

Dickens and his novels are one prompt to thinking about childhood in Victorian Britain. Another is writing for children. We think immediately of Lewis Carroll's *Alice in Wonderland*, published in 1865, and of the other writers who made up what is often called the golden age of literature for children in the later nineteenth and early twentieth century: Charles Kingsley and *The Water Babies*, George MacDonald and his fairy tales, Edith Nesbit, J. M. Barrie and *Peter Pan*, Kenneth Grahame's *The Wind in the Willows*, Beatrix Potter, and A. A. Milne's *Winnie the Pooh* stories. They, of course, were not the only writings for children: there was also a tradition that grew out of evangelicalism and was influenced by Dickens, in which children, preferably in poverty, redeemed sinning adults. *Jessica's First Prayer* by Hesba Stratton would have attracted more child readers than Lewis Carroll.

Fancy, or the world of the imagination, underlay the writings that make up this golden age of children's literature. But whereas Dickens, for example with the circus children in *Hard Times*, had been able to use fancy to confront the harsh world of facts, the writers of fiction for children seem rather too easily to want to escape into a world of fancy that is also an escape from the facts. It is difficult now to read them without wondering about the sources of their inspiration. Many of them seemed to have been trying in their investment in childhood to be compensating for a loss of faith in religion, so that childhood became a new place where faith could be found.[23] And if this were so, then Peter Pan with his wish never to grow up becomes emblematic of a curious view of the life cycle. Childhood becomes the best time of life, anything after it almost inevitably a decline. How different from those stages of life that had been depicted in the Middle Ages when young adulthood represented the prime of life.

More worrying, some of these writers, Lewis Carroll in particular, had a fixation with little girls. Carroll was not only a writer but also a photographer, and it is his photographs that have the power to shock. There is something apt in the fact that the Victorian obsession with childhood was paralleled by the rise of photography. Children have always featured heavily in photographs, to the extent that now about 70 per cent of photographs contain children. A photograph of a child captures a moment in time: briefly the present, it soon becomes the past and can be invested with all kinds of meaning, most potently nostalgia. Carroll's photographs, some of them of naked, young girls posed erotically, are most simply explained as paedophilia. They can also be seen as a means of access to a fantasy world of childhood that is an escape from the present. Carroll, whether he is accompanying Alice as she disappears into the rabbit hole at the beginning of her time in Wonderland, or is photographing little girls, is himself in a wonderland where he can shed his adulthood, perhaps return to the female self that he and others believed was the beginning of existence for all human beings.[24]

John Ruskin was as much obsessed with little girls as Lewis Carroll and for much the same reasons, and, as the premier art critic of his time, he was in a position to influence how children were depicted. In the 1850s he had delivered a fierce attack on the way that the seventeenth-century Spanish painter Murillo had painted beggar boys:

Look at those two ragged and vicious vagrants that Murillo has gathered out of the street. You smile at first, because they are eating so naturally, and their roguery is so complete. But is there anything else than roguery there, or was it well for the painter to give his time to the painting of those repulsive and wicked children? Do you feel moved with any charity towards children as you look at them? Are we the least bit more likely to take any interest in ragged schools, or to help the next pauper child that comes in our way, because the painter has chosen a cunning beggar feeding greedily?[25]

As an alternative Ruskin recommended William Hunt's paintings of healthy, peasant boys, but then later, in the 1880s, there was something even better, children painted as beautiful, 'the radiance and innocence of reinstated divinity showered again among the flowers of English meadows by Mrs Allingham and Kate Greenaway'. 'Reinstated divinity': there can be no greater indication of the value and weight some Victorians placed on childhood than this; children, at least as painted in this way, were divine. Kate Greenaway herself, who 'hated to be grown-up', set in train a tradition of depicting children that had many imitators. As her early twentieth-century biographers put it: 'Kate Greenaway interested us in the children themselves. She taught us more of the charm of their ways than we had seen before; she showed us their graces, their little foibles, their thousand little prettinesses, the sweet little characteristics and psychology of their tender age, as no one else had done before.' What this meant was blocking out anything unpleasant. Take her illustration for 'Hark, Hark, the dogs do bark, the beggars are come to town'. [Fig. 23] Far from being in a town, we see two girls standing within a garden looking out to a farmhouse where, at a safe distance, the beggars are grouped in a respectful pose. There is no sign of them being horse-whipped out of town.[26]

You could do this in an illustration for a nursery rhyme, but how could you depict the children you encountered selling flowers on the street or in other ways trying to make a living? Ruskin again gave the answer: 'I often see faces of children, as I walk through the black district of St. Giles's ... which, through all their pale and corrupt misery, recall the old "Non Angli", and recall it, not by their beauty, but their sweetness of expression, even though signed already with trace and cloud of the coming life.'[27]

These faces, with their 'sweetness of expression', were almost certainly the faces of girls. And in the late nineteenth century a number of artists made a living by turning out endless pictures of pitiful girls selling flowers. That there was beauty in the slums, in the children of the slums, became a kind of catchphrase. The job of the artist was to reproduce this for a mass audience, the more pitiful and ragged the child the better. Dorothy Tennant, wife of H. M. Stanley, the journalist who came across Livingstone in Africa, whose *London Street Arabs* was published in 1890, described to her readers how she worked:

> A good supply of rags is essential (carefully fumigated, camphored, and peppered), and you can then dress up your too respectable ragamuffin till he looks as disreputable as you can wish. If you have no rags to start with, and shrink from keeping them *by* you, the best way is to find an average boy, win his confidence, give him sixpence, and promise him another sixpence if he will bring you a boy more ragged than himself. This second boy must be invited to do the same, and urged to bring one yet more 'raggety'. You can in this way get down to a very fine specimen.[28]

The ragged child was as much an inhabitant of Wonderland as the primly dressed Alice as she appeared in artist John Tenniel's original drawings: the Alice of the Alice band. Both were adult fantasies. Both are testimony to the symbolic centrality of childhood in Victorian Britain. In Dickens, with immense power, in his successors with a drift into sentimentality and escapism, children became the verbal and visual way of giving expression to many of the anxieties they had about their civilization. You could, if only temporarily, escape from those anxieties by going to Never-Never-Land.

How did the evocation of this wonderland of childhood impact on the lives of children at work and in the streets? No greater contrast could there be than that between childhood as it was now thought it should be and as it actually was in the factories, mines and streets of industrial Britain.

Children at work

In the opening chapter of Charles Kingsley's *The Water Babies*, ten-year-old Tom is cleaning the chimneys in a grand house in the country. Getting lost among the maze of chimneys, he finds himself by mistake in a furnished room.

The room was all dressed in white – white window-curtains, white bed-curtains, white furniture, and white walls, with just a few lines of pink here and there ... Under the snow-white coverlet, upon the snow-white pillow, lay the most beautiful little girl that Tom had ever seen. Her cheeks were almost as white as the pillow, and her hair was like threads of gold spread all about over the bed. She might have been as old as Tom, or maybe a year or two older; but Tom did not think of that. He thought only of her delicate skin and golden hair, and wondered whether she was a real live person, or one of the wax dolls he had seen in the shops. But when he saw her breathe, he made up his mind that she was alive, and stood staring at her as if she had been an angel out of heaven ... And looking round he suddenly saw, standing close to him, a little, ugly, black, ragged figure, with bleared eyes and grinning white teeth. He turned on it angrily. What did such a little black ape want in that sweet young lady's room? And behold, it was himself, reflected in a great mirror, the like of which Tom had never seen before.[29]

We could understand this meeting of white and black in a number of ways: the female domain is being polluted by the male; it is a racial encounter in a society where blacks were few and, as here, stereotyped. But it is also a rare moment when the world of the well-to-do is invaded by the reality of working children.

The climbing boys featured large in the imagination of the middle classes of the late eighteenth and nineteenth century. They were, of course, much fewer in number than the children working in cotton factories or coalmines, but they were visible, and extraordinary rumours about them abounded: they were often, it was said, children of good families who had been stolen by gypsies and sold to the master sweeps. Charles Dickens, walking around London as a young man, wondered if the dirty and dishevelled climbing boys he encountered might be 'the lost son and heir of some illustrious personage'.[30]

Any romanticization of the climbing boy was cut short by those who came to know their real lives. The chimneys they had to climb were often very narrow, as little as 23 × 23 cm (9 × 9 inches): it is a task way beyond today's seven year olds. Even at the time, pinpricks to the heels or some lighted straw might be needed to persuade the boys to climb into the darkness. And if they inured themselves to the work, they were all too likely to fall victim to the occupational disease of the chimney sweep: cancer of the scrotum. From the late eighteenth century there were attempts to control the trade or, as a campaigning organization put it, to 'supersede the necessity of climbing boys' by substituting a machine for them.[31] Numerous Acts of Parliament were passed, one in 1864, only a year after the publication of *The Water Babies*. Like its predecessors, it proved deficient. In March 1875 a court heard how George Brewster, aged 11, had died while sweeping flues at Fulbourn Hospital in Cambridge. George was born in London. When his mother became ill, he was adopted by an elder brother then passed to another brother, and finally apprenticed to William Wyer, a master sweep. A post-mortem examination revealed that his arms were abraded, his head congested, and there was much black powder in his lungs and windpipe. He had died of suffocation. *The Times* devoted a leading article to George's death, Lord Shaftesbury presented yet another bill to parliament. It passed and it was effective, thus bringing to an end what *The Times* had called one of the worst 'public scandals of this Kingdom'.[32]

If some people in the early nineteenth century were beginning to envisage a world without climbing boys, most commentators and policy-makers at that date were still intent, as they had been in the eighteenth century, on ensuring that there were work opportunities for all the children of the poor. The problem was particularly acute for children in the care of the Poor Law, for if there were no work for these children to do they were a continuing expense. When the early factory masters, their factories dependent on water power and therefore sited in remote valleys in the north of England and the Midlands, were crying out for children to work the machines, Poor Law authorities in London saw a heaven-sent opportunity and began to dispatch cartloads of the children in their care. In 1832 a radical Manchester publisher put into the world, to give it its full title, *A Memoir of Robert Blincoe, an Orphan Boy, Sent from the Workhouse of St. Pancras, London, at Seven Years of Age, to Endure the Horrors of a Cotton-Mill, through his infancy and youth, with a minute detail of his sufferings, being the first memoir of the kind published*. Blincoe describes how 80 children, boys and girls, were sent to Lowdham mill near Nottingham, lured by false promises of roast beef and plum pudding. Horrified by the conditions, and working at least 14 hours every day, Blincoe attempted to escape but was captured. Thereafter

> Blincoe submitted sullenly and patiently to his fate; he worked according
> to his age and stature, as hard as any one in the mill. When his strength

failed, and his limbs refused their office, he endured the strap or the stick, the cuff or the kick, with as much resignation as any of his fellow-sufferers. In the faded complexions, and sallow looks of his associates, he could see, as, in a mirror, his own altered condition. Many of his comrades had, by this time, been more or less injured by the machinery. Some had the skin scraped off the knuckles, clean to the bone, by the fliers; others a finger crushed, a joint or two nipped off in the cogs of the spinning-frame wheels. When his turn to suffer came, the fore-finger of his left hand was caught, and almost before he could cry out, off was the first joint – his lamentations excited no manner of emotion in the specta-tors, except a coarse joke – he clapped the mangled joint, streaming with blood, to the finger, and ran off to Burton, to the surgeon, who, very composedly put the parts together again, and sent him back to the mill. Though the pain was so intense, he could scarcely help crying out every minute, he was not allowed to leave the frame.[33]

Long before the publication of Blincoe's *Memoir* in 1832, the cotton mills had come to rely on what was called 'free labour' rather than the indentured labour of the parish apprentices who were signed up for 14 years. But many thought this new system imposed as much cruelty on the children as parish apprenticeship. One of the critics of this unregulated labour market was Samuel Coleridge:

But *free* labour! – in what sense, not utterly sophistical, can the labour of children, extorted from the wants of their parents, 'their poverty, but not their will, consenting', be called *free*? ... It is our duty to declare aloud, that if the labour were indeed free, the employer would purchase, and the labourer sell, what the former had no right to buy, and the latter no right to dispose of; namely, the labourer's health, life, and well-being. These belong not to himself *alone*, but to his friends, to his parents, to his King, to his Country, and to God. If the labor were indeed free, the contract would approach, on the one side, too near to suicide, on the other to manslaughter.[34]

Joseph Hebergam, at the age of 17, gave evidence before a House of Commons Select Committee of 1831–2 and described this 'free labour'.

He had started work, he said, at the age of seven in a worsted spinning mill near Huddersfield, working from 5 a.m. to 8 p.m. with a break of 30 minutes at noon. One overlooker was 'kept on purpose to strap'. The report of his evidence then continues:

> Was the main business of one of the overlookers that of strapping the children up to this excessive labour? – Yes, the same as strapping an old restive horse that has fallen down and will not get up.
> Was that the constant practice? – Yes, day by day.
> Were there straps regularly provided for that purpose? – Yes, he is continually walking up and down with it in his hand.
> And his office is to strap you into labour? – Yes.

Moving at the age of ten to a woollen factory, where the hours of work were longer, and the discipline administered by fist and foot rather than strap, Hebergam recalled how 'I wished many times they would have sent me for a West India slave ... I thought ... that there could not be worse slaves than those who worked in factories.'[35]

We are at a rare moment in the history of childhood when children can be seen to be aware of their place in history and engaged in political activity. And it was not simply individual testimony. Periodic Acts of Parliament had been passed – in 1802, 1819, 1825 and 1829 – to put some limits to the exploitation of children in the cotton mills and factories, but for lack of enforcement procedures none of them had much impact. In the early 1830s the call for action was mounting. On 24 April 1832 thousands attended a meeting in the Castle Yard in York. They had assembled the previous night in Leeds, 24 miles away, and walked to York, 'not only men, but factory boys and girls, mothers with infants in their arms'. They carried banners, some inscribed simply, 'Father, is it time?': 'a cry which is often heard the night through in the crowded and wretched dormitory of the factory working-people, and which little children, more asleep than awake (dreading the consequences of being late), were often heard to utter'. One girl, on her death-bed, had started up, asked that very question and then sank back into her father's arms and died. Arrived in York, the demonstrators stood for five hours listening to the speeches calling for a Ten Hours Act. And then they had to face the walk back home again to Leeds and beyond. Later that year, in Manchester, hundreds of factory children lined up to greet Michael Sadler and Richard Oastler, two leaders of the campaign.[36]

The outcome of the agitation was the Factory Act, 1833. It did not meet the demand for a ten-hour day (that would have meant putting limits on adult labour), but it did for the first time appoint inspectors to enforce the provisions of the Act – only four of them for the whole of Britain, but their reports began to put in place a system of regulation that was further refined as the century progressed. Under the 1833 Act, no child under nine was allowed to work in a factory, and up to the age of 14 their eight hours of work was matched by time in school. So was born the half-time system, dominant in the north of England until 1918, with children half-time at school and half-time at work. [Fig. 26]

In the 1840s attention shifted to the work of children employed underground in the mines. Some of them, the trappers, controlled the air vents, others, a little older, were harnessed to the carts and pulled the coal through narrow tunnels away from the coalface. [Fig. 17] Revelation of what was happening, accompanied by drawings of the children at work, was deeply shocking, though perhaps as much for the near nakedness of workers of both sexes as for the conditions of work. Commissioners interviewed some of the children to find out the age at which they had started underground and their feeling about it. Here is Sarah Gooder, aged eight, in 1842, a trapper in the Gawber pit: 'It does not tire me, but I have to trap without a light and I'm scared. I go at four and sometimes half past three in the morning and come out at five and half past. I never go to sleep. Sometimes I sing when I've light, but not in the dark ... I don't like being in the pit. I am very sleepy when I go sometimes in the morning ... I would like to be at school far better.' Sarah's sisters Ann, aged 17, and Maria, 12, also worked in the pit, the girls' wages essential to supplement their father's.[37]

By the 1870s, if not before, contemporaries felt that the worst horrors of child labour were over, and that legislation was in force to bring abuses to light. In the late nineteenth and early twentieth century many people looked back in horror and disbelief at what one writer called 'the story of the martyrdom of childhood'.[38] There were, it is true, always apologists for what happened to children in the Industrial Revolution, and there still are. And some of the points they make are perfectly legitimate. Only a minority of working children was up the chimneys, down the mines or in the factories. Children were more likely to be working on the land or, especially if they were girls, as servants. Nor should it be assumed that work conditions in factories or mines were always the worst. The gang labour of children in agriculture or the long hours of children working for their families in so-called domestic industry were in their time equally notorious. But these points in a way simply spread the misery. The hours that children worked, the conditions of their work and the discipline to which they were subjected continue to make this a dark passage in the history of childhood in Britain.

It was little comfort to the children, but perhaps some to us, that so many writers expressed their outrage at what was happening. Sometimes, as in *The Water Babies*, the working child invades middle-class space: Tom could not be ignored. But more often it was reading about and imagining these children that stirred people. The work of the children seemed to run counter to nature. Here is Elizabeth Barrett Browning in the 1840s in her famous and often quoted 'The Cry of the Children':

> The young lambs are bleating in the meadows,
>   The young birds are chirping in the nest,
> The young fawns are playing with the shadows,
>   The young flowers are blowing toward the west –
> But the young, young children, O my brothers,
>   They are weeping bitterly!
> They are weeping in the playtime of the others,
>   In the country of the free.[39]

Seeing this overturning of nature – and seeing it in 'the country of the free', in Britain – some people, for the first time in history, began to imagine a world where children did not work at all – perhaps a mixed blessing, but one that still has resonance. In language that no previous century could have thought of, a Sheffield poet in the 1830s wrote how 'Ever a toiling *Child* doth make us sad'.[40] Many of his contemporaries were equally saddened and seriously alarmed by the children who often had no jobs and scraped a living on the streets.

Rescuing children

Henry Mayhew was an investigative journalist who in the middle years of the nineteenth century devoted much attention to the poor in London, and particularly to the children who lived and worked on the streets. His most famous interview was with 'the little watercress girl who ... although only eight years of age, had entirely lost all childish ways, and was, indeed, in thoughts and manner, a woman'. Mayhew found it difficult to adopt the right tone in getting her to talk, treating her as if she were a child, but eventually she opened up:

> On and off, I've been very near a twelvemonth in the streets. Before that, I had to take care of a baby for my aunt. No, it wasn't heavy – it was only two months old; but I minded it for ever such a time – till it could walk. It was a very nice little baby, not a very pretty one; but, if I touched it under the chin, it would laugh. Before I had the baby, I used to help mother, who was in the fur trade; and, if there was any slits in the fur, I'd sew them up. My mother learned me to needle-work and to knit when I was about five. I used to go to school, too; but I wasn't there long. Sometimes I make a great deal of money. One day I took 1s. 6d., and the creases cost 6d.; but it isn't often I get such luck as that. I oftener makes 3d. or 4d. than 1s.; and then I'm at work, crying, 'Creases, four bunches a penny, creases!' from six in the morning to about ten. All my money I earns I puts in a club and draws it out to buy clothes with It's better than spending it in sweet-stuff, for them as has a living to earn. Besides it's like a child to care for sugar-sticks, and not like one who's got a living and vittals to earn. I ain't a child and I shan't be a woman till I'm twenty, but I'm past eight, I am.

Mayhew thought anyone under 15 was a 'child'. The watercress girl at eight was no longer a child. At that age she had already been selling in the streets for nearly a year, having previously helped her mother in the fur trade and looked after an aunt's baby.[41]

By the time Mayhew conducted his interview, street children had already attracted much attention, and they were to continue to do so right through the nineteenth century. A plethora of institutions aimed to help them or control them, though some people seemed to feel that they should be left to enjoy themselves. One of the reasons for the interest in street children was that in the early nineteenth century children formed an exceptionally high proportion of the population. In 1826 there were 1120 children under 14 for every 1000 adults aged 25–60.[42] And it was in the rapidly growing cities of Victorian

Britain that these children were most visible. London, said a police magistrate, 'has got too full of children'.[43] The focus was first on what people were beginning to call 'juvenile delinquency'. Here is an 11-year-old boy, who's been thieving for three or four years and has already experienced four spells in prison, describing his entry into crime: 'I first began to steal apples with other boys, and then to pick pockets, being taught by my elder brother how to do it ... My mother has tried to keep me in, and has beat me; my step-father drinks. At times I have got clear off with as many handkerchiefs as I could carry, stowing them away in my trousers, and down my legs.'[44]

To try to curb the problem there was in London, from 1808, a Society for the Suppression of Juvenile Vagrancy, reconstituted in 1830 as the Children's Friend Society, formed, 'to rescue from early depravity children who are actually running wild about the streets'. In Portsmouth in 1818, a cobbler, John Pounds, founded a school for such children, his 'wagabonds' as he called them. Street children, however, were not an exclusively southern phenomenon. In Manchester an investigator in 1840 claimed that about 3650 children were lost each year 'and found straying in the streets by the police'. In that city, especially on Sundays, you could see a surprising number of 'shoeless, half-naked, uncombed, and dirty little urchins, who, from two to six years old and upwards, swarm in the streets, some grovelling in the dirt and mire, or collected in knots actively engaged in some idle amusement'.[45]

The alarm manifest here was often mixed with practical endeavours to bring some relief to the children. In Aberdeen, Sheriff Watson in the early 1840s was establishing industrial feeding schools that gained national fame. Out of all these initiatives came the 'ragged schools', open 'exclusively for children raggedly clothed'. [Fig. 19] Lord Ashley, who was and remained actively concerned for children in factories and mines, now turned his attention to these street children and to the remedies on offer through the ragged schools. There were, he thought, in London alone, more than 30,000 'naked, filthy, roaming, lawless, and deserted children'. Opening a ragged school was, as he recounted, a challenge:

> We have heard the various teachers narrate most graphically the drumming at the doors, the rattling at the windows, by those who demanded admittance; the uproar of their entry; the immediate extinction of the lamps; the dirt and the stones that flew in all directions, rendering this

service of love in no slight degree a service of danger. Oftentimes these lads got possession of the apartments; and, refusing either to learn or to retire, continued lords paramount until the arrival of the police. But patience and principle have conquered them all; and now we may see, on each evening of the week, hundreds of these young maniacs engaged in diligent study, clothed, and in their right mind.[46]

These children were the 'street Arabs' of Victorian Britain. The man who probably did most to put the phrase into circulation was the evangelical social reformer Thomas Guthrie in his *Plea for Ragged Schools* written in Edinburgh in 1847. Guthrie compared the children he saw to 'the wild Arab or wild ass of the desert', but it was normally people, the Bedouin Arabs, whom contemporaries had in mind when they talked about street Arabs. The Bedouin, travellers reported, were remarkable for their mobility and their independence. The children who attended ragged schools too often shared these characteristics, thought to be highly undesirable in children. 'The smallest offence to their freer than Arab feelings', reported one of Guthrie's correspondents, 'is cause enough for them to endeavour to escape from school, and to resume the more than savage life to which they have been habituated from their earliest infancy.'[47]

The teachers in ragged schools struggled on without making much impact on the concern about street children. An incident in the winter of 1869–70 marked what we would now call a step change in the level of concern. One cold night a teacher at a ragged school was about to set off home for the night when he noticed a little lad unwilling to leave:

> 'Come, my lad, had you not better get home? It is very late. Mother will be coming for you.'
>
> 'Please, sir, let me stop!'
>
> 'No, I cannot, I think it's quite time for you to get away now. Why do you want to stop?'
>
> 'Please, sir, do let me stay. I won't do no 'arm.'
>
> 'Well, but had you not better get home? Your mother will wonder what kept you so late.'
>
> 'I ain't got no mother.'
>
> 'Haven't got a mother, boy? Where do you live?'

'Don't live nowhere.'

'Do you mean to say, my boy, that you have no home, and that you have no mother and father?'

'That's the truth on't, sir; I ain't telling you no lie about it.'

'Well, but where did you sleep last night?'

'Down in Whitechapel, sir, along o' the 'aymarket in one of them carts as is filled with 'ay; and then I met a chap as I knowed this afternoon, and he told me to come up 'ere to school, as perhaps you'd let me lie near the fire all night. I won't do no 'arm, sir, if you let me stop.'

'[Are there other children sleeping out like you]?'

'Oh yes, sir, lots, 'eaps on 'em! More 'n I could count!'[48]

Jim Jarvis had left home when his mother died when he was about five. An old lady befriended him, and he got some work doing odd jobs for a lighterman on a barge, but ran away from his brutality. He helped another lady who kept a tripe and trotter stall, but was frequently without food, or lodging, and hassled by the police. The man to whom he was telling his story was Thomas Barnardo, who had arrived in London three years previously *en route* to work for the China Inland Mission, but brought to a halt by the child poverty he encountered in the capital city of the world's biggest empire. [Fig. 24] It was after midnight when Jim led Barnardo up to the roof near Petticoat Lane, where Barnardo saw 'eleven boys huddled together for warmth – no roof or covering of any kind was over them and the clothes they had were rags, which seemed to be worse than Jim's'.[49]

Barnardo's encounter with Jim Jarvis marks a moment when the movement to rescue children from poverty and neglect gains new momentum. Numerous organizations sprang up to give help. They were nearly all run on denominational lines. Barnardo was a Nonconformist, and his rescue of Jim Jarvis had the added piquancy that Jim was Catholic, saved from both destitution and papacy. The Waifs and Strays Society was founded after a young civil servant and Sunday-school teacher, Edward Rudolf, discovered that there was no free shelter for two homeless, young brothers other than in a Barnardo's home: immediately he set to work to create a parallel Church of England organization, which survives to this day as The Children's Society. For many years the picture on the society's collecting-boxes of a little boy and a younger girl in ragged clothing, asleep on a doorstep, opened the purses of Anglicans.[50]

The National Society for the Prevention of Cruelty to Children (NSPCC) surmounted these denominational hurdles. Its two main protagonists were a Roman Catholic, Cardinal Manning, and a Congregationalist, Benjamin Waugh. It is often said of the British that they were more concerned about cruelty to animals than cruelty to children. After all, the Royal Society for the Prevention of Cruelty to Animals (RSPCA) was founded in the 1820s, the merely National Society for the Prevention of Cruelty to Children only in the 1880s – though in Scotland it became a royal society. In fact, there is much evidence that cruelty to, and abuse of, children met with both legal and community sanction before the foundation of the NSPCC. Back in the seventeenth century Adam Martindale described how his own daughter, aged three and a half, gave testimony that resulted in the imprisonment of a man who had 'carnally known' the five-year-old daughter of his neighbour. There was an upward trend in the number of child-abuse cases coming before the courts in the late eighteenth and early nineteenth century. *The Times*, between 1785 and 1860, reported 385 cases of child neglect and sexual abuse, with only 7 per cent resulting in a 'not guilty' verdict. A London magistrate in 1830 acquitted, because of insufficient evidence, a shoemaker accused of intending to abuse girl children, but told the court that 'If I were the father ... and had a good horsewhip in my hand, I know where I should apply it.' Outside the court, the shoemaker 'was met by a posse of women, who began to hoot and pelt him, and a sturdy coal-heaver tripping up his heels rolled him for several yards in the kennel, to the no small delight of the bystanders'.[51]

The NSPCC wanted to get away from these community sanctions to a situation where the law gave protection to children. It campaigned hard for changes in the law and successfully steered through parliament a succession of what were known as 'Children's Charters', which reduced parental powers. For the NSPCC recognized that it was in the home that most abuse and neglect happened. If it were going to succeed, it needed the cooperation of the public, which it acquired. By 1910 the NSPCC had 250 inspectors, dealing with over 50,000 complaints, most of them originating with neighbours. The 'cruelty man', as he was called, was feared by some, trusted by most.[52]

NSPCC policy was to do everything possible to prevent the break-up of the home. But what was to be done with children for whom the home was non-existent or manifestly unsuitable? We have seen how in the seventeenth century troublesome teenagers were sent off to the American colonies. In the

1830s and 1840s attention turned to the possibilities in Australia. Many of the boys, who had their brushes with the law, welcomed the prospect of a new life in Australia, though the reality was not always what they had hoped for. Take Henry Underwood, who, interviewed in London at the age of 14, described how, some ten months previously, he had started out stealing 'provisions – such as bread and bacon'. He was transported in 1836 to a penal colony in Van Diemen's Land (modern Tasmania), one of over 10,000 juvenile convicts aged 18 and under sent there between 1803 and 1853. Once there, the records tell us how he was placed in solitary confinement for a variety of offences: talking at the muster, improper conduct at school, suspicion of secreting potatoes, fishing on the rocks contrary to orders. Then the punishment became physical: 25 stripes on the breech (lashes on the buttocks) for insolence, another 25 for disorderly conduct and then, in 1840, 14 days' hard labour in chains for further insolence. Minor theft in London ended in chain labour in Tasmania, a downward spiral all too frequent in these eloquent records.[53]

As the sense of alarm about children in the city grew, the empire seemed to have possibilities as a repository not only for young criminals but also for any of the children of the poor who had come into contact with Barnardo's or other rescue organizations or the Poor Law. The founder of the Salvation Army, William Booth, published in 1890 a famous book, *In Darkest England and the Way Out*. It contains a picture that you can unfold. At the bottom is a dark and raging urban sea, in which three million people are in danger of drowning if they haven't already done so. The Salvation Army lighthouse sheds light and hope on the scene, and its devoted workers are rescuing people to take them to the city colony where numerous institutions have been set up to help. They include Homes for Children, a Boys' Industrial Home and a Preventive Home for Girls (to prevent them from becoming prostitutes). The next step on the road to salvation is the Farm Colony where people are busy working the land. Then finally, at the apex of an arch, the colour now light rather than dark, there is the 'Colony across the Sea', the solution to the problems of modern urban life.

Between 1868 and 1925 some 80,000 British boys and girls, most of them under 14, were sent to Canada as agricultural labourers and domestic servants. Canada, said Barnardo, was 'a fair garden-like country, yielding abundantly', a description that may have rung a bit hollow for youngsters enduring the long Canadian winter. Once in Canada, the children were turned over to farms or homes, normally under some kind of apprenticeship system, the argument being that this would offer them, as it did, some kind of protection against cruelty or neglect. It was better than the alternative, adoption. As one girl succinctly put it, ''Doption, sir, is when folks gets a girl to work without wages.'

Even in favourable circumstances, life must often have been lonely and hard. The children showed signs of distress, cases of enuresis common. William White, a ward of the London Children's Aid Society, was placed at Grenfell, Assiniboia, in May 1892 at the age of 14. He became incontinent at night. His master had him sleep in the stable. Temperatures reached minus 45°C, William's feet froze solid, and he died on St Valentine's Day 1893 of gangrene after frostbite.[54] Events like the death of William White sometimes blew up into media scandals, and the proponents of child emigration were forced on to the defensive. But after lying low for a few years, the attractiveness of the empire would again come to the surface, and new schemes for emigration would proliferate.

For those rescued children who didn't cross the seas, the likely outcome would be life in an institution. Probably the worst fate was to be in a Poor Law institution, some children living with adults in the general mixed wards, others in what became criticized as barrack schools, vast buildings housing hundreds of children where, in a word coined by contemporaries, they became 'institutionalized'. There were attempts to remedy this by setting up 'cottage homes', the phrase disguising the fact that these were houses where some 15 or so children lived under the supervision and control of a house mother or father.[55] An alternative, particularly popular in Scotland, was to foster the children, a whole way of life emerging in which poor families in the Highlands supplemented inadequate incomes by taking in children from the Lowland cities.[56] Alongside these state initiatives were numerous schemes run by charities, orphanages and homes, which often came close to the institutions run by the state. Although a Prevention of Cruelty to Children Act, 1889, made it easier to remove children from parental care, some of the children in the charities' homes were there through a process that amounted, in Barnardo's case, to what he called 'philanthropic abduction'.[57] And once in such a home, Barnardo himself took the place of their parents. One girl, Ellen S, who had been at Barnardo's Barkingside home and then went out to service, wrote back to say how much she missed her friends and went on:

'Dr Barnardo gave me a Bible and a pledge card. How often I think now of what he said to me! I did ask him if he would still call me one of his daughters. And he said, yes, of course he would.'[58] To save the child, there had to be a complete break with the family.

Nineteenth-century cities swarmed with children. As those who encountered them or worked with them often noted, they were in many ways more attractive than rural children, quick-witted, cheeky, playful. Some were drawn to them. Here is essayist Charles Lamb in the early nineteenth century, describing a fall in the street:

> I scrambled up with pain and shame enough – yet outwardly trying to face it down, as if nothing had happened – when the roguish grin of one of these young wits encountered me. There he stood, pointing me out with his dusky finger to the mob, and to a poor woman (I suppose his mother) in particular, till the tears for the exquisiteness of the fun (so he thought it) worked themselves out at the corners of his poor red eyes, red from many a previous weeping, and soot-inflamed, yet twinkling through all with such a joy, snatched out of desolation, that Hogarth – but Hogarth has got him already (How could he miss him?) in the March to Finchley, grinning at the pieman – there he stood, as he stands in the picture, irremovable, as if the jest was to last for ever – with such a maximum of glee, and minimum of mischief, in his mirth – for the grin of a genuine sweep hath absolutely no malice in it – that I could have been content, if the honour of a gentleman might endure it, to have remained his butt and his mockery till midnight.[59]

For cartoonists in *Punch* and elsewhere this 'humour of the streets' was a stock topic. In Edinburgh Thomas Guthrie, watching the exuberance of the boys playing in the Grassmarket, reflected that 'God made childhood to be happy'. The street children added life to the Victorian street scene. [Fig. 20] Phil May, a late Victorian *Punch* cartoonist, introducing his collection of sketches entitled *Guttersnipes*, wrote, 'Children of the gutter roam about free, and are often hungry, but what would one not give for such appetites? ... Sometimes I wonder whether they don't lead the happier lives?'[60]

But for Ashley and Barnardo and the many others who devoted their lives to trying to rescue the street children, the happiness was only surface deep.

Over the children hung a sense of doom: their childhoods were short; they would grow up physically weak, their sense of morality similarly stunted. Looking back on it, we are amazed at the decisions the rescuers took on behalf of children, decisions that might remove children from their homes and from their homeland. Only the perceived scale of the problem could have led to such major initiatives. It was easy to be moved, as Barnardo was, by the plight of a Jim Jarvis, much less easy to see what to do about it. Some children were to their dying days grateful for their rescue; others resented and sometimes fought against it from the outset.

The habit of schooling

The number of children who needed to be rescued from street life was one factor prompting a move for compulsory schooling for children. There were, said the Registrar-General in 1851, just under one million 'healthy unemployed children between the ages of five and twelve'.[61] They should, he implied, be either at school or at work. As the century wore on, school became the favoured place for them. And yet long before schooling became compulsory in the 1870s and 1880s, most children did receive some schooling. [Fig. 15] Charles Shaw was born to a poor family in Tunstall in the Potteries in 1832, the year of the passage of the Great Reform Act.

> My education, such as it was, was like that of thousands in my day. I went to old Betty W.'s school, and as I had 'finished my education' when I was seven years old, I must have attended her school between three or four years. The school was the only room on the ground floor of her little cottage. It was about four yards square, with a winding, narrow staircase leading to the one bedroom above. The furniture was very scant, consisting of a small table, two chairs, and two or three little forms about eight inches high for the children to sit upon ... There was an alphabet, with rude pictures, for beginners. There must have been something intensely vivid about these letters in the alphabet, for to this day when I see the letters Q and S as single capitals I see them rather as when I first saw them in old Betty's alphabet ... Betty's next grade, after the alphabet, was the reading-made-easy book, with black letters, making words in two, three and four letters. The next stage was spelling, and reading of the Bible ... [T]hough she never taught writing, her scholars were generally

> noted for their ability to read while very young. I know I could read my
> Bible with remarkable ease when I left her school, when seven years old.

Rather than writing, successful readers were taught to knit stockings. Before
he had left old Betty's school, Charles Shaw had already started at another
school, the Sunday school. It was soon 'a life within my life', a counter
to the horrors he endured and witnessed as a young mould-runner in the
Potteries.[62]

It is often thought that, Scotland apart, most working-class children were
lucky if they got any schooling before the Forster Education Act, 1870. In fact,
most got some schooling. A majority went to Sunday school, many went to the
dame schools of the kind remembered with such affection by Charles Shaw,
and an increasing number went to the schools run by the two, big, voluntary
societies established in the early nineteenth century to provide education for
the poor. The biggest was the National Society for Promoting the Education of
the Poor in the Principles of the Established Church, its rival the non-denom-
inational but effectively Nonconformist British and Foreign Schools Society.
From the 1830s onwards these societies began to get government grants. It
soon came to be thought necessary to ensure that the money was well spent,
and the outcome was a system that became infamous – payment by results.
Joseph Ashby, at a National society school in Tysoe, Warwickshire, in the
1860s, described what happened:

> Two inspectors came once a year and carried out a dramatic examination.
> The schoolmaster came into school in his best suit; all the pupils and
> teachers would be listening till at ten o'clock a dog-cart would be heard
> on the road, even though it was eighty yards away. In would come two
> gentlemen with a deportment of high authority, with rich voices. Each
> would sit at a desk and children would be called in turn to one or other.
> The master hovered round, calling children out as they were needed. The
> children could see him start with vexation as a good pupil stuck at a word
> in the reading-book he had been using all the year, or sat motionless with
> his sum in front of him. The master's anxiety was deep, for his earnings
> depended on the children's work. One year the atmosphere of anxiety so
> affected the lower standards that, one after another as they were brought
> to the Inspector, the boys howled and the girls whimpered.

For boys like Joseph Ashby, school

> was so unreal ... There were 'object' lessons now and then – without
> any objects but with white chalk drawings on the blackboard ... Once
> there was a lesson on a strange animal called a quad-ru-ped – cloven-
> footed, a chewer of the cud; her house was called a byre (but in Tysoe
> it was not); her skin was made into shoes and from her udder came
> milk. It burst upon Joseph that this was one of the creatures he would
> milk after school, part of Henry Beasley's herd. He would milk three
> or four cows, and Robert Philpott, stronger and quicker in the hand,
> would milk the other six, though in school the latter was a famous
> dunce, always in trouble.'[63]

It was hardly surprising that many parents and children preferred the uninspected dame schools or, as they were sometimes called, the private adventure schools. These, alas, were not schools with adventure playgrounds, but schools run privately for profit, as a venture or speculation. Parents paid fees, but in return had some control. Children would attend when it suited their parents; harsh punishment would lead to a change of school. The curriculum was devoted to teaching basic skills, above all reading. There was nothing about the 'Principles of the Established Church'. Of course these schools ranged from the good to the bad, but that was probably not their main deficiency in the eyes of those who tried, successfully, to drum them out of business in the later nineteenth century. The problem was that they provided the children with no training in morality.[64]

There were many reasons for the move towards compulsory schooling. One was political. With democracy at least on the horizon after the passage in 1867 of the Second Reform Act, which gave the vote to most working-class men in the cities, it was important to 'educate our masters'. Another was a concern, which rumbles on to this day, that it was necessary to educate the future workforce if the economy were to be internationally competitive. But of course both these needs would have been met if the existing schools had been catering for all children and if the schooling they were giving were thought to be adequate. On both counts there were gaps. Too many children were neither at school nor in employment. There was more than a residue of that old fear, going back to Tudor times, of idle children. And then, the schooling that was on offer too often failed to inculcate habits of time-keeping, tidiness, respect and obedience. The only children in England and Wales who had to attend school before 1870 were those working under the Factory Acts and those in workhouses or otherwise in the care of the state. This hardly made it likely that compulsion would be attractive to working-class families. Caution was the order of the day.

The 1870 England and Wales Education Act did not make schooling compulsory. What it did was to allow for the establishment of board schools, financed out of the rates, in areas where voluntary provision was insufficient. And it allowed the school boards to make attendance compulsory. Compulsion for all children did not come until 1880. In Scotland, where attendance at school was more deeply entrenched, demonstrated in much higher literacy rates than in England and Wales, compulsion for all those aged between five and 13 came in 1872.

Compulsion seemed to many working-class parents like an intrusion into matters that were for the family. For 20 years, until 1891, parents had to pay for the privilege of compulsorily sending their children to school. It seemed a double whammy: paying for school and losing the income that might have come from the child's wages. For with compulsion came something else, full-time schooling. The only exemption was in areas, above all the textile districts of Lancashire and Yorkshire, where half-time school and half-time work had legal sanction. Previously, especially in agricultural areas, schooling was concentrated in the winter months, leaving summer for work. As it was, head teachers often adjusted the term dates to the vagaries of the harvests.

The imposition of compulsory schooling has to be seen as a 20- or 30-year period in which parents and children gradually became accustomed to what contemporaries called 'the habit of schooling'. School-attendance officers were at the forefront of this profound shift in expectations about schooling. Rather than being made to fit around work, school was now expected to have priority. Widespread habits and assumptions were under challenge. Working-class mothers had assumed as a matter of course that their daughters would help them with the weekly washing on a Monday and not attend school on that day. And daughters might also be required to look after younger siblings. At a school in Upper Holloway in the early days of the school board era, the headmistress reported difficulties in the school logbook: '17 Feb 1873 Numbers again small ... Parents say they would be glad to send but their girls' services at home cannot be dispensed with. 10 July 1873 It seems almost impossible to induce the parents to make an effort to send their girls regularly – they are kept at home for everything.' Teachers were often sympathetic to the absences. In a Deptford school at the turn of the century, a widowed washerwoman would regularly call through the classroom window to her eight year old, 'Come on out, Liz, I need you.' And the teacher would let her go.[65]

It required not only much persuasion but also frequent resort to the courts to habituate parents and children to school. In England and Wales in the 1880s there were nearly 100,000 prosecutions a year for non-attendance at school. After drunkenness, it was the second most common offence.[66]

Even if the majority of children began to attend school regularly, that did not stop them working before or after school, delivering newspapers or helping out in shops. And many of them couldn't wait for the day when they could leave school. The school-leaving age in England and Wales was gradually raised from ten when it was first introduced in 1880 to 11 in 1893 and 12 in 1899, though with complicated exceptions in rural areas, which meant that you had to reach a certain standard before you could leave. Flora Thompson remembered of her Oxfordshire hamlet in the 1880s that:

In those days a boy of eleven was nearing the end of his school days. Soon he would be at work; already he felt himself nearly a man and too old for petticoat government. Moreover, those were country boys, wild and rough, and many of them as tall as [Miss Holmes] was. Those who had failed to pass Standard IV and so could not leave school until they were eleven, looked upon that last year as a punishment inflicted upon them by the school authorities and behaved accordingly. In this they were encouraged by their parents, for a certain section of these resented their boys being kept at school when they might be earning, 'What do our young Alf want wi' a lot o' book-larnin'?' they would say ... Boys who had been morose or rebellious during their later schooldays were often transformed when they got upon a horse's back or were promoted to driving a dung-cart afield.[67]

Annie Wilson, born in Nottingham in 1898, who loved school, had to leave at the earliest possible moment to become an errand girl in a factory:

When I left school I wasn't quite thirteen. Because I should have
waited till the March when I was thirteen – but Dad had to go to the
Education Offices to say that I was thirteen – he went a few days before –
he didn't mean me to miss the chance for getting a job. And he got the
wrong date. And I went and got this job. And they made me go back
to school again for another week because I'd gone a few days before.
The schools didn't have everybody leaving at a certain time. You left
when you was thirteen.[68]

The pressures to earn for the family were powerful, but the pride that
came with doing so often considerable. Clifford Hills, born in 1904, had a job
before and after school as a kitchen boy from the age of nine and worked hard
in the summer holidays. His earnings paid for the weekend joint of beef. He
told an interviewer in the late 1960s that 'You must remember that boys from
nine to fourteen were men nearly in those days, you know.'[69]

James Brady, born in Rochdale in 1898, had the same sense of achieving
manhood through work:

The sheer force of economic necessity drove my astute mother to
pre-empt my twelfth birthday by a couple of weeks and find a job for
me as an alley-sweeper half-timer at Messrs Samuel Heaps and Sons'
flannelette factory ... It gave me satisfaction to know that I would soon
become a breadwinner to help the family budget ... I knew that when
I was thirteen I would have to say goodbye to my schooling at Spotland
Board School and become a full-timer at Heaps, working a fifty-five and
a half hour week for ten shillings and sixpence – a fortune for mother ...
[When that time came] I had to undergo the stimulating ritual of being
'lengthened', which meant changing baggy knickerbockers, long socks
and elastic garters which stopped your circulation, for long, smelly
corduroy trousers held up by stout leather braces. It also meant a new
heavy brown cap, with a button on top and a thicker scarf to keep the
icy blast out. This was the drab, but completely utilitarian attire of the
traditional Lancashire working-man which transformed you in a day
from boyhood to manhood. What a landmark in my life when Mum
took me down to the Co-op in Toad Lane to have me rigged out at
a total cost of fifteen shillings.[70]

Older children often resented the discipline of school, particularly as they neared the leaving age. In 1889 and again in 1911, both years when there were many strikes in the adult world, there was a spate of school strikes. Children demanded payment for the monitors who were often left to look after younger children and received little schooling themselves, an end to corporal punishment and shorter hours.[71]

When they grew up quite a number of children who had been at the board or national schools of the late nineteenth century and early twentieth remembered their schooling with some fondness. Amid the often harsh discipline, they recalled inspiring teachers or an introduction to literature that stayed with them through life. Girls especially were sorry to leave.[72] Whereas boys commonly thought of themselves as men once they left school, girls did not in the same way become women. Their most likely lot was to become a domestic servant or to work in a factory; marriage, probably a decade ahead, was their destiny. Their schooling had prepared them for it.

In the last 30 years of the nineteenth century board schools became dominant features of the urban landscape, their architecture letting in light, and the old single room divided into modern classrooms. Payment by results had gone in the 1890s though its effects lingered on. But new subjects could now be taught with more freedom, and the whole school experience improved. Despite all this, few working-class children could raise their eyes above the minimum leaving age. Even if they had the academic ability to proceed to secondary school – and entrance to it became easier after the 1902 Education Act – family expectations and family poverty often made it impossible. Robert Roberts was a bright boy in a poor neighbourhood in Salford. The school had a debate one day on the motion that the school-leaving age should be raised. Roberts made an eloquent speech in support. His opponent was brief and to the point: 'We should gerrout to work at fourteen and fetch some money in for us parents.' Only two votes were cast for Roberts, 48 for his opponent.[73]

By the early twentieth century both parents and children knew that schooling was compulsory, and that any prolonged resistance would lead to an appearance in court. Most accepted this situation without questioning. But in working-class families everyone knew instinctively that children's earnings were crucial to the family budget. If some Victorians came to believe that children should grow up happy, carefree and dependent, for the majority of children at that time that ideal was only a very partial reality.

Chapter Five

The Children of the Nation, 1900–1950

WAR LEFT AN INDELIBLE MARK ON BRITAIN in the first half of the twentieth century. The second and final South African or Boer War (1899–1902), the First World War (1914–18) and the Second World War (1939–45) exposed weaknesses in Britain as a world power and provided the energy and the incentive to try to remedy the defects. In wartime people looked to a better future ahead, and the future was the children. Their health, their education, their sense of citizenship all became matters of intense concern. Right-wing imperialists found common cause with socialists in arguing that something had to be done. The outcome, in and after the Second World War, was a welfare state in which children were of central concern. Rarely has there been such a close identification between childhood and the destiny of the nation.

It is tempting to think that this concern in what was widely trumpeted as 'the century of the child' amounted to the emergence of a child-centred society, one that gave priority to the best interests of the child. There were certainly many who placed great weight on the happiness of children, often associating it with improved health. Journalist and suffragist Evelyn Sharp in 1927 looked forward to a world where children acquire 'the habit of happiness … regard happiness as a right'. Even bureaucracy adopted the language of happiness, a 1931 Board of Education Committee Report urging that the aim of primary schools should be 'to aid children, while they are children, to be healthy and, so far as is possible, happy children'. In the horribly coy but much republished *Important People* of 1930 – the important people of course children – we are told that, rich or poor, children are now 'the personification of health and happiness'. Moreover, nowadays, writes Brenda Spender, 'we *like* children to be happy'. And, so it seemed to many, they were happier. In 1942, poet and children's writer Sylvia Lynd was confident that since Victorian days children had become 'happier'.[1]

But this positive, and self-congratulatory, note cannot disguise the fact that the children about whom there was so much concern in the first half of the twentieth century were rarely seen as individuals, more as a collective problem that if not solved would herald disaster. The institutionalization of children in need reached new peaks. Behaviourism, aiming to produce obedient and well-disciplined children – and future adults – was for many years dominant as a mode of child rearing. Only from the 1930s onwards did an alternative voice begin to be heard, one that tried to listen to what children were saying. Too often it was drowned out by an overriding concern for nation and empire.

'What is the meaning of Empire Day?'

Edna Rich, born in 1910, her father a labourer, remembered very well one lesson at her Bristol elementary school:

> I loved poetry, and the school was assembled and they stood me on top
> of the headmistress's desk and I had a Union Jack draped round me.
> And I had to recite, 'Oh, where are you going to, all you Big Steamers?
> To fetch England's own grain up and down the great sea. I'm going to
> fetch you your bread and butter.' And somehow or other it stirred a bit
> of rebellion in me. I thought, where's my bread, where's my butter?
> And I think it sowed the first seeds of socialism in me, it really did.'[2]

The poem Edna was reciting appeared on the front page of the history of England written by C. R. L. Fletcher and Rudyard Kipling, first published in 1911. Her response to the event is a useful reminder that the attempt to implant ideas in the heads of children can sometimes backfire: Edna did not buy into imperialism. Not all children were so resistant.

Children were deeply affected by Britain's acquisition of an empire on which the sun never set. That phrase dates back to the early nineteenth century. The victories at Trafalgar in 1805 and Waterloo in 1815 had made Britain the major world power. Britain ruled the waves. In the latter part of the nineteenth century and in the early twentieth century, it began to rule land as well. Between 1874 and 1902 Britain added to its empire nearly five million square miles and 90 million people, the advances in Asia and Africa now added to existing colonies such as Canada and Australia. Britain, its rulers became aware, had perhaps the greatest empire the world had ever known. Along with pride in the achievement of empire went growing anxiety as to its safety: Was Britain itself safe against invasion? Might the growing industrial power of Germany or of the United States topple Britain from its leading position? Above all, might the degeneracy of the race, signalled by the physical and moral deficiencies of working-class children in the cities of the United Kingdom, make Britain uncompetitive in a world where people had learnt from Charles Darwin that only the fittest would survive?

Empire and children were linked like mother and child, the empire often referred to as 'Mother Empire'. For the future of the British empire depended on its children. If they were ignorant of the imperial dream, or if they were indifferent to it, or if, like Edna Rich, they were hostile to it, then the future might be bleak. The first thing to do, then, was to ensure that children were brought up with a knowledge of empire, and the means to do this was to make use of the new compulsory elementary schools. Generations of children before Edna Rich had been told about the empire, about how it had been acquired, and about the nation's heroes and heroines. In the late nineteenth century an increasing proportion of these heroes were military or naval.[3] General Gordon, who had vainly defended Khartoum and lost his life in the process, was the most famous. In *Simple Stories from English History for Young Readers* in the 1890s, children read that 'Every boy and girl should be proud that Gordon was an Englishman, and should say to themselves: "I also will be a hero as Gordon was."' If you were looking for heroines, the most prominent names were Florence Nightingale, the Lady with the Lamp of the Crimean War in the 1850s, and Grace Darling, the lighthouse heroine who in the 1830s had risked her life to save the shipwrecked.

The turn-of-the-century war in South Africa was a wake-up call. The greatest empire the world had ever known struggled to defeat Boer farmers. In its aftermath, imperial enthusiasts established Empire Day when schoolchildren gathered to celebrate the empire. Many recalled it fondly as a day when there was a break with routine, and often some buns and oranges to eat. Robert Roberts in Salford remembered singing:

> What is the meaning of Empire Day?
> Why do the cannons roar?
> Why does the cry, 'God save the King!'
> Echo from shore to shore?
> Why does the flag of Britannia float,
> Proudly o'er fort and bay?
> Why do our kinsmen gladly hail,
> Our glorious Empire Day?
> *Réponse*
> On our nation's scroll of glory,
> With its deeds of daring told,
> There is written a story,
> Of the heroes bold,

In the days of old,
So to keep the deeds before us,
Every year we homage pay,
To our banner proud,
That has never bowed,
And that's the meaning of Empire Day!'[4]

This was empire as military conquest, nothing about a civilizing mission. Some children took exception. Vic Amey, born in 1896, remembered: 'On Empire Day we used to all go to the parish hall, sing "Flag of Britain" and all the rest of it. We had a vicar ... I remember him keeping on to us about the German navy, the strength of the German navy, and why shouldn't our navy be equipped with bigger guns. And, as I say, I was pretty bright and I thought it was pretty cheap at the time for a man of God to talk to us about our navy not being armed with big enough guns.'[5]

But if anything established empire in the minds of Britain's children, it was probably not so much these overt efforts at propaganda as the books and magazines that children read, the slides or, later, films that they saw and the toys that they collected or with which they played. Rider Haggard and G. A. Henty were simply the two best-known names amid the veritable army producing imperial adventure stories for the newly literate. Here are the opening lines of *Britons at Bay: The Adventures of Two Midshipmen in the Second Burmese War*, published in 1900:

'The licking we gave them the other day doesn't seem to have
frightened them much,' Arthur Drayton, midshipman on H.M.S. *Fox*,
said to his chum and fellow-middy, Harold Millett.
'They're cheekier than ever,' Harold replied ...
'If I were the Commodore,' Arthur declared, 'I wouldn't have any
more parley with the rascals. They've been insulting our flag and
ill-treating our countrymen for years, and now, instead of giving them
a jolly good thrashing, we're demanding compensation and getting
insulted for our pains every day. Why don't we land and capture the
town and take all the compensation we want?'
'The Commodore will do what is right,' replied Harold, who was not so
excitable and headstrong as Arthur. 'British interests are safe in his hands.'

'I should think they were. I didn't mean to suggest that they were not. The Commodore is a grand fellow, and it would be an honour to be blown to smithereens or go to the bottom in the same ship with him.'

In this story, set in the 1850s, Arthur and Harold are 'rather chubby-faced boys', still growing, hardly of an age to start shaving, their speech that of schoolboys. The boys who would be reading it would be of much the same age and be expected to identify with their bravado. Captured by the Burmese and told they are to be slaves of the queen, they promptly burst into 'Rule, Britannia!', proclaiming that 'Britons never, never, never shall be slaves'.[6]

Slide shows, films, toy soldiers, cigarette cards and almost any kind of merchandise came emblazoned with imperial motifs. It would have been very difficult for any child growing up in the early twentieth century not to have been infected by the ubiquity of empire. Nor did the First World War place the empire on the back burner. Far from it. In 1924 the new Wembley Stadium was the centrepiece of the vast British Empire Exhibition. From the 1920s onwards the emphasis was not so much on the glorious deeds that had won empire as on what is sometimes called 'produce imperialism': each and every part of the empire was associated with some product that bound mother country and empire together in an economic enterprise: wheat from Canada, tin and rubber from Malaya, cocoa from the Gold Coast and so on. Children were brought up on a map of the globe with pink the dominant colour and a knowledge of the trade routes that brought all this produce to the mother country.

India achieved independence in 1947, the Gold Coast became the independent Ghana ten years later, and soon most other African colonies followed suit. The empire became the commonwealth, something with much less hold on the public imagination. And yet until the 1960s the story of the empire played a central role in what might be called the conditioning of British children – as it did also of many children in the colonies.[7]

The empire was not simply an adventure playground in which children could fantasize about becoming heroes. It also offered a solution to some of Britain's most deep-rooted social problems. The emigration of children to the empire continued through to the 1960s. In 1925, Canada put a halt to further child immigrants, and the destination for children switched back to Australia, though other countries such as Southern Rhodesia were for a time much favoured. The numbers were never as great as in the heyday of child emigration to Canada but still considerable: Australia took 6000 children between 1912 and 1967, and in the post-Second World War period, which has been the focus of much recent attention, the total number of children who emigrated was 3000. In that final period of child emigration it was the Australians who were demanding the children rather than social services in Britain trying to offload their clients.[8] It was a common experience for children in institutions to be asked if they wanted to go to Canada, Australia or Rhodesia. One ten year old remembered:

> One evening I was called in by the then Mother Superior [of the children's home]. She was a strict lady and I thought I was going to be in for some kind of telling off. 'Have a seat, my child,' she said. Then she started talking about being sent to Australia. Blimey, I thought, have I been that bad to be sent away? Mother Superior went on to say that I had been chosen, that it was a wonderful opportunity, not some kind of punishment. But that night in bed, I cried. I was so frightened of leaving the only home I'd ever had, of leaving my school friends, my only sisters, of leaving my best friend Pearl, and never seeing any of them again.[9]

If some children left Britain for the dominions or colonies, other children from overseas were finding their way to Britain. They often faced prejudice and hostility, and found themselves caught midway between the culture of their home and the culture of Britain. Tom Barclay, who was Irish, recalled how in Leicester in the 1860s he and his friends were greeted:

> 'Hurro, Mick!'
> 'Ye Awrish Paddywhack!'
> 'Arrah, bad luck to the ships that brought ye over.'
> These were the salutes from the happy English child: we were battered, threatened, elbowed, pressed back to the door of our kennel amid boos and jeers and showers of small missiles.

Such a degree of hostility was likely, as it did, to throw Tom back on his Irish identity.[10] Jewish immigrants, perhaps as many as 150,000 between 1870 and 1914, faced similar reactions. Rose Kerrigan, brought up in Glasgow before the First World War, recalled how: 'We were waylaid quite often coming home from *cheder* [Hebrew school], especially on winter nights. My mother hid in a doorway one night when we were coming home. We'd come home crying 'cos these boys had hit us. We were running from them and my mother came out with an umbrella and gave them such a fright that they never came back.'[11]

Sometimes the overriding wish of the children of immigrants was to identify with the British. In his semi-autobiographical novel, *Children of the Ghetto* (1892), Israel Zangwill imagined the life of 11-year-old Esther Ansell who spoke Yiddish at home:

> The knowledge that she was a Jewish child, whose people had a special history, was always at the back of her consciousness; sometimes it was brought to the front by the scoffing rhymes of English children, who informed her that they had stuck a piece of pork upon a fork and given it to a member of her race.
>
> But far more vividly did she realize that she was an English girl; far keener than her pride in Judas Maccabaeus was her pride in Nelson and Wellington; she rejoiced to find that her ancestors had always beaten the French, from the days of Crécy and Poitiers to the days of Waterloo; that Alfred the Great was the wisest of kings, and that Englishmen dominated the world and had planted colonies in every corner of it; that the English language was the noblest in the world, and men speaking it had invented railway trains, steamships, telegraphs and everything worth inventing. Esther absorbed these ideas from the school text-books.[12]

The Anglo-Jewish establishment encouraged the kind of assimilation that Zangwill imagined Esther Ansell undergoing. The Jewish Free School was praised in 1895 as a 'factory of English citizens'.[13] War was soon to bring home the need for such citizens.

War and welfare

In the Boer War two out of five of those who volunteered to go to fight in South Africa were rejected because of poor physique. It was a shock. It came on top of an ongoing worry about city life and childhood. By the beginning of the twentieth century three-quarters of the population were urban dwellers, over 40 per cent of the population living in cities with more than 100,000 inhabitants.

It is difficult to exaggerate the gloom that many people felt about cities at the turn of the nineteenth and twentieth centuries, particularly as they affected children. Cities in history had always had higher death rates than the countryside, and by the late nineteenth century, the supply of willing migrants from the shires was drying up. William Booth, the founder of the Salvation Army, gave voice to widespread ideas: 'The deterioration of our population in large towns is one of the most undisputed facts of social economics. The country is the breeding ground of healthy citizens ... The town-bred child is at a thousand disadvantages compared with his cousin in the country ... To rear healthy children you want first a home; secondly, milk; thirdly, fresh air; and fourthly, exercise under the green trees and blue skies.'[14]

Doctors did nothing to relieve the gloom. Dr Freeman-Williams put it like this in 1890: 'The child of the townsman is bred too fine, it is too great an exaggeration of himself, excitable and painfully precocious in its childhood, neurotic, dyspeptic, pale and undersized in its adult state, if it ever reaches it.'[15]

What could be done for these stunted, overstimulated city-bred children? The future of Britain and of the empire was dependent on them. Not all of them could be emigrated to Canada. Some people thought that the genetic inheritance from one generation of urban dwellers to another was in decline, that there was what was called a 'degeneration of the race'. Others thought that the signs of physical decay could be remedied by environmental improvements. The debate came to a head in evidence given before the Inter-Departmental Committee on Physical Deterioration that reported in 1904. The environmentalist voice predominated but the committee's title helped implant a notion that physical deterioration was a fact. Many witnesses had in fact doubted this. The positive outcome was that there was now a head of steam behind moves for reform, and the voices calling for it were not only imperialists worried about the future of the race but also socialists and the many people involved in the schemes for the rescue of street children.

There was widespread agreement that even if environmental reform could improve life for city children they still needed to be brought in touch with the countryside, with nature. Here voluntary organizations made the running and had been doing so since the 1870s. Some enthusiasts tried to bring something of the countryside into the classroom or to turn small areas of urban waste into gardens. Margaret McMillan, an inspirational pioneer in child welfare and education, opened a garden in Deptford where girls spent the night asleep in the open air and received an education from nature.[16] But ideally city children would be taken out into the countryside. Edith Nesbit, in *Five Children and It* (1902), described the necessity: 'London has none of those nice things that children may play with without hurting the things or themselves – such as trees and sand and woods and waters. And nearly everything in London is the wrong sort of shape – all straight lines and flat streets, instead of being all sorts of odd shapes, like things are in the country ... This is why so many children who live in towns are so extremely naughty.'[17]

The organizers of children's country holidays were soon alert to the need, as they saw it, for careful planning. As one prominent social reformer, Mrs Barnett, put it, 'Children need to be taught to enjoy as much as they need to be taught to work.' She drew up a questionnaire for children, which quizzed them on such country matters as: 'When sheep get up from lying down, do they rise with their front or their hind legs first?' Or 'Do you think that the big pigs grunt as an expression of pain, or pleasure, or both? Do the little pigs show any sign of affection to each other?' But the children were not very good observers: only 32 out of 127 'were right as to the way sheep rise', only 20 could distinguish between a pig's grunts and squeals.[18]

The anxiety about city children ran alongside another that was difficult to separate from it: the enduring poverty of children. Seebohm Rowntree's study of poverty in York, undertaken in the late 1890s, is famous for introducing the concept of the life cycle. At certain points in that cycle, said Rowntree, you are much more likely to be in poverty than at others, the most vulnerable times being when you are a child and when you are old. Low wages, unemployment and ill health could be a cause of poverty, but the life cycle was at the root of it. We are in the same world as the Tudor Poor Law officials who wrote about families 'overburdened with children'.

Rowntree made brief notes on families, where the number of young children plunged the family into poverty. Here is one: 'Tailor. Married. Four rooms. Six children, school age or under. Apparently very steady and industrious. Home fairly clean and comfortable. Landlord has warned them to "look out for another house", as he objects to so many children.'[19] Rowntree was aware that the tailor's nameless six children would eventually become an asset to the family budget, but for the time being they were living in circumstances 'which cannot fail to arrest their mental and physical development'.[20]

The extent of poverty among children was continually brought to public attention. Exactly 100 years ago a Scottish doctor weighed and measured working-class children in Glasgow, dividing them up according to the number of rooms for each family. His findings were clear-cut and alarming: girls in one-room houses were 6 kg (14 pounds) lighter and more than 13 cm (5 inches) shorter than girls in four-room houses; for the boys the differences were only slightly less. The poverty that condemned people to live in cramped accommodation resulted in underweight children who were small for their age. On the eve of the First World War, nearly half of the schoolchildren in Reading were living in primary poverty – without an adequate income to meet basic necessities. Children there and elsewhere made up over half of all those living in primary poverty. After the First World War the surveys of poverty had to cope with the added problem of unemployment. New investigations in the 1930s found that between 21 and 43 per cent of all working-class children fell below their poverty lines. Rickets, the most obvious sign of early malnutrition, was found in as many as two out of three working-class schoolchildren.[21]

Right from the start of the century some reformers were saying that the only solution was for the government to pay family allowances to help meet the costs of children. Women were particularly active in this campaigning, Eleanor Rathbone an acknowledged leader, and they argued that the money should be paid to mothers.[22] It was women such as these who, nearly half a century after Rowntree's first study of York, in 1943, in the midst of war, reported on the continuance of poverty. The Women's Group on Public Welfare, a wartime foundation representing all the major women's voluntary organizations, argued that,

> The younger the child, the more likely it is to be living in poverty; the percentage so living is higher among the 'under fives' than in any older group of the population, higher still among the 'under fours', and so on. Poverty spells overcrowding with all its evils. The five-year-old enters school suffering from all the complaints which the school doctors and nurses will spend their time in combating during his school life. The under fives have been found lousier than any other group; evacuation showed that children of five were already set in bad habits of every kind ... An onslaught must be made on poverty by means of family allowances and minimum wages, and the children with unsatisfactory homes must be helped by letting them live day by day in a different environment; they must have nursery schools from the age of two years ... Nursery schools may be considered expensive, but the money spent on giving the child

these early years of happy, healthy life may be far less than what is now spent on combating the ill-health, dirtiness, delinquency and misuse of property which result from a bad start in life, while the lives actually saved and the efficiency conferred are beyond price. We cannot afford not to have the nursery school; it seems to be the only agency capable of cutting the slum mind off at the root and building the whole child while yet there is time.[23]

'[C]utting the slum mind off at the root': it is a nutshell summary of the thrust of much policy-making in the first half of the twentieth century. Of the three reforms recommended here, only one was implemented. A move on minimum wages beyond the initiatives taken by the pre-First World War Liberal government was never on the cards. Nursery schools, perhaps the most interesting policy proposal, had come into existence during the war to help release mothers to work for the war effort. Go back to the beginning of the twentieth century, and it is a surprise to find that children were going to elementary schools at the age of three. There was much criticism of these classes for babies, the influences in them, according to one observer, 'more military rather than maternal'.[24] Grants for them were reduced and five became the normal school-starting age. Now, in the 1940s, nursery schools were being promoted as the answer to almost all social problems, a rhetoric to be heard again only 60 years later, in the early twenty-first century. But the outcome at the end of the Second World War, amid fears that women might not return to the home to release jobs for men, was a closing of the wartime nurseries, and an emphasis on home as the place in which to bring up a child up to the age of five.[25]

But war did give added support to those who had for so long been campaigning for family allowances. The government was persuaded to support the measure in part because it seemed a way of restraining wage inflation after the war: if mothers were getting money for their children, there was an argument for keeping male wages down. So in 1946 family allowances came into being. The level at which they were set did not immediately lift masses of children out of poverty, but it helped relieve it, and set a precedent with which no subsequent government has dared tamper: that there should be an allowance paid for every child born.

School provided a site where the state could measure the effects on children of poverty and urban dwelling. Compulsory schooling in the late nineteenth century itself brought to light issues that had been until then largely dormant. Some children failed to thrive in the elementary schools. Sometimes it was for obvious reasons: they were blind, or deaf, or dumb or had some visible physical disability. An alarming number were diagnosed as epileptic. Others, in a language that was filtering into Britain from its origins in France, were thought to have low IQs or to be, in the phrase used at the time, 'feeble-minded'. The solution for all children labelled in one or other of these ways was thought to be the establishment of special schools, for the blind, the deaf, the epileptic, the feeble-minded and so on. An underlying worry was that this poor stock might breed and add to the degeneration of the race. As one authoritative figure, Dr Alfred Tredgold, put it in 1911: 'The feeble-minded, the insane and the epileptic have been allowed to mate to such an extent with healthy stocks that, although the full fruition of the morbid process may have been thereby delayed, the vigour and competence of many families has been undermined, and the aggregate capacity of the nation has been seriously reduced. The taint is, in fact, slowly contaminating the whole mass of the population.'[26]

The remaining children, now beginning to be thought of as 'normal', were not without problems. Some from poor families came so hungry to school that they could not concentrate. A variety of voluntary schemes to provide school meals already existed, and there was a move towards raising money through the rates for this purpose. Acts allowing this were passed in 1906 in England and Wales and in 1908 in Scotland. They were hugely controversial for they seemed to many to be taking away from the family one of its most fundamental activities, the buying, cooking and eating of food in the family home. Until the Second World War, only a small minority of children was fed at school. Edith Smith, born in 1901, her father dying when she was three, remembered what it was like to have school meals: 'I must have been eleven or twelve, and things were so tight that [mother] had to apply for me to have meals at school, which if people were very poor, they could have free. I remember the humiliation I felt, going to school to have breakfast. It consisted of two pieces of bread and jam and a cup of cocoa, and the dinner was always a stew of some kind. But I can feel now the humiliation, you know, of all my school friends knowing that my mother was too poor to feed me.'[27]

In the Second World War and its aftermath a much higher proportion of children had school dinners, but their response was never one of gratitude:

Splishy splashy custard,
   Dead dogs' eyes,
All mixed up with giblet pies,
Spread it on the butty nice and thick,
Swallow it down with a bucket of sick.[28]

Another important issue in the early twentieth century was the medical condition of children. In 1907 an Act enforced medical inspection of school-children. Those who prepared it knew that the inspections would reveal a lot of ill health, and would be followed by questions about what arrangements needed to be made to ensure treatment. By this time there were in fact chinks of light in the story of children's health. The mortality rates for children over the age of one had been in decline since the 1850s. The killer childhood diseases – scarlet fever, measles, whooping cough and diphtheria – were well known, and the overall trend in deaths was downward. There were other illnesses for which the remedies were fairly obvious if difficult to implement: the rickets that stemmed from poor diet and lack of sunlight, the nits that infested the heads of so many children and the teeth that rotted in early childhood.[29]

Children in the elementary schools of Britain thus found themselves standing in long queues to pass before the doctor, or to be inspected by the nit nurse or school dentist. The nit nurse loomed largest in school folklore, for her verdict could bring disgrace on a respectable family. [Fig. 25] Many children remembered the lengths their mothers went to, to prevent infestations and the outcome of failure. Grace Foakes, at a poor school in Wapping, recalled how: 'every day, without fail, my mother would undo our plaits and comb through our hair with a small-tooth comb. If we so much as scratched our heads, she would stop whatever she was doing and look to see if we had picked up anything.'[30]

For girls, school also became a site where they could be taught about their future roles as wives and mothers. To the nineteenth-century staple of sewing were now added classes in cooking and care of babies, what was soon to be called 'mothercraft'. These, it was hoped, would instil into the young standards of hygiene and care that would help in the ongoing campaign to reduce what seemed to many the biggest scandal in the health of children: the high mortality of babies. Each year a quarter of a million babies died before they reached their first birthday, a rate as high in 1900 as it had been in the worst days of the Industrial Revolution in the 1840s. The big killer was diarrhoea in the hot summer months. What contemporaries could not know, but we can now see, is that the situation was on the mend: a decline in the rate set in right at the beginning of the century and continued through to its end, so that by 2000 it was down from 150 for every 1000 live births to under ten. The reasons for this are complex, but probably have as much to do with improved diet for mothers and the spread of water-born sewage, as with the numerous campaigns targeted at unhygienic mothers.[31] War was always the stimulus for further efforts; the number of clinics doubled between 1914 and 1918, and the number of health visitors rose from 600 to over 2500.[32]

The Second World War had even more impact on the lives of children than the First World War. The evacuation of children from areas thought likely to be bombed was a massive exercise in social and political engineering. It would have been unimaginable without the experience garnered over many years in emigrating children and in taking them out to board in the country-side. To many there was a considerable silver lining in the prospect of evacuation in the Second World War. Now came the possibility of offering an experience of the country to a much wider range of the population than had been possible under voluntary efforts. As one enthusiast put it, 'the children of the nation are its most important asset and we have an unprecedented opportunity now of dealing with these children under country conditions, where they can grow strong and well.' The looming Battle of Britain was in this way seen as a blessing in disguise, at last an opportunity to get children out of the cities.[33] So it was that in September 1939, 826,959 unaccompanied schoolchildren and 523,670 mothers with pre-school children were evacuated. It was the most extraordinary and extensive intervention by the state in the lives of children and their families in history. [Fig. 30] For most of them it was short-lived. By early 1940, with the phoney war holding off the much-feared bombing of cities, about 80 per cent of the evacuees had returned.[34]

Some of those who remained in the countryside thrived in their new homes, finding it difficult at the end of the war to readjust to their own families. For others, the experience of evacuation was a nightmare. Here is how Reg O'Donoghue, born in London in 1933, remembered it:

I got no food, or very little food, from the woman that I was staying with. I can never remember having one meal in that house at all. I had to go out and fend for myself. I used to skulk around all day. I didn't go to school at all, I was too busy trying to find places, I suppose, to feed myself and keep out of trouble ... I spent my days sort of wandering around the back streets of Newton Abbot trying to find food. They never sent anybody from the school round to find out what the problem was. This went on for some time because I was vastly underweight. I had to scrounge for food from the army centre which was just close by. I quickly got to learn to go there at the right times when the meals were finished and the army corporal came out in his white apron and threw what was being left into a big dustbin. I used to have to climb up over the top. And I can remember I used to try and reach into the middle of what he'd just put in so that it hadn't touched the sides of the dustbin, and that's how I used to survive.

Eventually, Reg got on a train to go back to London but was stopped by police at Exeter, who were appalled at the state he was in and had him admitted to hospital. He was rescued by his mother and taken back to London. The countryside had done him no good at all.[35]

Reg O'Donoghue can be seen as one of a large number of children in the first half of the twentieth century who spent some or all of their childhood outside the parental home. Besides evacuees, there was a permanent core of families who, for whatever reason, failed to provide a safe home for children to grow up in. Huge efforts were made to improve the lot of these children. Government was at the centre of many of them, but voluntary organizations were also heavily involved.

The children at whom all this effort was directed rarely felt any gratitude for it. They didn't feel their individual needs were attended to. Many of them were bitter about their experiences. This was perhaps because the many adults working in this field, although they claimed to have the best interests of the child at heart, were also worried that the combination of the poverty and the personal characteristics of the children's parents made them and their children a danger to society. To put it another way, the emphasis was not entirely child centred.

There were around 100,000 children in the care of the child-welfare providers at any one time. [Fig. 27] In Scotland alone in the interwar period there were at least 275 institutions for homeless children and young persons.[36]

Accounts of life in these institutions suggested that it didn't make that much difference where you ended up. All worked on the stated or unstated assumption that your parents were to blame for your fate, and that you had probably inherited some of their worst characteristics. Regimentation, firm discipline, ghastly food and a lack of care on an individual basis were all too often how they were experienced.

Ed Cousins, born in 1916, was six when his father, a soldier, died, leaving his mother with three children to look after. Ed and his brother were taken to Barnardo's. 'We weren't physically abused,' he recalled. 'But not once can I remember any affection being shown. You had to accept a way of life so foreign, so disciplined ... I think I was always hungry.'[37]

Hetty Day was another whose father died, in 1929, when she was 18 months old, leaving a six-year-old sister, Hetty, and, born six months later, a brother, James. It was when James was born that Hetty was sent to Reedham Asylum for Fatherless Children.

> I missed my mother so much. We were severely treated. We were punished for talking, we had to sit and hold our tongues between our fingers if we talked when we shouldn't. If we talked after we'd been put to bed, they came and pulled the sheets over our heads, and I was always afraid of the dark. By the time I was four, I was no longer considered to be a child. I had to help look after the young ones, make the cots, just generally prove useful ... We had our clothes provided, orphan clothes, rough and durable. We were inadequately clothed, and always cold and hungry. The food was a penance. Monday, Wednesday and Saturday, we had watery soup, a slice of bread, and then a suet pudding with syrup. The smell of it was repelling. I often didn't eat it. We used to keep it and put it at the rat-holes, so the rats waxed fat on it.

As with many other children in institutions, the replacement of her name by a number seemed to Hetty to encapsulate the inhumanity. She was G80, her sister, G90, and her brother James, B52.[38]

Children were either cowed by the regimentation of these institutions, or they rebelled. Reg Chubb recalled how, at the Russell Coates Nautical School in Parkstone, Dorset, after the First World War, his seven-year-old brother got the birch for running away from school. He even helped with the punishment after his brother was caught on a train bound for London: 'I remember holding 'im down on the table meself, an' the rest of the school was all brought in to see the public flogging as an example to the rest if they absconded – they'd know what they was going to get ... They birched him six times. Four of us children held him down, two at hands an' two at legs, and a person in authority to give him the birch.'[39]

In Scotland the long-standing preference to board out city children with foster parents in the Highlands sometimes resulted in a close attachment between foster child and family. Two sisters boarded out on Barra had a confusing experience: 'I remember the night we got word of my mother's death in Glasgow. We felt very strange because our mother ... was in front of us. She was with us so we didn't feel we had suffered any great loss ... My mother came down saying how sorry she was that they'd heard that night that our mother had died. And we were all saying "But Mum, you're here."'[40]

But a fostered child might also be treated simply, as someone from Tiree remembered, as 'slave labour'. Peter, who spent much of his childhood boarded out in a village on the Moray Firth coast in the 1930s and 1940s, and was sent out to work on a neighbouring farm, remembered of his foster parents, who took in up to seven children at a time: 'They were obviously gaining something from sending us out to the farm to work, I mean we got nothing for it. We had to slave and do ... [T]here was no love, no, it was just no contact other than at mealtimes or getting told you go and scrub the floor or you polish the stair or clean the henhouse out, that was all.'[41]

By contrast with the organizations that either removed children from their families or looked after the children when their families were not able to, the National Society for the Prevention of Cruelty to Children (NSPCC) and the Royal Scottish Society for the Prevention of Cruelty to Children always sought to keep children in their families. Admirable as this might be in principle, it meant turning a blind eye to cases of physical and sexual abuse of children within the home, most of those known to us coming to light only years later. The NSPCC persuaded itself that the proportion of cases coming to it involving sexual abuse was in decline and almost negligible; so too were cases of violence against children. The 'neglect and starvation' that constituted the vast majority of the NSPCC's cases were dealt with by warnings and casework, and only very rarely were children taken into custody. But this could all too often mean that abuse was not picked up, and the consequences for a child could be long-lasting. Maud Wood, born in Bradford in 1914, was abused by her father from the age of ten:

> When I got home from school me mother used to be charring so there were just him in the house. I used to go out in the streets. I could throw it off when I went out to play, I never thought of it. It was an escape. I used to make up scenes from the silent films with the other children. They always had an 'appy ending and they always had me for the heroine, Pearl White. I were fastened up on the lamppost then one of the boys'd come and rescue me. When I got rescued with the hero I was wishing to God somebody would really come and rescue me. But then me father'd start calling me in to wash up about eight o'clock. When I 'eard, oh I can 'ear 'im in the distance now, I can 'ear him shouting, 'Maudie, come in and wash up.' I can 'ear it. I can 'ear it in me distant mind I can 'ear it. There was no delaying it and I knew I had to go in to him.'[42]

In the same year, 1946, that the Family Allowances Act was passed, government also moved towards a new policy for children in care. A committee under retired civil servant and principal of Newnham College, Cambridge, Dame Myra Curtis, reported on 'the care of children deprived of a normal home life'. It found that there were 125,000 children and young adolescents in care, and there was in many homes 'a lack of personal interest in and affection for the children which we found shocking'. Although it tempered its criticisms with some soothing praise, the report marked a sea change for children in care. In the Children Act of 1948 that followed the Curtis Report, every local authority had to set up a children's committee charged with furthering the best interests of children in care. Each committee looked specifically either to keep children in their families or restore them to the family unit, or to encourage the fostering solution. The large, institutional homes for children were now under threat.[43]

The focus of the initiatives for children that we have been considering has been on the physical health and welfare of working-class children. But war also prompted concern about their minds or, more specifically, about what kind and amount of schooling they were getting. It was no accident that each of the three wars ended with an Education Act. The 1902 Act increased the possibility for children from elementary schools to go on to receive a secondary education. The 1918 Act raised the school-leaving age to 14, and the 1944 Act, while also raising the school-leaving age, this time to 15, made secondary schooling compulsory for every child, in one of the three types of secondary school now established: the grammar school, the technical school and the secondary modern school. Doubtless each of these reforms would have happened without a war, but conflict focused the attention of policy-makers: it drove home the fact that the future of the nation was dependent on the skills with which its children were equipped.

Reality did not always accord with the optimism of the rhetoric. Jane Taverner, at elementary school in Exeter in the 1920s, had vivid memories of the scholarship exam she took for progression to secondary school:

> I was put in for the scholarship. I remember the rating I got because I didn't pass. I was fully expected to pass, but I didn't try because I knew that if I passed, I couldn't go. I wanted to pass, but you see it was no use, because although there was help, it wouldn't have been enough for our family. Actually, I didn't try and I was hauled over the coals. Headmistress had me in, didn't she? 'Why didn't you pass? What did you do?' And I suppose I didn't answer. 'I don't know,' I said ... I would have liked to have been a teacher but, you see, I knew what I was going to do and it was something I wasn't going to like. I had to go into service, for one thing to make room for the boys to sleep as they got older. And I had to go into service at fourteen.[44]

Jane Taverner's experience neatly captures how the state's hopes and expectations for its children could conflict with a child's awareness of the realities of his or her world: the poverty of the family, the expenditure that extra schooling would entail, the loss of the child's income, the lack of space in the house. The increase in the role of the state in children's lives, much of it a consequence of problems exposed by war, has to be set against the way children themselves experienced the changes. Children themselves were less aware than middle-class adults of the benefits that were being conferred upon them. For many of them, what stuck in the memory was the humiliation of being picked out by Nitty Norah, the homesickness of being an evacuee in the strangeness of the countryside or being caught between the need to contribute to the family and the wish to carry on in school.

In the latter part of the Second World War and in its immediate aftermath, the passage of the Education Act, 1944, the Family Allowances Act, 1946 and the Children Act, 1948, indicate the importance of childhood in the making of the welfare state. Children were of course also to benefit from the National Health Service. The six children of the tailor in York whom Rowntree observed would have had a better life had they been young in 1950 rather than 1900. It is in many ways a story of progress. People at the time often compared the present with the past, astonished at the improvements that had taken place. It was in 1942 that Sylvia Lynd could write that 'We have our temporary misfortunes; but the story of English children at the present hour is a story that moves towards a happy ending.'[45] It is, however, a measure of the progress that needed to be made that so many of the children in the first half of the century who came under the direct care of the state or of voluntary organizations felt so bitter about their experiences. The Family Allowances Act and the Children Act at the very least opened the prospect of better times for the next generation of children.

It was at the same time, in the 1940s, that ideas about how best to rear a child began to change. Before that, things were rather different.

'They'd some queer ideas at the clinic'

Katrina was aged eight in 1942 and living in a home run by child psychoanalyst Anna Freud, Sigmund's daughter. Someone heard her chatting away at night time: 'Teacher says there are angels and once when we were in the air raid shelter the Germans dropped bombs on us and we were very frightened. There was a lady in the shelter and she said there is a man sitting in heaven and he puts his arms out and he hides the people so that the Germans cannot bomb us. It is God. No German can do anything to us. Who made God? Who made everything? How did everything start?' Katrina settles down to sleep, but then laughs quietly to herself and whispers, 'Could God get wicked one day? Wouldn't it be funny if God would get wicked and Hitler good?' Another day, when someone asks, 'Whom will God help to win the war, Hitler or us?' Katrina answers, 'God will help both Hitler and us, because he likes all people.'[46]

Katrina's questioning reminds us of James Boswell's daughter, Veronica, in the eighteenth century posing similarly searching problems, to the consternation of her father. But, unlike Boswell, Anna Freud and her co-workers do not try to persuade Katrina that she is mistaken. They simply listen to what she is saying. It could hardly be said that such listening was universal in the advice on child rearing in the first half of the century. Rather, there was a tension between behaviourists, who taught control and regularity, and others who wanted parents to be alert to their child's wishes, anxieties and fears.

The infant-death rate, as high in 1900 as it had been in the 1840s, was the prompt for the concern about bringing up babies – and the answer to it was thought to lie in hygiene. Mothers were castigated for their negligence and their untidiness. Health visitors entered the working-class home to check on baby care. Mothers whose babies survived were rewarded. The mayor of Huddersfield famously offered a guinea to any mother whose baby survived its dangerous first year. In July 1917, Britain celebrated its inaugural National Baby Week, an occasion when healthy babies were prominently displayed.[47]

Hygiene came with the backing of science, which, with all the authority implicit in the word, laid down the rules for baby and child care. Adherence to hygiene itself required regular habits, and mothers were now taught to reach beyond that to ensure that the baby was regular in its habits. Early training, and adherence to scientific principles, was essential. And science now extended beyond the natural sciences to include psychology. Experts were on hand to advise on what this new science meant for child rearing. In the words of its most prominent figure, educational psychologist Cyril Burt, 'superintending the growth of human beings is as scientific a business as cultivating plants or training a race horse'.[48]

A mother's emotions were all too likely to get in the way of this training. In the United States, the influential behavioural psychologist John Watson, his authority crossing the Atlantic, was in no doubt that there were 'much more scientific ways of bringing up children [than by parents in individual homes] which will probably mean finer and happier children ... There is a sensible way of treating children. Treat them as though they were young adults ... Never hug and kiss them, never let them sit in your lap. If you must, kiss them once on the forehead when they say good night. Shake hands with them in the morning.'[49]

In Britain the *Mothercraft Manual*, with 12 editions between 1923 and 1954, advised mothers that: 'Self-control, obedience, the recognition of authority, and, later, respect for elders are all the outcome of the first year's training. To train the infant for the first year is comparatively easy but after that the child begins to resent authority.' Of all these forms of training, potty training was fundamental. Early training was of great importance, and from the third day 'the baby should be held with the back against the nurse's chest for not longer than two minutes; the cold rim should just be allowed to touch the child at the back of the anus, and very soon a reflex is established. Many nurses train their babies so that they have no soiled napkins after the first week or so, and very few wet ones.'[50]

New Zealander Dr Truby King, the guru for British mothers in the 1930s, told his readers that 'The leading authorities of the day – English, foreign and American – all agree that the first thing to establish in life is *regularity of habits* ... The establishment of perfect regularity of habits, initiated by "feeding and sleeping by the clock", is the ultimate foundation of all-round obedience.'[51] The goal, unquestioned it seems, is to instil into the child obedience. At a stroke it seems we are transported back into the world of the Puritans of the seventeenth century, though now without the concern for the child's salvation.

How did parents respond to this advice, and what was its impact on children? By and large, working-class mothers were less likely to adhere to the rules than middle-class mothers. Ivy Summers, born in Grimsby in 1901, and married to a fish splitter, had 12 children and took no notice of the new rules: 'if they was crying I used to pick 'em up and I used to do me work when they was asleep. But I never let them cry. Mind you, they was very contented ... They'd some queer ideas at the clinic ... of stripping a baby and laying him on a cold scales to weigh him. I said, "Put a bit of blanket on there, they'll get cold." They was full of ideas that was daft.'[52]

Olive Morgan, married to a bricklayer, had eight children born between 1934 and 1950. She describes the conflict between the advice given at the clinics and the traditional way of looking after babies in Wales: 'nursing the baby Welsh fashion, with the shawl wrapped around the baby, then around the mother and underneath the mother's arm was our way. The baby was close to the mother then and could hear the mother's heart beating. And they were curled up then. They loved that, they'd go to sleep that way. It always worked, it always kept my babies quiet.'[53]

Edith Broadway, by contrast, married to a cashier in an oil company, brought up her daughter, born in 1935, on Truby King methods.

I kept to the strict rigid routine of not cuddling her when I wanted to – you fed her, changed her, winded her and put her in her pram, and pushed her to the end of the garden and that was it. And you really didn't give the cuddles and the love and affection. If I kissed her it was on the back of the neck and nobody else was allowed to kiss her. That was something that we did bar, was kissing. I kissed her little body and I kissed her neck, but never kissing her as such ... Choosing the Truby King method meant that I didn't want a spoilt child, I didn't want a baby that was screaming every so often and expecting to be cuddled and nursed, and I wanted her to grow up to be obedient and to do as she was told. I suppose that's one's idea of a perfect child and it's wrong ... I wanted to love my baby, but this regime was very much against my desires and I'm sure loads of other mothers must have done and felt the same thing.[54]

We know that many mothers in later life regretted their adherence to Truby King's rules.[55] What of the babies themselves? We can hear them only occasionally. We know of Mary Davey, born in 1944, and brought up on Truby King principles. Put out in her pram on a bitterly cold day when she was 18 months old, she developed pneumonia and had to be admitted to hospital, her parents, according to the rules then adhered to, not allowed to see her, because seeing the parents was thought to upset the children: 'She was crying her eyes out ... I even had to plead with them to let her have a little counterpane ... that she used to hold when she slept, and suck her thumb ... I said she would never go to sleep unless she had it. So, the sister let her have it, but she had to hide it underneath the other covers so it wasn't seen.'[56]

Behaviourism, however, was not the only advice on offer in the first half of the twentieth century. Indeed, it was influenced itself by some of the new thinking that we can associate most readily with Sigmund Freud. Freud challenged any notion that sexuality played no part in childhood. He was not the first to do so: many psychiatrists had written about the sexual behaviour of children in the nineteenth century, generally seeing it as a departure from the norm.[57] For Freud, sexuality was of course unavoidable for all children. For some this was a cruel invasion of that sacred territory of innocence that had become associated with childhood. But it was perfectly possible to see child sexuality as natural, part of nature, and therefore no challenge to childhood innocence. The issue became not child behaviour but adult response.

Freud's ideas became known in shorthand, an indication of their influence. Phrases like the Oedipus complex or inferiority complex or penis envy or a slip of the tongue passed into everyday discourse. But, at a deeper level, Freud undoubtedly served to complicate childhood. And the more complex it came to seem, the more parents were felt to need, and needed, experts to tell them how to rear their children. Bedwetting or thumb sucking now became problems that were thought to require the skills of an expert to solve. In the 1920s the idea began to spread that if a child had a behavioural problem, the solution to it might lie not in strict routines and rules but in understanding his or her individual psychological make-up. It was this type of thinking that lay behind the Child Guidance Clinics that began to be set up in the later 1920s, 40 of them in existence on the eve of the Second World War.[58] The impact of the war itself on children furthered this move away from behaviourism. As we saw with Katrina, people began to listen to what children were saying.

An important change was taking place, its influence clear in the debates on corporal punishment. At the beginning of the century there was little challenge to the dominant view that corporal punishment was necessary in the rearing of children, whether in the home or the school, or as a punishment for crime. It was indeed seen as an important element in the making of the national character. As 'a lover of my country' put it in 1908: 'If we would maintain our position in the world as an imperial race, we must insist upon a virile training both in the home and the school, which shall raise up a people hardy, bold, accustomed to concentration of thought, firm of purpose and not afraid of struggle and difficulty. Such a people cannot be raised without discipline.'[59]

By the 1930s experts were almost universally of the opinion that corporal punishment was more likely to do harm than good. Britain was still a long way from ending the practice – that did not happen in schools until 1982, and in the home it is still allowable. Nevertheless, for the first time in our history, despite innumerable protests against its efficacy stretching back to the Middle Ages, children were now less likely than before to be beaten. Corporal punishment in magistrates' courts declined from over 2000 cases per year before the First World War to about 170 per year before the Second World War.[60] It is difficult to measure its incidence in the home. As late as 1938 the *Daily Herald*, a Labour-supporting paper, published without comment this letter from B. Sutton of Benfleet: 'Slap your daughters or your life will not be worth living! Particularly slap the elder, as she sets the example. I have two daughters. When one was 16 she said "Shan't" to me. I slapped her face, which was very humiliating to her, and hurt her pride. She never answered me back after.'[61]

The decline in corporal punishment was accompanied by a growing sense that if children had problems they were more likely to be problems of their minds – their anxieties, their fears, their wishes and their aspirations – than of their bodies. The psychological and psychoanalytical thinking of the 1930s, as we have seen, was already undermining behaviourism, and the Second World War furthered that process. It came to be thought that the personality type that would emerge from a Truby King-type upbringing, with its stress on obedience, would be more suited to the German Third Reich than to a country fighting for democracy. Further, studies of evacuated children and their fears showed how important the family was to emotional security. The ground had been laid for the phenomenal success of Dr Spock's *The Common Sense Book of Baby and Child Care*, published in 1946. This was followed up in the post-war years by studies on the malign effects on children of 'maternal deprivation', on the importance of children bonding with their mother or a mother-figure, the key person promoting this view being developmental psychologist Dr John Bowlby.[62] It was he, too, who began to question the practice of hospitals not allowing parents to visit their children – no small matter as some 685,000 children were hospitalized each year – a practice that so distressed Mary Davey and her parents. In 1952, Bowlby's colleague James Robertson produced a silent film, *A Two Year Old Goes to Hospital*, which was highly controversial but set in progress the moves that would eventually allow parents to visit their children.[63]

The first half of the twentieth century can be seen as a terrain on which a battle was fought between behaviourist and psychologically informed views of childhood. The victory went to the latter. Its impact was to place the spotlight on the family, not so much for its adherence or otherwise to the gospel of hygiene but for its ability to mould the character and personality of the children who were by now so firmly placed in its care. Children showed little awareness of the debates that raged around them. Their memories of childhood, unless they were living in institutions, were taken up more with the way they spent their time out of school and beyond the remit of the state.

Leisure and 'adolescence'

One of the most popular mid-twentieth-century skipping and ball-bouncing songs goes like this:

Charlie Chaplin went to France
To teach the ladies how to dance.
First he did the rhumba,
Then he did the kicks,
Then he did the samba,
Then he did the splits.[64]

The song captures the ways in which an activity that children had enjoyed for centuries could be infused with new material, drawn here from the most important commercial entertainment: the cinema.

If we think of children's lives outside the reach of school, the most important influence on them was their family. But children also had a culture of their own, much of it based in the street. As they grew older, the opportunities for involvement in the commercial world of leisure became greater, but to counter it there was a remarkable growth of organizations designed specifically for older children, the youth movements; these came imbued with new thinking about the dangers of adolescence.

The world in which the children were growing up was undergoing a major change. Mothers marrying in the 1870s had far more children than those born in the early twentieth century. More than one in ten of them had 11 or more babies, these families containing about a quarter of all babies born. For those marrying in the first decade of the twentieth century, and even more for those marrying later in 1925, the most common experience was to have only two or three children. In the 1930s demographers were seriously worried that the British population would decline because of what was seen as a failure on the part of women to fulfil their reproductive role.[65] For children and their families it was a change of the greatest importance. It had something to do with the decline in the death rate for babies and young children, which meant that you didn't have to have a lot of children in case some died in infancy. It may also have reflected the fact that with compulsory schooling children were of little use to the family economy until they were into their mid-teens. But the overriding cause seems to have been decisions by young mothers that they would try to avoid the ill health and the struggles that they had seen dominate the lives of their own mothers.[66] Child life changed in equal measure. Children were now unlikely to grow up with a bevy of siblings. Correspondingly they might expect more individual attention from their parents.

This meant that for more and more children home began to replace the street as the place where they spent time. It was driven in part by a concern to be respectable. But it was possible because homes themselves were becoming more comfortable and there was less overcrowding. The radio, almost universal by the end of the 1930s, had programmes especially geared to the child audience. *Children's Hour*, dating back to 1923, was described by Sir John Reith, the BBC's first director-general, as a 'happy alternative to the squalor of streets and backyards'. By 1938 six out of ten children aged five to 13 were listening to it.[67] Hobbies – stamp-collecting, model-building – and indoor board games were promoted. We can begin to talk about child-centred families, this becoming possible only when there were fewer children per family. [Fig. 29]

Despite these developments, and despite many predictions of its decline in importance, the street remained fundamental to the leisure hours of most children. [Fig. 28] As one observer of London children in the 1920s put it: 'The street is the cradle of the new-born babe, and the nursery of the toddler, and the playing field of the elementary school child; and running wild in it is responsible for much of the vitality and the wit and the insatiable curiosity that are found animating every grown-up London crowd.'[68]

Academic and cultural critic Professor Richard Hoggart, looking back in the 1950s to his own childhood in Leeds in the 1930s, described

the games of the street, with the lamp-post taking the place of the tree on a village green. Between five and thirteen, roughly, you play with your own sex. Games change as the year unfolds, following the products of the season (e.g. 'conkers'), or simply by the boys' own intuitively followed rhythm. At one time everyone is playing 'taws', with his marbles ranked in prestige according to age and killing power; quite suddenly marbles go and everybody wants a threepenny peashooter ... Hoops and shuttlecocks have almost entirely gone, and whips-and-tops are not so popular now; but 'piseball', 'tig', hopscotch across the flags and a great number of games involving running round the lamp-posts or in and out of the closet-areas, such as 'Cowboys and Indians', are still popular. Girls still like skipping-ropes, and almost peculiar to them is the game of dressing-up – trailing round the streets in grown-ups' cast-off clothes and old lace, as 'a wedding' ... There are outings with jam-jars to a dirty stream a mile or so away, for sticklebacks and red-throats ... Those who can cadge a few coppers from their mothers go to the public baths; or occasionally catch a tram to some remote part of the city where the children's playground is said to be good, and spend the whole day there with a few sandwiches and a bottle of pop between the lot of them.[69]

This street life is entirely without adult supervision, and reminiscent of the children's games described in the Middle Ages. And, in stark contrast to the twenty-first century, children can roam far and wide in the city and outside it.

When they first started earning both boys and girls tipped up their wages to their mother who might give them back something for spends. But often it was not much. One teenage girl in Scotland, already going out with her husband-to-be, described her life around the time of the First World War: 'Well, I didnae really need anything to spend, actually. There wasnae so many – well we didnae get so much to the pictures then and even at that it was the only place you could go ... I was only allowed out three times a week anyway. Half-past nine Sunday and ten o'clock through the week, sometimes half-past nine. And if I didnae do what I was told I was kept in and deprived of my nights out.'[70]

Her experience was by no means untypical. Nevertheless, despite these parental pressures, many young earners enjoyed the weekly monkey parade. This was how the one at Clapham Common was described in 1915:

After tea, the bright boys wash, clean their boots, and change into their 'second-best' attire, and stroll forth ... in company with others, up and down that parade until they 'click' with one of the 'birds'. The girls are out on much the same programme. They, too, promenade until they 'click' with someone, and are escorted to a picture palace or hall or chocolate shop ... As the boys pass the likely girls they glance, and, if not rebuffed, offer wide smiles. But they do not stop. At the second meeting, however, they smile again and touch hands in passing, or cry over the shoulder some current witticism, as: ''Snice night, Ethel!' or 'I should shay sho!' And Ethel and Lucy will swing around, challengingly, with scraping feet, and cry, 'Oooh!' The boys linger at the corner, looking back, and the girls, too, look back. Ethel asks Lucy, 'Shall we?' and Lucy says, 'Ooh – I d'no,' and by the time the boys have come down level with them ... 'Well – shall we stroll 'cross the Common?' 'I don't mind.' Then boys and girls move forward together ... They have 'got off.'[71]

Some boys in Birmingham, just starting work on the eve of the First World War, kept diaries of how they spent their time. Here is M. R., a boy in unskilled work, giving an account of his Saturday:

> Had to work hard this morning to finish a contract ordor.
> Had dinner at 1 p.m.
> Read the Birmingham Weekly Post till 2.30 then rote to London for a list of Banjo Music, went out to buy a cap and tie, come home and got ready for the night.
> After tea I change myself and went a walk around the town untill 8.30 and then went to the Empire.
> The top of the bill was George Mozart in his thumb-nail sketches, I think he was very good, as I take great interest in acting. Most of his sketches were different characters on the race course.
> The rest of the Bill was very good but I cant remember their names as I see so many Music Halls in the week I get them mixed up.

And here is K. L., describing a Sunday:

> Had bread and bacon and two cups of tea for breakfast. Got up at 9.50 got ready and went out. I went for my friends and we went on some waste ground and played football until about 2 oclock went home. In the afternoon we gathered together and saw some lads who live the other end of our street and asked them if they would play us at football this was agreed and we went on the ground and kicked off we were the winners of that match by a list of 8 goals to 5. After that we went to the coffee house and stayed there for a while and then went home to tea at 6.15. Went out in the evening for a short time and came back and began to read that book [a historical-adventure story by G. A. Henty given to him by the investigator].[72]

Football, the cinema and the music hall are their dominant interests. Each of them was thought to have harmful effects. In Nottingham in 1913, so it was claimed, the picture palaces had undermined the Band of Hope, the teetotal movement for children, cut borrowings from a children's lending library by 50 per cent, and 'Bands of boys, fired by the cowboy drama, have paraded the streets armed with pistols'. Young offenders up before the courts said that they had stolen to get money to go to the picture palaces.[73]

Complaints about the cinema continued unabated through the first half of the century, experts always sceptical about the claims. What no-one could doubt was cinema's importance for children: in Edinburgh in the 1930s seven out of ten children went at least once a week; in London 63 per cent of children under five were cinema-goers. Every week over four and a half million children went to the cinema. By the 1930s the prime time had shifted from the Saturday-afternoon matinee to special children's shows on Saturday mornings, with all the major chains of cinemas offering clubs for children to join. Boys went more often than girls.[74]

One reason the way the young spent their leisure hours attracted such attention was because of the anxieties that now surrounded 'adolescence'. There has probably never been a society that has not given some recognition to the onset of puberty and to the transition from childhood to adulthood. In previous centuries apprenticeship or entering into service, or in the nineteenth century starting work provided some means of external control over a period of life during which, it had long been recognized, boys in particular might become unruly. By the beginning of the twentieth century it was becoming obvious that these years would increasingly be spent in some form of education or training, the acquisition of adult status by earning money delayed. These years now became known as 'adolescence', stretching, according to its most prominent advocate, the American psychologist G. Stanley Hall, up to 25.

Hall held to a widely shared belief that human beings, as they grow up, experience in some way the different epochs of the development of the human race. Having got through the hunter–gatherer stage in early childhood, with the onset of puberty they had to pass through another phase of human history, and it was littered with obstacles. In Hall's words:

> The momentum of heredity often seems insufficient to enable the child to achieve this great revolution and come to complete maturity, so that every step of the upward way is strewn with wreckage of body, mind, and morals. There is not only arrest, but perversion, at every stage, and hoodlumism, juvenile crime, and secret vice seem not only increasing, but develop in earlier years in every civilized land. Modern life is hard,

and in many respects increasingly so, on youth. Home, school, church fail to recognize its nature and needs, and, perhaps most of all, its perils ... Sex asserts its mastery in field after field, and works its havoc in the form of secret vice, debauch, disease, and enfeebled heredity.[75]

Hall's thinking and language carried huge authority, and anyone with any kind of official responsibility for youth would have absorbed some of it, carrying, as it did, the imprimatur of 'science'.

A concern about adolescence was one influence in the enormous effort given to setting up youth organizations. The most famous of them was the Boy Scouts, originating in a camp organized by the Boer War hero, Robert Baden-Powell, on Brownsea Island in Poole Harbour in August 1907. But the Boy Scouts were late comers on the scene. The Boys' Brigade, formed in Glasgow in 1883, a dominantly Presbyterian organization, was followed up, before the end of the century, by the Church of England Lads' Brigade, the Jewish Lads' Brigade, the Catholic Boys' Brigade, and the less militaristic Boys' Life Brigade. Girls had been organized into the Girls' Friendly Society since the 1870s and in Scotland, from 1900, in the Girls' Guildry. Alongside these national organizations lay a multiplicity of local lads' clubs and church groups. All of these were trying to capture the loyalty of boys and girls when they left school, and, as everyone agreed, also left the Sunday schools and most probably any kind of formal religious allegiance. If the churches took the dominant organizational role, what has most struck later commentators has been the extent to which youth organizations seemed to be run on military lines, many of them uniformed and certainly adopting military terminology.

A survey in the 1960s found that one adult in three had belonged to the Boy Scouts or Girl Guides (the latter dating back to 1910), while nearly three out of five men had belonged to one or more uniformed groups when young.[76] If we add in the non-uniformed groups, it is clear that a considerable majority of children came under the influence of these youth organizations in the first half of the century. They are testimony to the efforts that volunteers were prepared to make to provide facilities where the young could enjoy themselves free from harmful influences; also to the fear of what might happen if young people were left alone to cope with the dangers of adolescence, commercial leisure and their own street culture.

17 The 1842 Royal Commission on Children
Employed in Mines and Manufactories printed
this scene from a pit in Lancashire. One boy in
front hauls and two behind push a wagon of
coals. The boys covered four to six miles a day
hauling in 'roads' that might be as low as
20 inches. In 1851 in England and Wales
there were 24,247 children under the age
of 15 working in coal mines.

18 *Many Happy Returns of the Day* (1856) by
William Frith. The birthday girl sits under a
celebratory arch. But the eye is drawn to the
father, looking away from his daughter to
grandfather who is absorbed in his paper
while waited on by a granddaughter. Frith
was perhaps intending to link the generations,
but he is also drawing attention to the gender
divide in the Victorian middle-class home.

THE WEATHER AND THE PARKS.—GLORIOUS NEWS FOR THE BOYS!

Billy Wilkins. "Hi! Look here! Come! Such a Lark! Here's a Perliceman fell on a Slide!"

19 *The Ragged School, West Street (previously Chick Lane)* by George Cruikshank. The ragged schools for the poorest children date from the 1840s. In the early days, as shown here, it was difficult to maintain order. The two groups in the centre are dutifully studious, but the girls on the right, and even more the boys on the left, are larking around and wrecking the furniture.

20 *Glorious News for the Boys!* by John Leech. City streets and parks were enlivened by street boys who had a reputation for finding humour in the misfortunes of adults, in this case a policeman falling on the ice. The police, says Leech, are the street boys' 'natural enemy', but he often seems to side with the boys. This sketch first appeared in *Punch* and later in a collection, *The Rising Generation* (1846–7).

Hark! bark! the dogs bark,
The beggars are coming to town;
Some in rags and some in tags,
And some in silken gowns.
Some gave them white bread,
And some gave them brown,
And some gave them a good horse-whip,
And sent them out of the town.

23 'Hark! hark! the dogs bark' by Kate Greenaway, in *Mother Goose* (1881). No one did more than Kate Greenaway to spread a romanticized and sentimental view of children. Here the beggars are not, as the words of the poem suggest, in town, but in the countryside, and the observing children have a dog and a garden gate to protect them from any danger. The beggars are respectful and unthreatening. No need for a horsewhip to send them out of town.

24 Barnardo had bought the Edinburgh Castle, previously a notorious gin palace, in 1872, and it became the centre of his London work, with a 'coffee palace' and a large mission hall where he regularly preached. Always alive to the need for publicity and fully aware of the power of the camera, Barnardo has here brought together a crowd of boys to wave their free meal tickets.

25 A cleanliness inspection at a London elementary school in 1911. Concern about children's health – or lack of it – escalated after the Boer War revealed the unfitness of adult recruits. Regular inspections in schools became the norm. Here a nurse looks for 'nits'. Respectable families took pains to avoid the disgrace of their children bringing back from school a card saying they had headlice.

26 'Half-timers' employed in Farnworth, Bolton, c. 1900. Until 1918 many children in the Yorkshire and Lancashire textile districts were 'half-timers', working in the mills for half the day and at school for the other half. The system had won almost universal support in the middle years of the nineteenth century but by its end there was a chorus of complaint from teachers and others. But to the embarrassment of the trade-union movement, workers consistently voted for its retention.

27 Infants at Muller's Orphanage, Bristol, in 1919. Orphanages never had enough 'orphans' to fill them – they became home to any children in need. George Muller had opened an orphanage in 1836. It came to hold 2000 children. Since the 1860s critics had warned of the 'institutionalization' of children kept in large orphanages, but it was only after the Children Act, 1948, that this one was closed down. In the first half of the twentieth century 100,000 children lived in institutional care.

LEFT

28 Residents of Little Collingwood Street, Bethnal Green, *c.* 1902. John Galt, a Scot, came to London in 1890 to work as a missionary for the London City Mission. In the early 1900s he took a series of photographs, mainly of the East End, that he had made into lantern slides to illustrate lectures publicizing the work of the mission. This posed photograph places slum dwellers in their street environment, the children flanked by adults.

LEFT

29 Children have been, and are, extensively used to advertise goods and services. The practice probably started in the late nineteenth century when Millais's painting *Bubbles* was used to advertise soap. Now about half of all advertisements with photos feature a child. The Prudential neatly plays on the mid-twentieth-century elevation of the child to the centre of the family. She towers above her adoring parents who are, literally, about to invest in her.

BELOW

30 Evacuated children at a camp run by the Hertfordshire Boy Scouts, 1944. The Second World War offered the opportunity to get poor children out of the unhealthy cities into the fresh air of the country, an aim on the policy agenda of reformers for over half a century. Here the results, obviously posed, look entirely positive. Note the clean shoes and stockings of the children – bare feet are a thing of the past.

31 'Boys reading comics' from *Picture Post – Children of the Streets* (1954). Comics were the reading of choice for nearly all children in the mid-twentieth century. Forerunners date back to the late nineteenth century, but the modern format, with speech bubbles, came with the *Dandy* in 1937, and the *Beano* in 1938. They were joined after the war by the slightly more upmarket *Eagle* in 1950, and its companion, *Girl*, started in 1951.

32 From the 1950s, Peter and Iona Opie carried out extensive research into children's games, language and songs. They and their co-workers across the country spent hours in school playgrounds, and revealed that what children said and did could often be traced back centuries. Here the Opies have become the participants, the children perhaps slightly bemused by this strange adult behaviour.

Children, however, were not dragooned into uniform. The youth organizations would have shrivelled on the bough if what they were offering did not attract young people. School was compulsory; the clubs and brigades were not. To join the Boy Scouts you needed to have 15s (75p) for the uniform, way beyond the reach of most working-class boys but not beyond their dreams. Having nicked a copy of Baden-Powell's *Scouting for Boys* from a barrow in Manchester's Shudehill Market, Syd Carey and his friend Robert Roberts wanted to join the Scouts. Roberts was the more respectable of the two:

> [I] went to offer our services at St John's, a troop in a lower-middle-class district beyond the tramlines, and duly reported back.
> 'Stuck up!' I said. 'I was the only one with clogs on!'
> 'But they didn't tell you to piss off?' asked Syd hopefully.
> 'You got to go to their church regular ... and buy a uniform inside a month.' This killed all hope.[77]

Failure to win entry, or some sense that you were not respectable enough for one of the uniformed youth movements, could breed ridicule of them. All over the country the Boys' Brigade would be met by some version of this song: 'Here comes the Boys' Brigade / All covered with marmalade. / A tuppenny ha'penny pill-box, / And a half a yard of braid.'[78] None of this stopped boys and girls wanting to join, the key attraction perhaps being the annual camp. The worries about adolescence that so exercised their elders seem to have passed over their heads.

By the mid-twentieth century the home, the street, commercial attractions like the cinema and youth organizations competed for the attention of children. How they spent their time would depend to a large degree on their parents' status and sense of respectability. Children would have been fully aware of this, but probably blind to the debates about the future of the nation which reverberated around the way they spent their leisure time as much as they did about all other aspects of their lives.

CHAPTER SIX

Post-war Childhood

MORE THAN HALF A CENTURY after the end of the Second World War, many people talked as if they were living in 'post-war Britain'. Wars have replaced the reigns of monarchs as the means of dividing up history. There are, of course, other ways of splitting up this tranche of time. One much used marker is the coming to power of Margaret Thatcher's Conservative government in 1979, considered the end of the consensus between the Labour and Conservative parties of the 1950s, 1960s and 1970s. Certainly, Thatcher's governments deeply affected the lives of children for they placed many of them in the relative-poverty category. Yet the key divide probably came rather earlier with the oil-price crisis of 1973; it presaged the much tougher economic times that lay ahead.

The period up to 1973 was one in which young people made the transition to adulthood in a remarkably short space of time. The average age of marriage for women, which had been 24.6 in 1951, fell to 22.6 in 1971, historically an all-time low. Men, too, were getting married much younger.[1] This was made possible by a buoyant youth-labour market and increasing prosperity. They were the years when the Conservative prime minister Harold Macmillan could say, in 1957, 'You've never had it so good.' He was reflecting what many people felt. Mothers in the early post-war years were fully aware that a higher standard of living enabled them to look after their children in a quite different way from that of their own mothers. But after 1973 the job market for the young became much more difficult, and job-creation schemes multiplied in an attempt to reduce youth unemployment. The age of marriage went up and its incidence down. Young people became dependent on their parents much longer. Children's attitudes and expectations changed to take account of these new, and unwelcome, circumstances.

Most families for some 30 years after the end of the war could be allocated by sociologists to one of five social classes according to the occupation of the father: professional and managerial, white collar, skilled manual, semi-skilled manual and unskilled manual. The first two, roughly one-third of the population, constituted the middle classes, the last three the working classes. Class, as it had long been, was the most important indicator of how a child would be raised and what its life-chances were. But a whole variety of changes were rendering this less and less useful as a way of understanding Britain. The decline of manual working-class jobs was one factor. Another was the increasing participation in the economy of married women as wage earners.

And yet another was the impact of immigration. The Irish continued after the Second World War to provide the biggest contingent, but they were soon followed by large numbers of people from continental Europe and then, heralded by the arrival at Tilbury on 22 June 1948 of the *Empire Windrush*, by immigration from the Caribbean and Asia. Immigrants brought with them their own cultures of family structure and child rearing.

Many children's lives were deeply affected by the high divorce rate of the post-war years. In the late 1930s there were only 7500 divorces a year. The number shot up to 60,000 a year in the immediate aftermath of the Second World War, fell in the 1950s and then began an apparently inexorable rise, from 32,000 in 1961 to 74,000 in 1971. There was an accompanying rise in one-parent households. By the late 1970s there were nearly 1.5 million dependent children, 11 per cent of all children, living in one-parent families.[2]

But change in the structure of the family was even more rapid in the later twentieth century and early twenty-first. The family was still held up as the model environment for children but itself bore little resemblance to the back-of-the-cornflakes-packet ideal. By the mid-1990s only one-quarter of households consisted of a couple with dependent children. Divorce, illegitimacy, single-parent families, children with step-parents, all made matters much more complex. In 2004, 149,300 children under 16 experienced the divorce of their parents – down from the peak year, 1993, when there were 176,000, but very much higher than in the 1950s and 1960s. By 1995 over one-third of children were born out of wedlock: it had been less than one in ten 20 years earlier. In 2005, 24 per cent of all children, nearly one in four, were living in lone-parent households – up from 7 per cent in 1972.

Homelessness became a problem. Shelter, the national campaigning charity for housing and homelessness, estimated in 1998 that there were 100,000 children homeless at any one time. This was linked to the fact that over one-third of all children were living in families with no full-time wage earner. In what is historically a very short time period, 20 or 30 years, the contours of the family changed dramatically.[3]

The kiddy and the pork chop: childhood 1950–1973

In Bethnal Green, in London's East End, Mrs Glass in the 1950s described the difference between her parents' generation and her own thus: 'Dad used to be very strict with us, we're different with our boy. We make more of a mate of him. When I was a kid Dad always had the best of everything. Now it's the children who get the best of it. If there's one pork chop left, the kiddy gets it.'[4]

There are few things more important in family life than food. In working-class families in the nineteenth century and early twentieth, everyone agreed about the pecking order. Fathers came first, children next and mothers last. Now, in the 1950s, fathers seem to have given place to children; the child has become 'a mate'. Mothers in the 1950s and 1960s became acutely aware that the way they were bringing up their children differed from how they themselves had been brought up.

Mrs Glass was one of the participants in a famous study of the 1950s that compared Bethnal Green and the new model town of Dagenham on London's eastern outskirts. In a nutshell, they found a community in Bethnal Green and isolated families of parents and their children in Dagenham. And of course the future was Dagenham. In Bethnal Green grandmothers were involved in child care on a daily basis, and young mothers were in constant touch with one another. But for the families moved out to Dagenham, grandmother was still in the East End, and mother and the children tended to live behind net curtains. These new homes were becoming much more attractive places in which to spend time. Children began to get their own bedrooms. Radio had already helped bring entertainment into the home, but on nothing like the scale of television, which spread rapidly in the 1950s. At the outset there was a brief revival of community, the house with the television set becoming a magnet for the neighbours, but that soon passed. The nuclear family of father, mother and the children was driven in on itself.

The decades in the middle of the twentieth century witnessed one of the most important changes in the history of childhood. Until then, it had been assumed as a matter of course in the great majority of families that children would start earning as soon as they could and would contribute their wages to the family economy. They would tip up their earnings to their mother, who might give them something back for spends. As everyone knew, once the children started earning, the family as a whole enjoyed a better standard of living. In innumerable families across the country some kind of negotiation, spoken or unspoken, went on, the teenage worker torn between the sense of family needs and the wish to be able to spend on her or his own account.

In the post-war world the balance began to swing decisively in favour of the teenage worker. It was in the 1950s that sociologists started talking about

'the teenage consumer'. There is in fact much evidence of teenagers as consumers throughout the twentieth century, but undoubtedly they had more
money at their disposal in the 1950s than they had had earlier.[5] They were
both earning more and contributing less to the family economy. What made
this possible was a rise in living standards: the higher earnings of the male
head of the household now began to make life less of a pinch. In addition,
some wives were beginning to enter the labour market, normally part-time
and in low-paid jobs, and what was often called their 'pin money' made its
contribution to the family budget. The flow of cash that throughout history
had gone from children to parents now began to change direction: parents
spent on their children. The change was more than simply economic. Parents
were beginning to think that their children might be able to have a better life
than they had had and were willing to make sacrifices to help this to happen.
An American historian, Viviana Zelizer, has described this process as a 'sacral-
ization of childhood'. Family life began to be centred on the children, the
parents investing in them emotionally as well as financially, their hopes insep-
arable from the happiness and success of their children.[6]

This consciousness of a change of generation can be seen in the history of
pocket-money, which first began to be spoken about in the later nineteenth
century. It only became an issue in the mid-twentieth century – and that
because it was the poor who were most generous to their children. A wartime
survey found that, 'school children in the poorer districts had far more pocket-
money than those of the better class ... These children spend their money
largely on sweets, ice-cream and comics ... [The] sweets [are] often of the most
wretched quality [and the comics] generally poor to a degree.'[7]

By the first half of the 1950s most parents were giving their children
regular pocket-money by the time they started going to school. In the late
1960s it still seemed to be true, as in the 1940s, that poor parents spent more
on pocket-money than the well-off.[8] But the poorer you were, the greater the
range of goods you were expected to buy with it. Parents varied in how they
distributed money to their children, the one common factor being that they all
did it. Mothers described what they did – or had done when their daughters
were younger – in Swansea in the 1960s. At one end of the spectrum, there
was a mother who said, 'I give them money when they ask for something and
I never comes back from the shops without something for them – sweets
and that. They moan sometimes that they don't get pocket-money like other

children, but I tell them, "Look how much more in fact you get than the other kids."'

At the opposite end, the attitude was, 'I think it's very important in bringing up children to be strict on routine. I always gave them pocket-money every Friday – I wasn't allowed to forget it – they bought whatever they wanted with it.' But the most common attitude was expressed by another mother: 'Her father gave her [a few shillings] every week and if she wanted more, she came and asked me. Spoilt she was!'[9] Children had come to occupy a new place in the working-class home.

By the 1960s, too, over half of all seven year olds were earning money from their parents for doing odd jobs, the child taking the initiative in negotiating this extra income.[10] What in previous generations would have been an expected contribution to the family now became an opportunity to earn some money. Most children were exempt from any requirement to help. In the 1960s in Nottingham less than one-third of seven year olds were expected to do regular jobs and, particularly if you were a girl, the lower you were in the social scale, the less you were expected to do.[11] Mothers took on the whole burden. 'I used to ask if she wanted me to help and she said, "Help me by keeping out of the way!"' One young woman who had had to help clearly felt she was picked on. She used to bath her brother and sister on Saturday nights until she was 17: 'And I used to stay in every Tuesday evening to do the ironing, and to do the washing up. My mother had a big womb op. a few years ago – and she rather played up on it. She's *got* to do [the housework] now and so she *does* it. It was very inconvenient for my mother to let me get married – I did a lot of work.'[12]

Alongside pocket-money and small earnings, children were becoming adept at extracting money from their parents: pester power, perhaps dating back to the eighteenth century, was now more vigorous, or, as one observer put it, there was a 'pressure towards the material indulgence of children'. A mother in Nottingham described how, 'I think myself you give in to your own where you couldn't have it – you think to yourself, well I didn't get this, and I'll see that he gets it. I think that's the whole attitude of a lot of people.'[13]

If there were tensions between the generations, there was also a relationship between parents and children of a kind that could not have been imagined earlier. Children now found it much easier than in previous generations to talk to their parents. We have seen how in earlier centuries a prime virtue enjoined on girls was silence, and we all know the injunction that children should be seen and not heard. In many households the silence of the children remained the norm in the first half of the twentieth century. Mrs Peters in Lancashire recalled how you spoke when you were spoken to: 'I remember we had relatives in and they were talking about something and I spoke up. I'll never forget it. Dad turned right quickly on me, "Children should be seen and not heard." I can see him to this day pointing at me. I know I went crimson. I thought, I'll watch my step another time. They were kind and good, but firm. You'd to toe the line.'[14]

One indication of this pre-Second World War lack of communication between mothers and daughters was that girls were left in complete ignorance about menstruation. Mrs Calvert, born in Preston in 1919, remembered: 'When I had been to the toilet I thought, oh, what have I done? I never thought anything and I were turned fifteen. I told her that I had all colour on m'pants. All she said was, "In my bottom drawer you will find some cloths. Put them up against you and keep warm and keep away from lads." That's all my mother ever told me about anything.'[15]

Boys were equally ignorant. Robert Roberts remembered a conversation he had with his school friend Eddie Franklin:

Franklin: 'I see that there girl on the front row – Cissie Craven – has started her periods. That's another one!'
Roberts, lying: ''S right. She told me. Have *you* begun yet?'
Franklin, startled: 'Me? N-No! Not yet ... What's "periods"?'
Roberts: 'If you don't know, don't come pretendin' to us that you *do* – see?'[16]

By the second half of the century, however, this had changed. Here is a shop manager's wife in Nottingham in the 1960s talking about her daughter Jennifer, aged 11:

When I was Jennifer's age I didn't know – I was never told – and I don't think that's right. I think they *should* know as soon as they start to ask anything – I mean they *ought* to be told. Same as when your periods start – well, when mine started, oh, I was frightened to death, I didn't know *what* was the matter with me; and of course I didn't tell my mother until she found out. Well, Jennifer *knows*, and so of course she's *not* frightened ... Well, as I say – she's just started, this week in fact, the first signs of it started; well, she came straight away and told me. Well, I don't think there's anything if she wanted to know she wouldn't come and ask me; and if it came to it, I don't think she'd mind telling her Daddy, if I wasn't here. You see, they *can talk*.[17]

But in this brave new world children's talk could be wearing on the parent. A lorry driver's wife said of her son: 'He's got a terrible habit that he'll just talk and talk and talk and talk, until in the end you can hear his voice going through you, you know. I usually tell him to be quiet then. He'll say "All right" – and he just keeps right on! He doesn't take a bit of notice. He just keeps on, and on, and on, and on.'

Or as a railwayman's wife put it: 'It's her ordering me about. She'll want some water for her paint; I say "Wait a minute, will you, please?" "I want it *right away*, Mummy!" And she's on and on all the time until I go to get it her ... I mean, when we was kiddies, we had to do as we was told, didn't we?'[18]

These parents, and many others like them, were conscious that parenting for their generation was quite unlike it had been for their own parents. And, though there were pleasures, there were also frustrations, which often found a vent in smacking the child. Over two-thirds of parents interviewed in the 1960s smacked their four year olds somewhere between once a day and once a week, some guilty that they did so. And what led them to smack was what they perceived as the child's disobedience or defiance.[19] One mother, talking of her seven-year-old daughter and the other neighbourhood children, said: 'Well, it's a strange sort of rudeness – *disrespectful* rudeness – and I find it hard to cope with, because I would have never *dreamt* of talking to my mother like that, you know; not even *thinking* that way! ... I've just come to the conclusion that children today are *like* this ... This relationship with parents, it's completely different – and I'm not sure which is best.'[20]

There seems little doubt that children were behaving differently towards their parents than they had in previous generations, and that mothers, on whom the burden of parenting fell, were finding this often stressful. Mothers had almost certainly picked up from magazines or the radio some notion of the dangers of 'maternal deprivation' but found the level of commitment now expected wearing.

Most parents who were interviewed in the 1950s, 1960s and 1970s thought their children were having a better upbringing than they had had. They were comparing their own childhoods, often spent in the Depression years in the 1920s and 1930s and scarred by high unemployment, with the better post-war times. But in a more diverse Britain, some parents had a different reference point and a different set of attitudes. Many immigrants felt like Conroy, who had been born in Grenada, brought up in St Lucia and came to south London at the end of the 1950s when he was in his early twenties. His mother had died when he was very young and then his father, and he went to live with an elder sister who worked him very hard. Nevertheless he felt:

> I think my childhood happier than my kids. Plenty ... Them kids more demanding than I was in my childhood. In this country, you have to give them everything they want ... You have to give them money whenever they go out ... when they go to school. Here you have to buy everything ... In the morning, if I going to school, I go slipping in by my sister and get a cup of milk ... You didn't want sweets in the West Indies, you have a June plum and that's it ... And if you got plenty and your friends poorer than you, you hand it out.'[21]

Conroy felt the same pressures from his children that British-born parents experienced.

Until the early 1970s it seemed likely to many that the British economy, although subject to a pattern of stops and starts, would continue to grow, and that families would continue in much the same way as they had been doing. But in fact a major change was in store.

Modern childhood: a prison or a garden?

A 12-year-old girl in the early 1990s, asked to describe what she did when not at school, wrote: 'I help a lot at home because my mum and my dad are at work until about half past six, so when I get home I usually tidy the kitchen and living room, then cook dinner for mum and dad and then I sit down and do my homework until they get home.'[22] For much of the twentieth century there had been loud voices proclaiming that childhood should be a time of happiness, of freedom from cares, whether at school, at play or at home. The home, it was assumed, would have a breadwinning father and a stay-at-home mother. In the later twentieth century this ideal began seriously to unravel.

The modern era of childhood in Britain began in the early 1970s. It has been marked by three things. First, a prolongation of childhood, of which the first sign was the raising of the school-leaving age to 16 in 1972. This came at the same time as the previously buoyant youth-labour market entered very stormy waters and it became difficult for young school leavers to find jobs, something that further increased their dependency on their parents. In the 1950s and 1960s children had made remarkably quick transitions from childhood to adulthood, marrying in their early twenties. Now the transition to adulthood became infinitely protracted.

Second, alongside this dependency, children were being expected to contribute in significant ways in many family situations: where both parents worked, in single-parent homes, in homes where other family members had need of care and in some ethnic-minority families. Third, it was a period when the rights of children came to be asserted with increasing force. Children were not alone among subordinate sections of society in demanding to be heard. The feminist movement provided the most powerful exemplar for those asserting children's rights, not least because the restrictions against which children and their advocates began to protest were so similar to those that had prevented women from playing a full role in society.

Modern childhood is the story of the relationship between dependency, contributions to the family welfare and rights. It has presented children with experiences and challenges unprecedented in history. We can see the change from the 1950s and 1960s, and the increased dependency, by looking at the age at which children left home. In the late Middle Ages and in the early modern centuries, roughly up to 1800, the most common age of leaving home was around 14. Some, particularly those living on small farms, or in the middle classes, stayed longer. But most left at about 14 to become servants or apprentices, and, having left home, they did not return there to live. The fundamental reason for this was that there was no way of earning money while they remained at home. In the Industrial Revolution, it made more sense for teenage workers to stay at home, certainly from the point of view of their parents who benefited from the wages they brought in. The habit grew up of leaving home only to get married, and that might not be till your mid-twenties. This situation lasted through to the 1970s, the only change being that young people were earning enough to enable them to get married younger, and they took advantage of this to leave home earlier.

From the 1970s onwards the pattern has changed. Housing and economic difficulties have made it much more difficult to leave home. A typical pattern became for a teenager, who had left school and was working, to leave home, find it too expensive to live independently and then return home. There is now no one decisive break from home, and the pattern of graduates of 21 or more returning to live at home has become the stuff of television sitcoms. And all studies of adult children living at home show that, even if they make some contribution to expenses, they never pay the market rate. They are subsidized by, and dependent on, their parents.[23]

Changing patterns like this make it very difficult to know when childhood now ends. Mary Carpenter, a major figure in the mid-nineteenth-century attempt to rescue street children, a woman with a considerable public profile but living in her adulthood in the parental home, said that it was only in her fifties, when her mother died, that she felt that she was 'emerging from childhood'.[24] It seems likely that children in the late twentieth and early twenty-first century who remained at home retained something of this feeling that they were still children. The school leaving age might be 16, but a rapidly increasing number of young people remained in full-time education beyond that age, and the financing of it weighed more and more heavily on parents. It is difficult to think of any other period in history when children have remained dependent on their parents to such an advanced age, the only possible exception being for upper- and middle-class girls in the eighteenth and nineteenth centuries who did not get married.

We have seen that in the immediate post-Second World War period the flow of resources began to go from parents to children. Children began to expect to keep their earnings or at least most of them. In the later twentieth century, however, there was accumulating evidence that children were contributing more to the family's welfare than many people expected.

First, researchers in the 1980s and 1990s found that schoolchildren were undertaking a considerable amount of waged labour. The general view was that child labour belonged to the nineteenth century or, at worst, to the very early twentieth century. What these studies showed was that between one-third and one-half of children aged 13 to 15 were in some form of paid employment. Some of them worked in jobs that had long been designated as being for children, like delivering newspapers, but others worked in shops, hotels, door-to-door selling, garages and building sites. A significant minority of these children, perhaps as many as a quarter, worked more than ten hours a week, on top of 30 hours at school.[25]

Second, there was evidence that children in some immigrant communities were also often hard at work. One of the best documented of these is the work of children in family-owned Chinese take-aways. The children played a crucial role, not simply as supplementary workers but also because their skills in language and in understanding British culture could help overcome their parents' lack of them. These children rarely questioned that work in the take-away would be expected of them; indeed there was no separation between shop and home. As one young Chinese boy, Foon, put it when asked how he had got involved in working in the shop: 'I don't know. They've never asked us. It's almost as though it's just expected. We just watched and learned when we were young ... When we came back from school, we came back to the shop and hung around. That's where the TV was – at the counter, in the shop. We didn't have a TV upstairs [their living quarters].'[26]

Third, it also became apparent that children were playing a much larger role in the domestic economy than had been assumed; largely because their mothers were at work, or they had only one parent living in the home. When children in the early 1990s were asked to write essays on what they did when they were not at school, over half of the girls and nearly one-third of the boys mentioned time spent on domestic work. Some of them were paid for this work. They were like the 12-year-old girl who tidied and then cooked the evening meal for her parents. A 15 year old wrote: 'I do help my mum with the housework. I polish, change the sheets, hoover and clean the bathroom every Saturday. And when we are on half term or holidays I clean the house every day for my mum. I wash up every night and sometimes cook the meal.'

A 15-year-old boy, living with his father, shows that these sorts of jobs are not confined to girls: 'I put the shopping away with the help of my brother. That is on the days when my dad does the shopping. The rest of the days I do the washing up and the hoovering and my bedroom with my brother's help, when we have done our work we can go out but we have our dinner then wash up ... our dad sometimes does dinner but we would do it normally.' A 13-year-old girl also bucks gender stereotyping, describing how 'As I don't have a Father because he died I help with a lot more things, eg clean car, do bins, and mechanical or handy work, fixing things.'[27]

Children tend to explain the amount of domestic work they do by referring to their parents' work patterns. If in the immediate post-Second World War world mothers gained some sense of purpose and self-esteem by taking sole responsibility for the home, in the late twentieth century many of them were working in the labour market, and reliant on their children to contribute. Children were well aware of this. A 13-year-old boy describes how: 'In the holidays I get up at about 10.00 am (I am very lazy) then I will have breakfast then do the daily chores because my Mum and Dad both work. The daily chores: putting out the washing, cleaning the house, tidying rooms, going to the shops, cooking meals (for my younger brother).'[28]

Children also act as carers for other family members, particularly younger siblings but also grandparents and parents. Some 175,000 children are reported as acting as carers in Britain.[29] A 14-year-old girl wrote, 'I sometimes go round my nan's on Saturday. To help her get her shopping because she is quite old and finds it difficult to carry her shopping in by herself. I also do her hoovering and clean out her bird for her.' Another describes how she has been caring for her mother since she was about eight: '[Mum] had very bad depression at the time, and used to take it out on us by hitting us – not good memories. As the eldest, I got used to shopping, taking my younger brother and sister to school, cooking, cleaning ... Like most young carers, I would still care even if I had the choice not to.'[30]

Julie, who is 16 and has a brother in very poor health, says:

I am the only one who can give him emotional support when he is feeling down. Our parents drive him round the bend (surprise surprise!) and it's me who's left to make him smile when he's going through hard times. It's me who is there to make him laugh when there's absolutely nothing to laugh about. However much work it is to achieve this, it's always worthwhile for the smiles and look he gives me ... Being a young carer teaches you so much, perhaps taking away childhood, but often giving you an awareness of life and how precious it is. Some would say I've had to grow up too fast, but I believe I've made more of my life because of it.[31]

On the one hand, then, children are now more dependent on their parents, and for longer, than children in the past. On the other, many of them are making a crucial contribution to the welfare of the family. How does this square with the increasing assertion of their rights?

We can trace a concern with the rights of children back to the nineteenth century when it seemed to many middle-class observers, under the influence of romanticism, that there were far too many 'children without childhood'. A child, they asserted, had a right to childhood. They were rarely explicit about what might constitute childhood, but at its heart lay the right to a home life, the right to play, the right to be protected and the right to be dependent. Children's rights became defined almost as the opposite of adult rights: if adults, faced with unemployment, claimed a right to work, children had a right not to work.[32]

Some of this thinking began to find its way into legislation. There was an attempt to map out the kind of territory that children should inhabit, and the kind of contacts they should or should not have. The Children Act, 1908, for example, made it illegal for children to go into pubs – it had until then been common for fathers to send their children off to fetch home a pint. Children were also breaking the law if they were found in possession of tobacco. If they did commit some offence, then they would, from 1908 onwards, appear in special children's courts.

The first formal statement of children's rights, approved by the League of Nations in 1924, was drawn up by an Englishwoman, Eglantyne Jebb, the founder of Save the Children: it asserted the duties of adults towards children. After the Second World War, the United Nations in 1959 agreed a Declaration of the Rights of the Child, in which the emphasis was again on the duty of adults to protect, feed and educate children.

In the 1970s a very different note began to be heard. If romanticism had helped to shape the view that children should be protected and dependent, it could also draw on another strand within its repertoire, an emphasis on the development of the individual and on the sacredness of her or his experience. In this individual development the different ages of life needed to cohere. From this it could easily be argued that children, if they were to develop into good adults, needed above all freedom so that their innate potentialities could grow and develop – anything else might stand in the way of growth.

This cast of thinking was first evident in what became known as progressive education, itself a reaction against the rote learning and discipline associated with most schools. Its most prominent advocate in twentieth-century

Britain was A. S. Neill. Of Summerhill, the school he founded in 1921, he said that they set out to make a school in which they would allow children freedom to be themselves. To do this, they had to renounce all discipline, direction and suggestion, all moral training and religious instruction: 'We have been called brave, but it did not require courage. All it required was what we had – a complete belief in the child as a good, not an evil being. For over forty years, this belief in the goodness of the child has never wavered; it rather has become a final faith.'[33]

Neill's statement of belief is a perfect encapsulation of the romantic belief in childhood goodness. Out of his experience, and that of others, and influenced by the radical ideas of the 1960s, came the children's liberation movement of the late 1960s and early 1970s. Its focus was precisely on the restrictions and lack of liberty associated with the ideal of childhood: school uniforms, school discipline, restrictions on sexual behaviour and indeed on anything that seemed to belong to the adult world. A symptomatic text (and title) was John Holt's *Escape from Childhood* (1974). For Holt childhood was an institution that took powers to

> lock the young into eighteen years or more of subserviency and dependency, and make of them ... a mixture of expensive nuisance, fragile treasure, slave and super-pet ... Most people who believe in the institution of childhood as we know it see it as a kind of walled garden in which children, being small and weak, are protected from the harshness of the world outside until they become strong and clever enough to cope with it. Some children experience childhood in just that way. I do not want to destroy their garden or kick them out of it. If they like it, by all means let them stay in it. But I believe that most young people, and at earlier and earlier ages, begin to experience childhood not as a garden but as a prison ... I am not saying that childhood is bad for all children all the time. But Childhood, as in Happy, Safe, Protected, Innocent Childhood, does not exist for many children. For many other children, however good it may be, childhood goes on far too long.[34]

As a movement with any kind of organization, children's liberation was short-lived – probably, like so many phenomena associated with the 1960s, we shall come to see it as killed off by the more difficult economic times consequent on the oil-price rise of 1973. But it left an important residue. Books on children's rights spilled from the presses, and they all had to engage with the challenge laid down by Holt and his fellow liberationists. Going beyond protection, it became axiomatic that children should be seen as human beings with rights to autonomy and self-determination, and to participation in decisions that concerned them.[35] This was written into the 1989 UN Convention on the Rights of the Child that laid stress on a child's right to participate in decisions affecting her or him.

Evidence of the impact of this thinking is all around us. Barnardo's, for example, has radically changed its attitude to the children in its care. Instead of encouraging them to break all contact with their birth families, it now provides facilities to enable them to re-establish contact. In family disputes, too, children now have a right to bring proceedings against their own parents.

Children in the early twenty-first century stand, often uncomfortably, in the middle of a triangle. On one side lie the rights that they know they now have, on another their sense of obligation to subordinate their own wishes to those of the family, and on the third side the awareness that they are economically dependent on their parents. It is difficult to predict in any particular case, or for society as a whole, how the tensions in that situation will work out.

The disappearance of childhood?

In the 1950s, a 12 year old from Spennymoor in County Durham reported:

> When I get home from school there is usually some little girls out of the infants school playing in the street, and their special little rhyme is:
>
> > 'Little fatty doctor, how's your wife?'
> > 'Very well, thank you, she's alright.'
> > 'Can she eat a twopenny pie?'
> > 'Yes sir, yes sir, and so can I.'

She would have been astonished to know that in the early nineteenth century two boys meeting one another would have this interchange:

> > 'Doctor! Doctor! How's your wife?'
> > 'Very bad, upon my life.'

'Can she eat a bit of pie?'

'Yes, she can, as well as I.'[36]

How far was this centuries-old world of childhood able to survive in the second half of the twentieth century? The challenges it faced were numerous: increasing regulation of play, and worry about the dangers to children playing outside in the street unsupervised, the advent of television in the home and the targeting of children by toy-makers who themselves concentrated on spin-offs from television programmes. Some people argued that childhood itself was undermined by these developments.

The 12 year old from Spennymoor was one of 5000 children in 70 schools across Britain who contributed to a project devised by Iona and Peter Opie. [Fig. 32] The aim was to record the beliefs children held, the language they used, the games they played and the songs they sang. The results were set out in three volumes, the later ones adding in more children and more up-to-date material. In *The Lore and Language of Schoolchildren* (1959), *Children's Games in Street and Playground* (1969) and *The Singing Game* (1985), the Opies provided us with a unique record of the culture of children in the second half of the twentieth century. What we learn from it is that children are, to an extraordinary extent, custodians of a rich heritage, one generation of children passing on to the next words, games and songs. It is not a sterile tradition, children change or add to the canon, but much of what they are doing has deep roots in history.

Adults have long been convinced that this traditional culture of children is in decline. But in fact, as the Opies reported, it was perhaps no coincidence that the games whose decline was most pronounced were those that were best known to adults and therefore the most often promoted by them, while 'the games and amusements that flourish are those that adults find most difficulty in encouraging (e.g. knife-throwing games and chases in the dark), or are those sports, such as ball-bouncing and long-rope skipping, in which adults are ordinarily least able to show proficiency.'[37]

Daring games are widespread. A 13-year-old Scots girl tells how they meet in the street after dark:

Sometimes the question master tells you to go to a wifie's window and knock on it and cry, 'Are you in, Nellie?' and then run along and knock at the wifie's door and act as you're walking up the street, and say that a boy did it and went away round the corner. Then the question master says you have to throw water on the wifie's door-step and she threatens you, 'I'm going awa for the Bobby,' and she shammies she's going away for the police. Then you play your game on another auld wifie until the other wifie come back. Then sometimes you're dared to go and tie the wifies' doors together (of course it's the wifies you do not like) and knock on them and run awa, and the auld wifies come out both together. What a laugh you get when they come out and discover the string tied to the door.

Such dares, like the common 'Last Across', a dare to cross a road when traffic was coming or a railway line with a train approaching, could end in disaster.[38]

Children, in these games and in other activities, seem deliberately to pit themselves against the adult world, often to subvert it. It can be seen in the parodies of hymns and of other texts that adults revere.

> Jesus loves me, I don't think,
> He took me to a skating rink.
> He drank whisky, I drank beer,
> Jesus loves me – I'm a leer.[39]

A study of children in northeast England suggested that children lived in a world that was an inversion of the adult world. In adult language 'kets' meant rubbish; for children it signalled the most desirable things you could think of, for example the kind of sweets you knew that adults disapproved of, and that carried names suggesting they were inedible: Syco Discs, Fizzy Bullets, Supersonic Flyers, Robots, Traffic Lights, Golf Balls and Car Parks. These were sweets that you would lick, take out of your mouth, perhaps swap with a friend, as the colour changed from vibrant green to shocking pink. This was the world of childhood. Begin to be attracted by the thought of a brown and carefully packaged After Eight and you were leaving childhood behind you.[40]

The Opies' work suggested that children were retaining a culture that most people assumed was being swept away by commercial attractions. They themselves were alert to changes, but if the culture they described was under threat, the chief danger, they thought, came from authority figures who were destroying the wild habitat in which children were most happy. Many children in and after the Second World War delighted in bomb sites. A Peckham child in 1955 described how 'In my neighbourhood the sites of Hitler's bombs are many, and the bigger sites with a certain amount of rubble provide very good grounds for Hide and Seek and Tin Can Tommy.'[41] But in the 1960s everything began to be tidied up, to be replaced by adventure playgrounds and play leaders, developments for which the Opies had nothing but contempt. As they put it in 1969, 'nothing extinguishes self-organized play more effectively than does action to promote it.'[42] And the anxieties about safety outside the home, from traffic and from strangers, already present in the 1960s, began to escalate.

In 1971 eight out of ten seven or eight year olds were allowed to go to school on their own, 20 years later fewer than one in ten. At the age of nine most children in 1971 were allowed to cross roads on their own, to go on non-school journeys on their own and to use buses. In 1990, only half were allowed to cross roads, only one-third to go on non-school journeys and less than one in ten to use buses. The median age at which children were allowed to do these things had risen by two and a half years; what you could do on your own at seven in 1971, you had to wait until you were nine and a half to do in 1990.[43] The world the children inhabited was drawing in on itself, and the chances of the world that the Opies described surviving correspondingly diminished.

The dangers that the Opies pointed to have been fully in evidence since they wrote, but most people argue that there has been something even more potent undermining this traditional child culture, and that has been the media. And the new media, it was argued, were destroying childhood itself.

In 1982 an American, Neil Postman, published a book with the title *The Disappearance of Childhood*. Postman argued that modern childhood rose with the invention of print. Learning to read was a difficult task that you had to be taught. It required sitting in a classroom slowly building up a skill, from letters to sounds, from sounds to words, from words to sentences and so on. The visual media required no such prolonged training: everyone, immediately, could make some response to a picture. Children at a stroke were on a par with adults. The boundary line that adults had been able to draw, separating off childhood from what came after it, disappeared from sight. The change was evident not only in the media but, for example, in clothing and food as well. Children's clothes ceased to mark them off in quite the same way as they used to do; indeed adults began to copy children's fashions.[44]

Looked at historically, television, videos and the internet, each in turn produced forebodings of their impact on children little different from the cinema, the penny dreadfuls (cheap, sensational serials or tales) of the nineteenth century, or those chapbooks that we saw so exercising a Tudor Puritan. The response to the cinema bears a remarkable similarity to reactions to more recent media. Year after year there was alarm in the press and in parliament that films were sapping the morals of children; year after year experts who investigated these claims poured doubt on them. The alarmists imagine the child's mind as a sponge, children absorbing every message and every nuance from what they see on a screen. The sceptics see children taking from what they see what they want, ignoring the rest and also having a critical judgement rather greater than is imputed to them.[45]

What cannot be doubted is that a market for children's toys grew up around films and television – or, put another way, that films and television were themselves produced with an eye to the accompanying marketing opportunities. Even before the Second World War, film producer Walt Disney was making most of his money from merchandise, mainly models of his famous cartoon characters. Most toys sold are linked in some way to what a child has seen. The market in children's consumer goods is huge, an estimated £10 billion a year in the United Kingdom at the end of the twentieth century. Parents on average now spend £715 each year on toys for each one of their children.[46]

From early in the twentieth century toy manufacturers realized that they would sell more if they focused on the child as purchaser rather than some well-meaning adult. They played on children's known wish to collect sets of objects or to have a model of a character they knew from a cartoon. Children's comics were one way of reaching this new market. [Fig. 31] Of course it would only work if there were some disposable income that the child could cadge from a parent, and this began to be the case. On top of this, major occasions for expenditure on children, such as birthdays and Christmas, were given increasing importance.

Many people in the late twentieth and early twenty-first century felt distinctly uneasy about the linked phenomena of the growth of the child-consumer market and the amount of time children spent in front of a television set – more time than at school in some cases. It seemed, if nothing else, that children were being manipulated into a kind of passive subservience to these market forces. It was also felt that they were being exposed too young to things about which they shouldn't yet know.

And yet children, as the more sophisticated research showed, were capable of interpreting what they saw in their own terms. Children were in a way caught between two forces. Often more media-savvy than their parents, they had access to the world of the internet. At the same time their access to the world outside their own homes was sharply diminished. With the visual media, they could think of themselves as adults. In the home and its surrounds, their childhood was being prolonged. It is no coincidence that what is often called the second golden age of children's literature focused very much on growing out of childhood.

In the first golden age in the late nineteenth and early twentieth century children were presented with ideal worlds – a secret garden or Badger's kitchen – where they could live out their lives as children. It had been followed by a period in which the most noted author was Arthur Ransome, his world, too, one where there were idealized childhoods, children having adventures largely free from adult supervision. But after the Second World War, the tone changed. Adults begin to be challenged. In Mary Norton's *The Borrowers* (1952), the borrowers are tiny people living below the floorboards of a big house inhabited by 'human beans'. Arrietty, the child, is virtually imprisoned. The way to the upper world is barred by gates, to keep cats and other predators out but also to keep Arrietty in. Eventually, Arrietty goes upstairs and begins to escape from the prison of childhood. The same theme is pursued in Philippa Pearce's *Tom's Midnight Garden* (1958) where the garden inevitably represents childhood, and Tom wants to remain there for ever. But he is in for a shock, as Hatty, the girl with whom he plays, herself grows old very fast. Tom learns that 'Nothing stands still, except in our memory.' You can't stop growing up. In this second golden age, in these books, or in those of Alan Garner or Roald Dahl or Philip Pullman or J. K. Rowling, children have the chance to live in a world governed by very different forces than those of the market or the media: by magic, by a challenge to, or an overturning of, the values of the adult world.[47]

The culture that the Opies described was one in which children passed on to one another rhymes, songs and games. Often children thought that what they were doing was their own invention, the words of their song their own.

Nearly always they were old. The Opies also knew that most of their adult contemporaries thought that this world of children had disappeared, destroyed by the forces of modern life. But those contemporaries were wrong. And despite all the forces for change since the Opies did their research, many of the old rhymes, songs and games survive. In 1994 a girl in Sheffield, asked for her favourite 'dip', the way of choosing who starts a game, recited:

> Ickle ockle
> Chocolate bottle
> Ickle ockle out
> If you want a chocolate bottle
> Please walk out.

The Opies recorded numerous versions of this jingle, tracing it back 80 years.[48] We can be pretty confident that the girl's mother in the 1960s, her grandmother at the end of the 1930s and very probably her great-grandmother in the early years of the century had used the same dip to start a game.

In short, children's long-standing ability to live their own culture, to invert the adult world and to turn upside down its most cherished values and objects, has not completely disappeared. Some outward markers of childhood, probably having more to do with middle-class ideas about appropriate food and clothes for children than with the invention of print, may have crumbled, but if the appeal of the second golden age of children's literature is any guide, children still like to set themselves up in some kind of opposition to, or tension with, the adult world. Children can now explore this stage of growing up in literature as well as in their own language, lore and games.

Curiously, too, if childhood itself is under threat, it may be in part because adults want to rejoin it. As publishers have shrewdly noted, books that sell well with children can often also be marketed for adults. Certainly the boundary between childhood and what comes after it is now more fluid than it once was. Yet, children often continue to feel powerless in their relationships with their parents and the state.

A hit they call a smack: children, parents and the state
Some 88 per cent of adults in Britain think that a parent should have the right to smack a child. The government goes along with this. Children are rarely

asked what they think about smacking, but they tend to have a rather different view from adults and government. Here is a seven-year-old girl: 'It's parents trying to hit you, but instead of calling it a hit they call it a smack.' Or a seven-year-old boy: 'And sometimes if you smack, if it was an adult like my daddy, he can smack very hard ... He can smack you like a stone ... and you'll cry.'[49] Children's lives are in many ways shaped by the interactions between their parents and the state. What has this meant for children in post-Second World War Britain?

In the second half of the twentieth century there was a move away from the idea that the best thing for some children was that they should be taken out of parental custody and placed in the care of the state or of some approved voluntary organization – and perhaps sent off to a new life in Canada or Australia. In nearly all circumstances, it came to be thought, it was in the best interests of the child to stay with its birth family. The studies of the behaviour of evacuated children and the parallel concern that 'maternal deprivation' was so harmful to children caused a major rethink. As the Home Office put it just after the Second World War: 'To keep the family together must be the first aim, and the separation of a child from its parents can only be justified when there is no possibility of securing adequate care of a child in its own home.'[50]

The Home Office in the 1940s would have had a clear idea of what constituted a family: a breadwinning father, a stay-at-home mother and the children. In the early post-war period actual families bore some resemblance to this ideal model. Of course father might have a drink problem, or mother might be negligent and careless, or the children might be delinquent. The family then became a 'problem family', and all kinds of agencies set about offering it advice and treatment. But that the family was best for children remained unquestioned. In the rhetoric of politicians, families, 'hard working families', remained the bedrock of the state, the place where children should be brought up. Parents were now frequently reminded of their responsibilities as well as of their rights, but wherever the emphasis lay, few doubted that it was they who should make decisions for their children.

There were, however, increasingly problems for those who thought that children growing up with their families were in a sense taken care of and not really something the state needed to worry about. The first of these was that so many children seemed to be living in poverty, a theme that has run through our history. The children in poverty in the late twentieth century had more material resources available to them than those living in the sixteenth century. Nevertheless they were poor relative to the rest of society. And under the Conservative governments of the 1980s and 1990s their numbers escalated. In 1979 one in ten children was living in poverty and by the late 1990s nearly one in three. In the early 1990s over four million children inhabited households with incomes that were 60 per cent or less of the median income. Britain had child-poverty rates higher than in any other country in the European Union (EU), and, among industrialized countries, rates that were exceeded only by those in the USA and Russia. The reasons for this increase in child poverty in the 1980s and 1990s included high rates of unemployment, a large rise in the number of single-parent families, in which the incidence of poverty is much greater than in two-parent families, and the raising of benefits in line with prices rather than wage levels. New Labour in 1997 set itself an ambitious target of halving child poverty by 2010. By 2006, 700,000 children had been lifted out of poverty, but this was less than was needed to meet the target of reducing child poverty by a quarter by then.[51]

The lives of many children have been scarred by their poverty. A poor child is much more likely than a well-off one to die from an accident or a respiratory disease like bronchitis or pneumonia.[52] But the impact of poverty goes beyond what is easily measurable. As one analyst, Carey Oppenheim, put it in 1996: 'Poverty means going short materially, socially and emotionally ... spending less on food, on heating and on clothing than someone on an average income. However, it is not what is spent that matters, but what isn't. Poverty means staying at home, often being bored, not seeing friends, not going to the cinema ... It impinges on relationships with others and with yourself ... It stops people being able to take control of their lives.'[53]

This analysis is confirmed by the account of two sisters, Kelly, aged ten, and Amy, 13, discussing what it was like to be poor in the late twentieth century:

> Kelly: We haven't got that much money to, to get food and go shopping ... The fridge is just bare. It's just horrible ... I'm worried about my mum, all of us are – because of all the things she's going through. She's got six kids, three bedrooms and six kids, it's just horrible ... She's on tablets right now. We look forward to go to school, because it's better at school, it's warm and it's got heaters and everything.

Amy: [T]here's these kids, I weren't listening to them, but they, it really got to me. I had these Airtech trainers … and, they went to me, 'Oh, look what you're wearing … you ain't got named trousers and all that and named trainers … you ain't got nothing' and it just made me upset.[54]

A second problem with putting so much faith in the family lay in some awkward statistics. It was in the family that a child was most at danger. The NSPCC reckons that in each generation of children over 1000 will be killed before they reach adulthood, most at the hands of violent or neglectful parents or carers. In 2001 alone, 65 children under seven were killed by parents or carers. One solution to this, and to other reasons for birth families failing to cope, is to remove children from their families and to foster them out. And it is a policy that is in many ways successful. If you ask children who now live in foster homes how they are finding the experience, most of them are pretty positive about it. They wish that they had been told more about their foster families before going to live with them, but they on the whole reckon they are better looked after than they were before; they feel safer, they do better at school, and they are becoming more independent. Asked to name the worst things about being fostered, one-third answered, 'Nothing'.[55]

But think how the experience of being fostered, or in a children's home, or in some way under the care of the state is known to most of us, and you are likely to think of one or more of these names: Dennis O'Neill, Maria Colwell, Jasmine Beckford, Victoria Climbié or indeed quite a number of others. These children had two things in common: they were all killed in post-war Britain; each of their deaths provoked outrage and rethinking of where children should stand between their families and the state.

Dennis O'Neill died aged 13 from acute cardiac failure after being beaten on the chest and back while in a state of undernourishment. He and his ten-year-old brother were boarded out in the care of Reginald and Esther Gough in Shropshire. They came to court in 1945 and were followed quickly by a parallel Scottish case: the ill-treatment by John and Margaret Walton in Fife of two children boarded out in their care, Norman and Harry Wilson, aged 12 and ten. The indictment against them alleged that

they wilfully assaulted and ill-treated them in such a manner likely to cause them unnecessary suffering and injury to their health. They were also charged with having beaten and thrashed them with a wooden spoon or spurtle or similar instrument, and with a cane and electric cable, knocked them to the ground and kicked them, pulled their lips with a pair of pliers, tied Harry Wilson to a chair and thrashed him with an electric cable and cane, placed him on the crossbar of a pulley, raised him to the ceiling and caused him to fall from the crossbar to the ground, tied him to the seat of a lavatory, placed his feet against a wringer and frightened him by placing him in a dark cupboard contrary to the Children and Young Persons (Scotland) Act 1937, Section 12.[56]

Maria Colwell was killed by her stepfather in 1973. She had been in foster care with her aunt for five years, but when she was six years and eight months, against her own wishes she was returned to her mother and stepfather. In the last nine months of her life, 30 complaints about her treatment by her mother and stepfather were made. None of them prevented her stepfather battering her to death in January 1973. Four-year-old Jasmine Beckford was starved and battered to death by her stepfather in 1984, another case where social workers had been too trusting of parents. Victoria Climbié, eight, died of hypothermia in 2000 after suffering months of abuse and neglect. There were at least 12 occasions when the agencies involved in her protection could have intervened to save her.[57]

What these cases have in common is a child caught between two opposing ideologies: the first believes that the family is the proper place for children to be brought up in, that it should be allowed to police itself and that the state should keep its prying eyes out. This view received powerful reinforcement when parents in Cleveland in the mid-1980s and in the Orkneys in the early 1990s successfully argued that the state had trampled over their parental rights when it removed children from their care on suspicion that they had been sexually abused within the home. The second ideology considers that the state has an overriding duty to care for endangered children and, in appropriate circumstances, act in the best interests of a child even when that means removing parental rights. Children have little say, their side of the story rarely heard, in these disputes. And if the state did act on their behalf, there was absolutely no guarantee that it would provide adequate protection. A succession of cases in the late twentieth century revealed systematic physical and mental abuse of children in so-called children's homes.

The difficulties for the state were made more severe from the 1960s onwards when experts began first to talk about 'the battered-child syndrome' and later about the sexual abuse of children in the home. There had been a convenient silence about sexual abuse of children after a flurry of concern in the late nineteenth and early twentieth century. For most of the twentieth century, the NSPCC and its Scottish counterpart focused their attention on negligence, and the vast majority of the cases with which they dealt were in working-class homes. But sexual abuse might be found anywhere, and how could it be monitored and exposed? The Cleveland and Orkney cases showed the difficulties.[58]

To focus on the children who died is of course to give a one-sided view of children in relation to their families and the state. There were many cases with happy outcomes. Yet it is the murdered children, their wounded bodies exposed to us, their words unheard, that stick in the public mind and determine the tenor of public discourse about childhood and the state.

Only a minority of children get caught up in violence in the home or are placed in care. What all children experience is school. And at school the state and parents formed some kind of alliance to determine what children should do. The 1944 Education Act put children in a situation where a minority would pass the 11-plus and go to a grammar school, and the majority would fail and go to a secondary modern school. This soon came under attack, and there was a move towards comprehensive schools. These were in place in most of Britain by the end of the 1970s. But if this seemed to have drawn the sting that had condemned so many 11-plus failures to a sense that education was not for them, the experience of school for children soon became caught up in another issue. The 'winter of discontent' of 1978–9 gave added force to what many political commentators were saying: that Britain, compared to its continental European rivals, was failing as a state and as an economy. Recovery seemed to lie in large part in an education system that would train its young for entrepreneurial or technical roles in a revived economy. At the same time, it was said, the young needed to be taught about the history of Britain and the lessons it held for the present. The outcome was the national curriculum, introduced in 1988, much modified since, but providing from then onwards the structure for all that goes on in school. In addition, it was felt, pressures had to be put on schools to, as it were, produce the goods. What needed to be ended was the type of experience recorded in the 1970s where a group of boys are describing school:

Joey: Of a Monday afternoon, we'd have nothing right? Nothing hardly relating to school work, Tuesday afternoon we have swimming and they stick you in a classroom for the rest of the afternoon, Wednesday afternoon you have games and there's only Thursday and Friday afternoon that you work, if you call that work. The last lesson Friday afternoon we used to go and doss, half of us wagged out o' lessons and the other half go into the classroom, sit down and just go to sleep, and the rest of us could join a class where all our mates are.

Will: ... What we been doing, playing cards in this room 'cos we can lock the door.

PW [interviewer]: What's the last time you've done some writing?

Will: When we done some writing?

Fuzz: Oh ah, last time was in careers, 'cos I writ 'yes' on a piece of paper, that broke me heart.

PW: Why did it break your heart?

Fuzz: I mean to write, 'cos I was going to try and go through the term without writing anything. 'Cos since we've cum back, I ain't dun nothing. [It was half-way through term.][59]

The solution to this kind of situation was to set up league tables, measuring school performance, all this in the name of offering parents information about the schools to which their children might go. On top of this there were nation-wide tests to measure the performance of cohorts of children at set ages. Children were subjected to an almost constant regime of testing, the preparation for the test consuming the energies of pupils and teachers. If there is a historical parallel, it perhaps lies in the way elementary schools in the nineteenth century under the payments-by-result scheme geared everything to the visit of the inspector.

From the perspective of children, what is striking about the changes in schooling in the last quarter of a century is that school is seen to serve the needs of parents, anxious about their children's futures, and of the state, worried about how it will compete in a global economy. We are accustomed to think that in the late nineteenth and early twentieth century children were rescued from wage-earning work so that they could enjoy school. That was always a bit of a myth. But now, from the perspective of the early twenty-first century, it can look as if it were made illegal for children to participate in one form of work, earning wages, and compulsory for them to engage in another form of work, this time unpaid: school. And to do so until they were 16.

It would of course be wrong to conclude from this that there are not many children who enjoy their schooling and find it a positive experience. But it is hardly in any sense an experience that they have chosen. The state and their parents call the shots. On schooling the two often seem in alliance. On other issues they can fall out badly – witness the history of the Child Support Agency. If families lived up to the ideals held out for them, the state could leave them to their own devices. But families, inevitably, don't always do this. And even if they try to, they can be undermined by forces largely outside their control, like unemployment. It is a condition of modern life that governments will intervene in family life. What is surprising about childhood in modern Britain is that, despite all the talk about children's rights, the voice of children is rarely heard in the issues that concern them most intimately. And those voices are worth listening to: '[I]nstead of calling it a hit they call it a smack.'

The present and the past

We started out in the seventh century with a child's grave. And there have been many more child graves in the centuries that followed. But in the twenty-first century, children's graves are almost a thing of the past. This decline in the chances that a child would die in the first few years of life is one of the most important changes in the history of childhood, and it places us in a privileged position. Only a century ago, the decline had hardly begun to make itself felt. It was in the twentieth century that there was progress.

By the beginning of the second half of the century it was very rare for a child to have to confront the death of a sibling or, in its school years, of a parent. Compare this with what had been a common experience for nearly all children in the whole of preceding history. Here is Mrs Peters, born in Lancaster right at the end of the nineteenth century, describing the death and funeral of her sister who had died in hospital:

> They brought her back home, and she was in the front room, the coffin was on chairs. A dreadful time. I was scared stiff. The neighbours came and the children from school as well. You didn't seem to want to deprive

them of it. I only had one look and I thought well it's not my sister. She must have been in pain, torn at her little face. They'd put cotton wool in her nostrils and granny said, 'You must go in.' Fancy making you do things like that in those days, and she said, 'Now just touch her.' I remember putting my hand on her forehead and it was stone cold. I remember shuddering. I didn't ever go in again. They collected at school and we were all dressed up in little black dresses.

Mrs Peters was recounting this event in the 1970s, conscious that such things no longer happened; not only the deaths but also the neighbours and the children from school coming in to view her dead sister.[60] Grief, like much else, became private, something for the family alone.

One of the features of recent years has been the concern to eliminate even further the deaths of, or serious injuries to, children. In many ways this has indeed been an extraordinary success. If we compare the numbers of children killed in road accidents in 1922 with those in 1986, we find that, for every 100,000 children, only half as many were killed in 1986 as in 1922, despite a vast increase in the number of cars. Death rates for all accidents for children under 15 fell from 17.5 for every 100,000 children in 1970 to 4.5 at the end of the century. No-one can fail to be impressed by these figures. But if we ask the cause of them, we may begin to count the cost of achieving this decrease. It is primarily because children's mobility outside the home has become seriously restricted. The 'home habitat' of a typical eight year old has shrunk by a factor of nine in one generation.[61]

A concern for safety, for assessing and managing risk, has become a dominant concern for many adults in their dealings with children. And children have taken on this concern. When some 700 children, mostly aged ten, were asked recently what they thought was of most importance in their upbringing, they placed highest of all, 'stay safe'.[62] It is difficult to imagine that this would have been the highest priority for any previous generation of children.

There are other things to suggest that childhood now is quite different to what it has been in the millennium and more that we have traversed. One is that children now live in a multicultural society. To an extent that has always been true. British history can be written as a history of immigration: in earlier centuries Anglo-Saxons, Danes, Normans, Jews, Italians, Huguenots and blacks (a substantial presence in eighteenth-century London). We have seen how Irish and Jewish immigration in the nineteenth and early twentieth century posed all kinds of difficulties for the children, caught as they were between cultures. And for many people in Britain, for centuries there had been cultural divides that shaped childhoods, the most obvious of them those between Protestants and Catholics or among Protestant denominations. In Scotland, Episcopalians used to be taunted with:

> Pisky, Pisky, say 'Amen',
> Doon on yer knees and up again

To which the reply was:

> Presby, Presby, canna bend,
> Sit ye doon on man's chief end.[63]

But the plurality of cultures in twenty-first-century Britain is something new. Perhaps the most striking way of appreciating that is by looking at how the many children of mixed race experience their lives. Nearly all of them, 85 per cent, say they have experienced racism.[64] This is how some of them encountered it:

> When I was about 4, at my state school, people used to take the mickey out of me, and, like, make childish, racist remarks. They didn't mean to be horrible to me, but it was hurtful all the same, and it upset me.

> Well, when I was in infant school, because my mum used to work at the junior school in the same building, people found out that she was my mum. One boy turned round and said, 'Oh, your mum is a black bitch,' and that really hurt me, and I just ended up by beating him, and I really got into trouble because they said that I started it, but after I had beaten him up I felt a lot better about it.[65]

When they were a bit older, children adopted a number of different strategies to deal with racism, deliberately ignoring it, tackling it directly, excelling in almost everything to avoid exposing themselves to it or taking pride in their parentage. A girl of eight put it this way:

I had an argument with my friend, and then the whole school weren't talking to me, she had that kind of power. And I got called pick and mix, mixed blessings, breed, and they would imitate Africans and you know say, 'Your dad comes from the jungle.' It upset me a lot ... And I thought, Oh, God, why do they have to say that to me, but then I thought about it, I thought, Well, I'm a bit of both, so in a way I'm better than you, I'm black and I'm white, and I can't ever be racist, so I thought of that and I just really took no notice of it.[66]

No generation before our own has had to concern itself with the obesity of children. In 1997, 9.6 per cent of children under ten were obese; by 2003 it had risen to 13.7 per cent, one out of every seven children. Nine out of every ten schoolchildren, it is said, are set to become 'couch potatoes'.[67] All this is new. Indeed in some ways it seems to be the reverse of what used to be. Only 100 years ago, what worried doctors was not that young children in the poorer classes were overweight, but that they were underweight and small for their age.

But if we stop for a moment and think of this obesity, it may be simply the modern symptom of an age-old problem. In previous centuries poor children didn't get enough to eat. We may remember the children in Langland's *Piers Ploughman* feeding off a loaf of beans and bran until the next harvest. Now food is more plentiful, but the cheaper it is the more likely it is to make you obese. Obesity, like underweight before it, is one of the consequences of poverty. And the poverty of children has always been with us.

Child crime is also a theme that has run through our history. What could you do with the child criminal or potential criminal when it was no longer possible to ship him or her off to the colonies? There was assumed to be a link with poverty: the deprived child all too often became the depraved child. Policy veered between two extremes: on the one hand, treat crime as a cry of distress and seek above all to rehabilitate the offender. On the other, stamp down on juvenile crime by punishing the offender. The difference can be seen in the unending debate about the age at which a young person could be said to be criminally responsible, a debate that started in Anglo-Saxon England. The 1963 Children and Young Persons Act raised the age of criminal responsibility from eight to ten. In 1969 another Act proposed to raise it yet further from ten to 14, but the Labour government that sponsored this lost power in the 1970 election, and the incoming Conservatives did not implement it. The ideology, however, at this time was clear. Court should be a last resort for a child committing an offence.

From the 1970s onwards the tide flowed the other way, with the emphasis more on the punishment of the offender than his or her rehabilitation. This came to a head with the murder of James Bulger in 1993. James was murdered by other children, two ten year olds, and they were put on trial for murder at Preston Crown Court. Just 25 years earlier, in 1968, in Newcastle, another child murderer, 11-year-old Mary Bell, had been put on trial for strangling two young boys and, like Robert Thompson and Jon Venables, was found guilty. But something had happened between 1968 and 1993 to make the response to these two murders very different. Press reporting of the Mary Bell case was restrained, its emphasis on how she could be rehabilitated: her father was a drunkard, her mother a prostitute, and few people were into blaming Mary for what she had done. Thompson and Venables, by contrast, were put on trial in the full glare of publicity. Watching it, many observers came to the view that what they were seeing was, in a word, 'evil': not the trial, but the boys. And they were not just freaks: evil was all around us. In the words of one columnist, Janet Daley in *The Times*: 'What happened to him [James Bulger] seems to me not an incomprehensible freakish accident but simply the worst possible example of amoral childish viciousness; horrible precisely to the degree that it was childlike – random, aimless and without conscience ... If we are all "guilty", it is of refusing to accept the naturalness of evil.'[68] 'The naturalness of evil': Locke, Rousseau and the romantic poets must have turned in their graves as they heard the rebirth of a doctrine that they thought had been silenced.

Five years after the Bulger trial, the 1998 Crime and Disorder Act repealed the ancient principle of *doli incapax*, that children between ten and 13 were presumed to be not capable of criminal behaviour unless the prosecution could prove otherwise. In the late twentieth and early twenty-first century children were being punished under the criminal-justice system in ways that would have seemed unimaginable in the optimism of post-war Britain: there was provision for 'Detention and Training Orders' for children aged ten and over; 12 year olds could be put into 'secure accommodation'.[69]

There are, then, sometimes surprising linkages with the past in our present position. Sometimes they stare us in the face. Walk into almost any toy-shop or children's clothes shop, and the thing that is most striking is the gendering of what is on display. The dominant pink directs us immediately to the girls' side, the more sombre colours to the boys'. The gendering of childhood has been a constant theme throughout the centuries, childhood becoming the place where we learn how to be feminine or how to be masculine. The rare moments in the past where being a child has seemed to be more important than gender tend to leave us confused. We can't easily adjust to old Victorian photographs of three-year-old boys in dresses. We forget that it was only in the 1930s that colour coding – blue for a boy, pink for a girl – became a norm. We are as hooked on the gendering of childhood as any generation in history.

We are also, at least in theory, still hooked on the main tenets of the romantic view of childhood. In day-to-day dealings with children we may ignore it, determined that our children will be well behaved and oriented towards achievement, towards the goal of adulthood. But at a deep level we have absorbed the view that children have a right to a childhood, and that means a time in life when we are protected and dependent and happy. A happy childhood is something we see as essential for a good adulthood. It's true that many recent best-sellers describe unhappy childhoods: we love reading about them and marvel at the way in which the author has overcome the huge disadvantages of an unhappy childhood or sympathize if there has been failure. But these unhappy childhoods, we know, should never have happened; they are, we hope, the exception that proves the rule.

And yet the happiness of childhood is also fragile. We think of smiling happy children whose lives have been brutally ended, of Jessica Chapman and Holly Wells, in their Manchester United strips, just before they were murdered at Soham; of the children of Dunblane, mown down by a mad gunman; or of Sarah Payne, playing with her brothers and sister in a cornfield, and abducted and killed. Perhaps no other generation of adults has been so conscious of the vulnerability of children, of their exposure to risk. Statistically, we know, the dangers of such deaths are no higher than in the past, but that is not how it is perceived. The cost of maintaining the ideal of the happy childhood is high, not so much in monetary terms as in the protective barriers with which we surround children, perhaps thereby reducing their chances of happiness.

We have encountered anxious parents in the past. We have seen them tormented by their children's illness or death, worried about the best way to bring them up, anxious about their behaviour when they leave home. But there has probably been no previous generation of parents that has been quite so constantly concerned for their children and their future as our own. Our worries are evident in the numerous TV programmes that tell others or us how to parent: *Supernanny, Bad Behaviour, House of Tiny Tearaways* and so on.

This anxiety at a family or individual level is evident also at a political level. Children, we are constantly reminded, are the future. It is in a way an axiom, and we are not the first to think in this way. The Puritans, in their different way, were fully aware that the quality of a future generation would depend on their ability to imbue their children with a sense of the need for salvation. In the eighteenth century, just like now or in the 1930s, publicists and politicians worried whether we were having enough children. In the early twentieth century, when so many feared 'the degeneration of the race' unless something was done to improve the state of the children, the future was imagined in terms of its children. Our own worries link child and nation in similar ways. Just as in the early twentieth century, children, it is said, need to know the history of their nation and need to know its political system. They need to be educated to be citizens. They need to be educated to play their part in the economic future of the nation.

It is at this stage in our story that it is tempting to ask whether it holds any lessons for the present and the future. Probably not in terms of predicting the future, for the future always turns out to be different from how we imagine it will be. But there is one striking difference between childhood now and childhood as it has been lived for most of the last millennium that may be worth reflecting on. Children in the past have been assumed to have capabilities that we now rarely think that they have. The assumption was made in the past out of necessity: children were needed to help the family survive. No-one would now want to see a child of eight selling watercress on the streets, or a child of three or four, if we can believe Defoe, meeting the costs of its upkeep through its labour. We certainly wouldn't want to put our seven year olds up a chimney to clean it. But children could do these things. So fixated are we on giving our children a long and happy childhood that we downplay their abilities and their resilience. To think of children as potential victims in need of protection is a very modern outlook, and it probably does no-one a service.

Notes

INTRODUCTION

1   Henry Mayhew, *London Labour and the London Poor*, 4 vols (London, 1864), vol. I, pp. 157–8.

2   Nicholas Tucker, *What is a Child?* (Glasgow, 1977).

3   Ivy Pinchbeck and Margaret Hewitt, *Children in English Society*, vol. II (London, 1973), p. 351.

4   Quoted in Patrick Collinson, *The Birthpangs of Protestant England: Religious and Cultural Change in the Sixteenth and Seventeenth Centuries* (Basingstoke, 1988), p. 78.

5   *Observer*, 29 May 2005 and 26 March 2006.

6   R. Waugh, *The Life of Benjamin Waugh* (London, 1913), p. 296.

7   Quoted in Claudia Nelson, *Boys will be Girls: The Feminine Ethic and British Children's Fiction, 1857–1917* (New Brunswick, NJ and London, 1991), p. 17.

8   Carolyn Steedman, *The Tidy House: Little Girls Writing* (London, 1982), pp. 69–75; A. O. J. Cockshut, 'Children's diaries', in Gillian Avery and Julia Briggs (eds), *Children and Their Books* (Oxford, 1989), pp. 382–98.

CHAPTER ONE
The Middle Ages

1   Sally Crawford, *Childhood in Anglo-Saxon England* (Stroud, 1999), pp. 94–6; G. Drinkall and M. Foreman, *The Anglo-Saxon Cemetery at Castledyke South, Barton-on-Humber* (Sheffield, 1988), pp. 73, 180.

2   Crawford, *Childhood in Anglo-Saxon England*, p. 117.

3   Florence Warren (ed.), *The Dance of Death* (London, 1931), p. 71.

4   Crawford, *Childhood in Anglo-Saxon England*, pp. 25, 30–2.

5   Drinkall and Foreman, *Anglo-Saxon Cemetery*, pp. 15–16.

6   Quoted in Mathew S. Kuefler, '"A Wryed Existence": attitudes toward children in Anglo-Saxon England', *Journal of Social History*, 24 (1990–1), p. 828.

7   Crawford, *Childhood in Anglo-Saxon England*, pp. 175–7.

8   Ibid., pp. 175–7.

9   John Sommerville, *The Rise and Fall of Childhood* (Beverly Hills, London and New Delhi, 1982), pp. 52–6; St Augustine, *Confessions*, trans. with introduction and notes by Henry Chadwick (Oxford, 1991), pp. 29–34.

10 Danièle Alexandre-Bidon and Didier Lett, *Children in the Middle Ages, Fifth to Fifteenth Centuries* (Notre Dame, IND, 1999), pp. 24–9.

11 Crawford, *Childhood in Anglo-Saxon England*, p. 175.

12 Nicholas Orme, *Medieval Children* (New Haven, CT and London, 2001), pp. 28–9; Barbara A. Hanawalt, *The Ties That Bound: Peasant Families in Medieval England* (Oxford, 1986), p. 173.

13 Mark 10: 14–15; Matt. 18: 10.

14 Alexandre-Bidon and Lett, *Children in the Middle Ages*, p. 22; Crawford, *Childhood in Anglo-Saxon England*, pp. 92–3.

15 *Magna Vita Sancti Hugonis: The Life of St Hugh of Lincoln*, 2 vols, ed. Decima L. Douie and David Hugh Farmer (Oxford, 1985), I, pp. 129–32.

16 Mary Martin McLaughlin, 'Survivors and surrogates: children and parents from the ninth to the thirteenth centuries', in Lloyd de Mause (ed.), *The History of Childhood* (London, 1976), pp. 120–1.

17 Shulamith Shahar, *Childhood in the Middle Ages* (London, 1990), p. 96.

18 *Two Sermons Preached by the Boy Bishop*, Camden Society, new series 14 (1875), pp. 15, 21.

19 B. A. Kellum, 'Infanticide in England in the late Middle Ages', *History of Childhood Quarterly*, I (1973), pp. 98–116, 367–88; R. H. Helmholz, 'Infanticide in the Province of Canterbury during the fifteenth century', *History of Childhood Quarterly*, II (1974–5), pp. 379–90.

20 Eadmer, *The Life of St Anselm, Archbishop of Canterbury*, ed. R. W. Southern (Oxford, 1972), pp. 37–8.

21 Jenny Swanson, 'Childhood and childrearing in *ad status* sermons by later thirteenth century friars', *Journal of Medieval History*, 16 (1990), pp. 309–18.

22 Luke Demaitre, 'The idea of childhood and child care in medical writings of the Middle Ages', *Journal of Psychohistory*, 4 (1977), pp. 461–90.

23 J. A. Burrow, *The Ages of Man: A Study in Medieval Writing and Thought* (Oxford, 1986).

24 H. E. Butler (ed.), *The Autobiography of Giraldus Cambrensis* (London, 1937).

25 Eadmer, *The Life of St Anselm*, pp. 38–9.

26 McLaughlin, 'Survivors and surrogates', pp. 136–7; Swanson, 'Childhood and childrearing', p. 327.

27 Orme, *Medieval Children*, pp. 52–5; Charles Phythian-Adams, *Desolation of a City: Coventry and the Urban Crisis of the Late Middle Ages* (Cambridge, 1979), pp. 224, 233–4.

28 *Two Sermons Preached by the Boy Bishop*, p. 23.

29 Ibid., p. 26.

30 William Nelson (ed.), *A Fifteenth Century School Book* (Oxford, 1956), pp. 13–14.

31 Edith Rickert (ed.), *The Babees' Book: Medieval Manners for the Young* (London, 1933), p. 41.

32 Ibid., pp. 123–6.

33 Ibid., pp. 5–6.

34 Frederick J. Furnivall (ed.), *Manners and Meals in Olden Times* (London, 1868), part 2, pp. 32–3.

35 *Guardian*, 9 November 2005.

36 Barbara A. Hanawalt, 'Childrearing among the lower classes of late medieval England', *Journal of Interdisciplinary History*, VIII (1977), pp. 14–15, 17.

37 Ibid., pp. 15–16; Hanawalt, *Ties That Bound*, pp. 180–1; Eleanora C. Gordon, 'Accidents among medieval children as seen from the miracles of six English saints and martyrs', *Medical History*, 35 (1991), pp. 150, 157, 159.

38 Gordon, 'Accidents', pp. 158, 160.

39 Hanawalt, *Ties That Bound*, p. 177; 'Childrearing', pp. 16–17.

40 Gordon, 'Accidents', pp. 158–9.

41 Hanawalt, 'Childrearing', pp. 11–21; *Ties That Bound*, p. 157.

42 Hanawalt, *Ties That Bound*, p. 183.

43 Gordon, 'Accidents', pp. 160–1.

44 *The Golden Legend of Jacobus de Voragine* (New York, 1969), p. 17.

45 Kuefler, 'A Wryed Existence', p. 827

46 Crawford, *Childhood in Anglo-Saxon England*, p. 139.

47 Kuefler, 'A Wryed Existence', p. 827

48 Butler, *Autobiography of Giraldus Cambrensis*, p. 35.

49 Beatrice White (ed.), *The Eclogues of Alexander Barclay* (London, 1928), p. 184.

50 Nicholas Orme, 'The culture of children in medieval England', *Past & Present*, No. 148 (1995), pp. 68–9.

51 Ibid., p. 52.

52 Ibid., pp. 67–8.

53 Shulamith Shahar, 'The Boy Bishop's Feast: a case-study in church attitudes towards children in the High and Late Middle Ages', in Diana Wood (ed.), *The Church and Childhood* (Oxford, 1994), pp. 243–60; Orme, *Medieval Children*, pp. 188–9; *Two Sermons Preached by the Boy Bishop*, p. xx.

54 Rickert, *Babees' Book*, pp. 123–4.

55 Barbara A. Hanawalt, *Growing Up in Medieval London: the Experience of Childhood in History* (Oxford, 1993), pp. 78–9.

56 Hanawalt, 'Childrearing', p. 21.

57 Orme, 'Culture of children', p. 62.

58 John Stow, *A Survey of London*, ed. C. L. Kingsford, 2 vols (Oxford, 1908), I, pp. 92–3.

59 Swanson, 'Childhood and childrearing', p. 327; Orme, 'Culture of children', p. 60.

60 Demaitre, 'The idea of childhood', p. 466.

61 Gordon, 'Accidents', p. 159.

62 Demaitre, 'The idea of childhood', p. 481; *Oxford Dictionary of English Proverbs*, 3rd edn (Oxford, 1970), p. 120.

63 Geoffrey Chaucer, *The Canterbury Tales*, trans. Nevill Coghill (Harmondsworth, 1951), p. 249.

64 *The Oxford Book of Children's Verse* (Oxford, 1973), p. 11.

65 Jo Ann Hoeppner Moran, *The Growth of English Schooling 1340–1548: Learning, Literacy, and Laicization in Pre-Reformation York Diocese* (Princeton, NJ, 1985), p. 180; Hanawalt, *Growing Up in Medieval London*, p. 82.

66 Crawford, *Childhood in Anglo-Saxon England*, p. 149.

67 Nicholas Orme, *English Schools in the Middle Ages* (London, 1973), pp. 11–42.

68 Chaucer, *Canterbury Tales*, pp. 185–7.

69 Orme, *English Schools*, pp. 61–2.

70 Ibid., p. 128.

71 Ibid., pp. 87–117; Moran, *Growth of English Schooling*, p. 151.

72 Moran, *Growth of English Schooling*, p. 31.

73 Ibid., p. 34.

74 Orme, *English Schools*, pp. 187–8.

75 Ibid., pp. 188–9.

76 Moran, *Growth of English Schooling*, pp. 163–7, 237–79.

77 Ibid., p. 221.

78 Furnivall, *Manners and Meals*, p. 2.

79 Orme, 'Culture of children', p. 77.

80 Nelson, *Fifteenth Century School Book*, pp. 1–2.

81 Orme, *English Schools*, p. 135.

82 Ibid., pp. 52–6.

83 Moran, *Growth of English Schooling*, pp. 175–6.

84 Orme, *Medieval Children*, pp. 281–9.

85 *Merry Jest of the Friar and the Boy* (London, 1626); Orme, *Medieval Children*, pp. 293–4.

86 Orme, *Medieval Children*, p. 288.

CHAPTER TWO

The Reformation and Its Aftermath

1 Alexandra Walsham, '"Out of the mouths of babes and sucklings": prophecy, Puritanism, and childhood in Elizabethan Suffolk', in Diana Wood (ed.), *The Church and Childhood* (Oxford, 1994), pp. 285–99.

2 Ibid.

3 Susan Hardman Moore, '"Such perfecting praise out of the mouth of a babe": Sarah Wight as child prophet', in Wood, *Church and Childhood*, pp. 313–24; Nigel Smith, 'A child prophet: Martha Hatfield as *The Wise Virgin*', in Gillian Avery and Julia Briggs (eds), *Children and Their Books* (Oxford, 1989), pp. 79–94.

4 Philippa Tudor, 'Religious instruction for children and adolescents in the early English Reformation', *Journal of Ecclesiastical History*, 35 (1984), pp. 391–413; Ian Green, '"For children in yeeres and children in understanding": the emergence of the Elizabethan catechism under Elizabeth and the early Stuarts', *Journal of Ecclesiastical History*, 37 (1986), pp. 397–425; John Philip Morgan,

Godly Learning: Puritan Attitudes Towards Reason, Learning, and Education, 1560–1640 (Cambridge, 1986), p. 153.

5 'The Catechism of Thomas Becon', in *The Works of Thomas Becon*, ed. John Ayre, 3 vols (Cambridge, 1844), vol. II, pp. 9–10.

6 Tudor, 'Religious instruction', pp. 393–4.

7 Michael Lynch, *Scotland: A New History* (London, 1991), pp. 258–9.

8 Quoted in Christopher Hill, 'The spiritualization of the household', in *Society and Puritanism in Pre-Revolutionary England* (London, 1964), p. 447.

9 Robert V. Schnucker, 'Puritan attitudes towards childhood discipline, 1560–1634', in Valerie Fildes (ed.), *Women as Mothers in Pre-Industrial England* (London, 1990), pp. 108–16.

10 Morgan, *Godly Learning*, pp. 169–70.

11 William Gouge, *Of Domestical Duties: Eight Treatises* (London, 1634).

12 Ralph A. Houlbrooke, *The English Family 1450–1700* (London, 1984), p. 149.

13 William Sloane, *Children's Books in England and America in the Seventeenth Century* (New York, 1955).

14 Quoted in Gillian Avery, 'The Puritans and their heirs', in Avery and Briggs, *Children and Their Books*, p. 97.

15 Ibid., p. 113.

16 In *Sunday Scholars' Magazine* (Oxford, 1821). Quoted in ibid., p. 113.

17 Ralph Houlbrooke, 'Death in childhood: the practice of the "good death" in James Janeway's *A Token for Children*', in Anthony Fletcher and Stephen Hussey (eds), *Childhood in Question: Children, Parents and the State* (Manchester, 1999), pp. 37–56; Avery, 'Puritans and their heirs', pp. 109–13.

18 Walsham, '"Out of the mouths of babes and sucklings"', pp. 298–9.

19 Houlbrooke, *English Family*, p. 129.

20 *The Diary of John Evelyn*, 6 vols, ed. E. S. de Beer (Oxford, 1955), III, pp. 206–10.

21 Ben Jonson, *Poems*, ed. Ian Donaldson (Oxford, 1975), pp. 26–7.

22 Alan Macfarlane (ed.), *The Diary of Ralph Josselin 1616–1683* (London, 1976), pp. 201–3.

23 Paul S. Seaver, *Wallington's World: A Puritan Artisan in Seventeenth-Century London* (London, 1985), pp. 87–8.

24 Linda Pollock, *A Lasting Relationship: Parents and Children over Three Centuries* (Hanover and London, 1987), pp. 72–3.

25 Ibid., p. 96.

26 Houlbrooke, *English Family*, pp. 135–6.

27 Pollock, *Lasting Relationship*, p. 73.

28 *The Life of Adam Martindale, Written by Himself*, Chetham Society, old series, 4 (1845), p. 154.

29 Pollock, *Lasting Relationship*, pp. 224–5.

30 Lawrence Stone, *The Family, Sex and Marriage in England 1500–1800* (London, 1977), pp. 109–11.

31 Ibid., p. 112.

32 Sara Heller Mendelson, 'Stuart women's diaries and occasional memoirs', in Mary Prior (ed.), *Women in English Society 1500–1800* (London, 1985), p. 196.

33 Christopher Brown and Hans Vlieghe, *Van Dyck 1599–1641* (London, 1999), pp. 83, 295–7.

34 Rosemary O'Day, *Education and Society 1500–1800: The Social Foundations of Education in Early Modern Britain* (London, 1982), p. 6.

35 Ibid., p. 7.

36 *The Autobiography of Henry Newcome*, 2 vols, ed. R. Parkinson, Chetham Society (1852).

37 Pollock, *Lasting Relationship*, pp. 264–5.

38 *The Autobiography of William Stout of Lancaster, 1665–1752*, ed. J. D. Marshall, Chetham Society (1967), pp. 68–73.

39 Margaret Spufford, 'First steps in literacy: the reading and writing experiences of the humblest seventeenth-century spiritual autobiographers', *Social History*, 4 (1979), p. 410.

40 Ibid., pp. 415–17.

41 *The Diary of Samuel Pepys*, ed. R. C. Latham and W. Matthews, 11 vols (London, 1995), VIII, p. 338.

42 Spufford, 'First steps', pp. 415–17.

43   Ibid., p. 418.

44   Ibid., p. 420; Ilana Krausman Ben-Amos, *Adolescence and Youth in Early Modern England* (New Haven, CT and London, 1994), pp. 51, 57–8.

45   Spufford, 'First steps', p. 425.

46   Ben-Amos, *Adolescence and Youth*, pp. 55–6.

47   Jocelyn Dunlop and R. D. Denman, *English Apprenticeship and Child Labour: A History* (London, 1912), pp. 27–71.

48   Ben-Amos, *Adolescence and Youth*, pp. 84–108.

49   Ibid., pp. 63–4.

50   Keith Thomas, *Rule and Misrule in the Schools of Early Modern England* (Reading, 1976), pp. 21–2.

51   Ibid., pp. 22–6.

52   Ibid., pp. 8–16.

53   Ibid., p. 7.

54   Morgan, *Godly Learning*, pp. 185–6.

55   O'Day, *Education and Society*, p. 37.

56   Thomas, *Rule and Misrule*, p. 14.

57   Pollock, *Lasting Relationship*, pp. 224–5.

58   Ibid., pp. 249–50.

59   David Cressy, *Education in Tudor and Stuart England* (London, 1975), p. 109.

60   Ivy Pinchbeck and Margaret Hewitt, *Children in English Society*, vol. 1 (London, 1969), p. 31.

61   Ibid., p. 33.

62   Ibid., pp. 28–30.

63   Ibid., pp. 11–12.

64   *Oxford Dictionary of English Proverbs*, 3rd edn (Oxford, 1970), p. 120.

65   Cressy, *Education*, p. 111.

66   Anthony Fletcher, *Gender, Sex and Subordination in England 1500–1800* (New Haven, CT and London, 1995), p. 368.

67   Pollock, *Lasting Relationship*, p. 153.

68   Ibid., p. 226.

69   Ibid., p. 222.

70   Fletcher, *Gender, Sex and Subordination*, p. 366; John Lawson and Harold Silver, *A Social History of Education in England* (London, 1973), pp. 121–2; O'Day, *Education and Society*, p. 187.

71   Pollock, *Lasting Relationship*, p. 223.

72   Lawson and Silver, *Social History of Education*, p. 122.

73   Ben-Amos, *Adolescence and Youth*, pp. 133–55.

74   Elizabeth Melling, *Kentish Sources, Vol. 4, The Poor* (Maidstone, 1964), pp. 30–2.

75   Ibid.

76   Nicholas Orme, *Medieval Children* (New Haven, CT and London, 2001), pp. 88–9.

77   Pinchbeck and Hewitt, *Children in English Society*, I, pp. 96–7.

78   Paul Slack, *Poverty and Policy in Tudor and Stuart England* (London, 1988), pp. 83, 97.

79   Pinchbeck and Hewitt, *Children in English Society*, I, pp. 95–6.

80   Paul Slack (ed.), *Poverty in Early Stuart Salisbury*, Wiltshire Record Society, vol. XXX (1975), p. 89.

81   W. K. Jordan, *Philanthropy in England 1480–1660* (London, 1959), p. 174; Margaret Pelling, 'Child health as a social value in early modern England', *Social History of Medicine*, I (1988), pp. 142–3.

82   Pinchbeck and Hewitt, *Children in English Society*, I, pp. 131–3.

83   *Diary of Samuel Pepys*, V, p. 289.

84   Pelling, 'Child health', pp. 135–64.

85   Slack, *Poverty and Policy*, pp. 65–6, 71.

86   Richard M. Smith (ed.), *Land, Kinship and Life-Cycle* (Cambridge, 1984), p. 71.

87   John Cary, *An Account of the Proceedings of the Corporation of Bristol in Execution of the Act of Parliament for the Better Employing and Maintaining the Poor of that City* (London, 1700), pp. 13, 19–20.

88   Pinchbeck and Hewitt, *Children in English Society*, I, pp. 105–7.

89   Slack, *Poverty and Policy*, pp. 172–3, 179.

90   Melling, *Kentish Sources: The Poor*, pp. 71–2, 112–13.

Chapter Three
The Eighteenth Century

1   Ruth K. McClure, *Coram's Children: The London Foundling Hospital in the Eighteenth Century* (New Haven, CT and London, 1981), pp. 229, 237–8.

2   Ibid., p. 14.

3 *The Foundling Museum* (London, 2004), pp. 14–15.

4 McClure, *Coram's Children*, pp. 123, 126.

5 Ibid., pp. 47–8.

6 Ibid., p. 134.

7 Ibid., pp. 78, 124; A. Levene, 'The origins of the children of the London Foundling Hospital, 1741–1760: a reconsideration', *Continuity and Change*, 18 (2003), pp. 201–36.

8 McClure, *Coram's Children*, p. 102.

9 Hugh Cunningham, *The Children of the Poor: Representations of Childhood since the Seventeenth Century* (Oxford, 1991), pp. 23, 33–4; M. G. Jones, *The Charity School Movement* (Cambridge, 1938), p. 72; M. Dorothy George, *London Life in the Eighteenth Century* (Harmondsworth, 1966), p. 219.

10 Cunningham, *Children of the Poor*, pp. 38–44.

11 William Blake, *A Selection of Poems and Letters*, edited with an introduction by J. Bronowski (Harmondsworth, 1958/ repr. 1972), pp. 34, 43.

12 Report from the Committee Appointed to Review and Consider the Several Laws which Concern the Relief and Settlement of the Poor, repr. in *House of Commons Sessional Papers of the Eighteenth Century* (Wilmington, DE, 1975), vol. XXXI, pp. 4, 7.

13 Cunningham, *Children of the Poor*, p. 32.

14 'Report from the Select Committee on the Poor Laws', Parliamentary Papers, 1817 (462), VI, pp. 14–16.

15 Jenny Uglow, *The Lunar Men: The Friends who made the Future 1730–1810* (London, 2002), pp. 182–8; Geoffrey Summerfield, *Fantasy and Reason: Children's Literature in the Eighteenth Century* (London, 1984), pp. 148–53.

16 James L. Axtell (ed.), *The Educational Writings of John Locke* (Cambridge, 1968), pp. 98–104.

17 Hugh Cunningham, *Children and Childhood in Western Society since 1500*, 2nd edn (Harlow, 2005), pp. 43–4.

18 *Educational Writings*, p. 143.

19 Ibid., pp. 143, 145, 148–51, 159.

20 Ibid., p. 141.

21 Ibid., pp. 255–60.

22 Ibid., 55–6, 114, 116.

23 Samuel Richardson, *Pamela*, 4 vols (Oxford, 1929), IV, pp. 297–371.

24 Jean-Jacques Rousseau, *Émile*, ed. P. D. Jimack (London, 1974), p. 1.

25 Ibid., pp. 1, 54, 58.

26 Ibid., pp. 5, 80.

27 Ibid., pp. 43–4.

28 Ibid., p. 322.

29 Stella Tillyard, *Aristocrats: Caroline, Emily, Louisa and Sarah Lennox 1740–1832* (London, 1995), p. 239.

30 Linda Pollock, *A Lasting Relationship: Parents and Children over Three Centuries* (Hanover and London, 1987), pp. 218–19.

31 Lawrence Stone, *The Family, Sex and Marriage in England 1500–1800* (London, 1977), pp. 436–7.

32 Pollock, *Lasting Relationship*, p. 149.

33 Ibid., pp. 78–9, 105, 140.

34 Ibid., p. 144.

35 K. C. Phillipps, *Language and Class in Victorian England* (Oxford, 1984), pp. 160–2; *Oxford English Dictionary*.

36 Pollock, *Lasting Relationship*, p. 155.

37 Randolph Trumbach, *The Rise of the Egalitarian Family: Aristocratic Kinship and Domestic Relations in Eighteenth-Century England* (New York, San Francisco, CA and London, 1978), p. 187.

38 Pollock, *Lasting Relationship*, p. 58.

39 Trumbach, *Rise of the Egalitarian Family*, pp. 198, 223.

40 Ibid., p. 226; Stone, *Family, Sex and Marriage*, pp. 424–5.

41 *Educational Writings*, pp. 123–4.

42 Stone, *Family, Sex and Marriage*, p. 410; Pollock, *Lasting Relationship*, pp. 55, 83.

43 Jenny Uglow, *Hogarth: A Life and a World* (London, 1997), pp. 353–4; J. C. Steward, *The New Child: British Art and the Origins of Modern Childhood 1730–1830* (Berkeley, CA, 1995), p. 86.

44 Pollock, *Lasting Relationship*, p. 186.

45 *The Autobiography of Francis Place (1771–1854)*, ed. Mary Thale (Cambridge, 1972), pp. 47–8.

46 Ibid., pp. 52–3.

47 Samuel Bamford, *Autobiography*, 2 vols, ed. W. H. Chaloner (London, 1967), vol. I, pp. 40, 90.

48 Ibid., pp. 94–5.

49 *A Memoir of Thomas Bewick Written by Himself*, ed. Iain Bain (Oxford, 1979), p. 11.

50 *Autobiography of Francis Place*, p. 55.

51 Nicholas Orme, *Medieval Children* (New Haven, CT and London, 2001), pp. 167–76.

52 *Educational Writings*, pp. 237–9.

53 J. H. Plumb, 'The new world of children in eighteenth-century England', *Past & Present*, 67 (1975), p. 88.

54 Ibid., pp. 88–90.

55 Ibid., p. 91.

56 *The Life and Struggles of William Lovett* (London, 1967), p. 3.

57 Summerfield, *Fantasy and Reason*, pp. 79–80.

58 Ibid., pp. 76–7.

59 Percy Muir, *English Children's Books 1600–1900* (London, 1954), p. 65.

60 Summerfield, *Fantasy and Reason*, p. 84.

61 Ibid., p. 36.

62 Plumb, 'New world of children', pp. 85–6; Peter Borsay, 'Children, adolescents, and fashionable urban society in eighteenth-century England', in Anja Müller (ed.), *Fashioning Childhood in the Eighteenth Century* (Aldershot, 2006), pp. 53–62.

63 *Autobiography of Francis Place*, pp. 45, 51.

64 *18th Century Children at Home* (London, 1965), p. 12.

65 Blake, *A Selection of Poems and Letters*, pp. 37–8.

66 William Wilberforce, *A Practical View of the Prevailing Religious System of Professed Christians in the Higher and Middle Classes in this Country, Contrasted with Real Christianity*, 3rd edn (Glasgow, 1829), p. 109.

67 Paul Sangster, *Pity my Simplicity: The Evangelical Revival and the Religious Education of Children 1738–1800* (London, 1963), p. 31.

68 R. Lonsdale (ed.), *Eighteenth-Century Women Poets* (Oxford, 1989), pp. 505–6.

69 Cunningham, *Children of the Poor*, pp. 36–7.

70 T. W. Laqueur, *Religion and Respectability: Sunday Schools and Working Class Culture 1780–1850* (New Haven, CT and London, 1976); A. P. Wadsworth, 'The first Manchester Sunday Schools', in M. W. Flinn and T. C. Smout (eds), *Essays in Social History* (Oxford, 1974), pp. 107–8.

71 Blake, *A Selection of Poems and Letters*, p. 27.

72 Peter Coveney, *The Image of Childhood* (Harmondsworth, 1967), p. 68.

73 'Intimations of Immortality from Recollections of Early Childhood', in *The Oxford Book of English Verse*, ed. Arthur Quiller-Couch (Oxford, 1912), pp. 609–16.

74 B. Garlitz, 'The Immortality Ode: its cultural progeny', *Studies in English Literature*, 6 (1966), pp. 639–49.

75 Dror Wahrman, *The Making of the Modern Self: Identity and Culture in Eighteenth-Century England* (New Haven, CT and London, 2004), pp. 287–90.

76 'Intimations of Immortality', p. 612.

77 Summerfield, *Fantasy and Reason*, pp. 101–4.

78 *The Letters of Charles and Mary Anne Lamb*, ed. Edwin W. Marrs Jr, II (Ithaca, NY and London, 1976), p. 82.

79 Summerfield, *Fantasy and Reason*, pp. 49–58, quoting p. 55.

80 Bamford, *Autobiography*, I, p. 41.

CHAPTER FOUR
The Victorians

1 M. V. Hughes, *A London Child of the 1870s* (Oxford, 1977), pp. 33, 16.

2 Clare Rose, *Children's Clothes since 1750* (London, 1989), pp. 95–6; P. N. Stearns, 'Girls, boys, and emotions: redefinitions and historical change', *Journal of American History*, 80 (1993), pp. 36–74.

3 Stana Nenadic, 'Middle-rank consumers and domestic culture in Edinburgh and Glasgow 1720–1840', *Past & Present*, 145 (1994), pp. 122–56.

4   Linda Pollock, *A Lasting Relationship: Parents and Children over Three Centuries* (Hanover and London, 1987), p. 180.

5   Ibid., p. 181; John Tosh, *A Man's Place: Masculinity and the Middle-Class Home in Victorian England* (New Haven, CT and London, 1999), pp. 79–101, 147.

6   Tosh, *Man's Place*, pp. 82–3, 147–9; John R. Gillis, *A World of Their Own Making: A History of Myth and Ritual in Family Life* (Oxford, 1997), pp. 101–3.

7   Quoted in Malcolm Andrews, 'Childhood', in Paul Schlicke (ed.), *Oxford Reader's Companion to Dickens* (Oxford, 1999), p. 90.

8   John Lawson and Harold Silver, *A Social History of Education in Britain* (London, 1972), p. 301.

9   An Old Boy [Thomas Hughes], *Tom Brown's School-Days* (London, n.d.), p. 218 ('Fever in the school').

10 Pollock, *Lasting Relationship*, p. 200.

11 J. R. de S. Honey, *Tom Brown's Universe: The Development of the Victorian Public School* (London, 1977), pp. 139–40, 153.

12 Henry Newbolt, 'Clifton Chapel' in *Collected Poems 1897–1907* (London, 1910?), pp. 128–30.

13 Tosh, *Man's Place*, pp. 170–94.

14 Pollock, *Lasting Relationship*, p. 241.

15 Carol Dyhouse, *Girls Growing Up in Late Victorian and Edwardian England* (London, 1981), pp. 41–3.

16 Ibid., pp. 44–54.

17 Ibid., pp. 67–8.

18 Charles Dickens, *Oliver Twist* (Harmondsworth, 1985), pp. 56–8.

19 J. M. Goldstrom, *The Social Content of Education 1808–1870: A Study of the Working Class School Reader in England and Ireland* (Shannon, 1972), p. 170.

20 Hugh Cunningham, *The Children of the Poor: Representations of Childhood since the Seventeenth Century* (Oxford, 1991), pp. 169.

21 Charles Dickens, *The Old Curiosity Shop* (Harmondsworth, 1972), p. 308.

22 Andrews, 'Childhood', p. 88; Malcolm Andrews, *Dickens and the Grown-Up Child* (Basingstoke, 1994), pp. 36–7; Emily Shore

quoted in A. O. J. Cockshut, 'Children's diaries', in Gillian Avery and Julia Briggs (eds), *Children and Their Books* (Oxford, 1989), p. 390.

23 Humphrey Carpenter, *Secret Gardens: A Study of the Golden Age of Children's Literature* (London, 1987).

24 Catherine Robson, *Men in Wonderland: The Lost Girlhood of the Victorian Gentleman* (Princeton, NJ, 2001), pp. 129–53.

25 John Ruskin, *The Stones of Venice* (1851–3), in *The Library Edition of the Works of John Ruskin*, 39 vols (London, 1903–12), X, pp. 228–9.

26 Cunningham, *Children of the Poor*, pp. 152–3, 159.

27 John Ruskin, *Time and Tide* (1867), in *Library Edition of Works of Ruskin*, XVII, p. 406.

28 Mrs H. M. Stanley (Dorothy Tennant), *London Street Arabs* (London, 1890), p. 7.

29 Charles Kingsley, *The Water Babies* (London, n.d.), pp. 25–6.

30 'The First of May' in *Sketches by Boz* (London, 1836)

31 Cunningham, *Children of the Poor*, pp. 51–64.

32 K. H. Strange, *Climbing Boys: A Study of Sweeps' Apprentices 1773–1875* (London, 1982), pp. 30–2.

33 *A Memoir of Robert Blincoe, an Orphan Boy; Sent from the Workhouse of St. Pancras, London, at Seven Years of Age, to Endure the Horrors of a Cotton-Mill* (Firle, Sussex, 1977), p. 35.

34 Quoted in Cunningham, *Children of the Poor*, p. 71.

35 House of Commons Select Committee on the Bill to Regulate the Labour of Children in the Mills and Factories of the United Kingdom, Parliamentary Papers, 1831–2, vol. XV, p. 161.

36 Alfred [Samuel H. G. Kydd], *The History of the Factory Movement*, 2 vols in one (New York, 1966), I, pp. 235–57.

37 Children's Employment Commission, Parliamentary Papers, 1842, vol. XVI, pp. 252–3.

38 Sylvia Lynd, *English Children* (London, 1942), p. 40.

39 'The Cry of the Children', *Selected Poems of Elizabeth Barrett Browning*, ed. M. Forster (London, 1988), p. 179.

40 Quoted in Cunningham, *Children of the Poor*, p. 51.

41 Henry Mayhew, *London Labour and the London Poor*, 4 vols (London, 1864), vol. I, pp. 157–8.

42 E. A. Wrigley and R. S. Schofield, *The Population History of England, 1541–1871* (London, 1981), pp. 443–50.

43 Joy Parr, *Labouring Children: British Immigrant Apprentices to Canada, 1869–1924* (London, 1980), p. 28.

44 Heather Shore, *Artful Dodgers: Youth and Crime in Early Nineteenth-Century London* (Woodbridge, 1999), p. 138.

45 Cunningham, *Children of the Poor*, pp. 103–4.

46 'The Ragged Schools', *Quarterly Review*, 79 (1846), pp. 127–41.

47 Cunningham, *Children of the Poor*, pp. 106–7.

48 *The Christian*, 22 Aug. 1872 and 29 Aug. 1872, quoted in Gillian Wagner, *Barnardo* (London, 1980), pp. 30–2.

49 Ibid., pp. 32–4.

50 John Stroud, *Thirteen Penny Stamps: The Story of the Church of England's Children's Society (Waifs and Strays) from 1881 to the 1970s* (London, 1971).

51 *The Life of Adam Martindale, Written by Himself*, Chetham Society, old series, 4 (1845), p. 154; Louise A. Jackson, *Child Sexual Abuse in Victorian England* (London, 2000), esp. pp. 20–1, 38; Linda A. Pollock, *Forgotten Children: Parent–Child Relations from 1500 to 1900* (Cambridge, 1983), pp. 91–5.

52 G. K. Behlmer, *Child Abuse and Moral Reform in England, 1870–1908* (Stanford, 1982); Brian Ashley, *A Stone on the Mantlepiece: A Centenary Social History of the RSSPCC* (Edinburgh, 1985); Harry Ferguson, 'Cleveland in history: the abused child and child protection, 1880–1914', in

Roger Cooter (ed.), *In the Name of the Child: Child Health and Welfare, 1880–1940* (London, 1992), pp. 146–73.

53 Shore, *Artful Dodgers*, pp. 57, 71, 136–7.

54 Parr, *Labouring Children, passim*, esp. pp. 83, 107.

55 Lydia D. Murdoch, 'From barrack schools to family cottages: creating domestic space for late Victorian poor children', in Jon Lawrence and Pat Starkey (eds), *Child Welfare and Social Action in the Nineteenth and Twentieth Centuries: International Perspectives* (Liverpool, 2001), pp. 147–73.

56 Lynn Abrams, *The Orphan Country: Children of Scotland's Broken Homes From 1848 to the Present* (Edinburgh, 1998).

57 Parr, *Labouring Children*, pp. 67–70; Wagner, *Barnardo*, pp. 214–36.

58 June Rose, *For the Sake of the Children: Inside Dr Barnardo's: 120 Years of Caring for Children* (London, 1987), p. 68.

59 Charles Lamb, *The Essays of Elia*, ed. A. Ainger (London, 1921), pp. 151–2.

60 Thomas Guthrie, *Seed-Time and Harvest of Ragged Schools* (Edinburgh, 1860), p. 8; Cunningham, *Children of the Poor*, pp. 114–19, 154–7, 161.

61 Hugh Cunningham, 'How many children were "unemployed" in eighteenth- and nineteenth-century England?', *Past & Present*, 187 (2005), p. 213.

62 Charles Shaw, *When I was a Child* (1903; Firle, Sussex, 1977), pp. 1–10.

63 M. K. Ashby, *Joseph Ashby of Tysoe 1859–1919: A Study of English Village Life* (London, 1974), pp. 18–19.

64 Phil Gardner, *The Lost Elementary Schools of Victorian England* (London, 1984).

65 Anna Davin, *Growing Up Poor: Home, School and Street in London 1870–1914* (London, 1996), pp. 101–3.

66 J. S. Hurt, *Elementary Schooling and the Working Classes 1860-1918* (London, 1979), pp. 203–4.

67 Flora Thompson, *Larkrise to Candleford* (London, n.d.), pp. 195, 207.

68 Thea Thompson (ed.), *Edwardian Childhoods* (London, 1981), p. 95.

69 Ibid., p. 56.

70 John Burnett (ed.), *Destiny Obscure: Autobiographies of Childhood, Education and Family from the 1820s to the 1920s* (London, 1982), p. 305.

71 Stephen Humphries, *Hooligans or Rebels? An Oral History of Working-Class Childhood and Youth 1889–1939* (Oxford, 1981), pp. 90–120.

72 Jonathan Rose, *The Intellectual Life of the British Working Classes* (New Haven, CT and London, 2002), pp. 146–86.

73 Robert Roberts, *A Ragged Schooling: Growing Up in the Classic Slum* (Manchester, 1976) pp. 171–2.

CHAPTER FIVE

The Children of the Nation, 1900—1950

1 Evelyn Sharp, *The London Child* (London, 1927), p. 37; *Conflict and Change in Education: A Sociological Introduction; Block Four Progressive Education: Unit 17 Progressive Ideals* (booklet prepared by Kevin Brehony for an Open University course) (Milton Keynes, 1984), p. 28; Brenda Spender, in J. H. Dowd, *Important People* (1930; London, 1948), p. 14; Sylvia Lynd, *English Children* (London, 1942), p. 8.

2 Stephen Humphries, *Hooligans or Rebels? An Oral History of Working-Class Childhood and Youth 1889–1939* (Oxford, 1981), p. 43.

3 Stephen Heathorn, *For Home, Country, and Race: Constructing Gender, Class, and Englishness in the Elementary Schools of Victorian England, 1880–1914* (Buffalo, NY and London, 2000); Valerie E. Chancellor, *History for their Masters: Opinion in the English History Textbook 1800–1914* (London, 1970).

4 Robert Roberts, *The Classic Slum: Salford Life in the First Quarter of the Century* (1971; Harmondsworth, 1973), pp. 142–3.

5 Humphries, *Hooligans or Rebels?*, p. 38.

6 Henry Charles Moore, *Britons at Bay: The Adventures of Two Midshipmen in the Second Burmese War* (London, 1900), pp. 1–2, 8–9, 29.

7 John Mackenzie, *Propaganda and Empire: The Manipulation of British Public Opinion, 1880–1960* (London, 1984).

8 Geoffrey Sherington, 'Fairbridge Child Migrants'; Patrick A. Dunae, 'Gender, generations and social class: the Fairbridge Society and British child migration to Canada, 1930–1960'; Shurlee Swain, 'Child rescue: the emigration of an idea'; Kathleen Paul, 'Changing childhoods: child emigration since 1945', all in Jon Lawrence and Pat Starkey (eds), *Child Welfare and Social Action in the Nineteenth and Twentieth Centuries: International Perspectives* (Liverpool, 2001), pp. 53–143.

9 Philip Bean and Joy Melville, *Lost Children of the Empire* (London, 1989), quoting p. 138.

10 Anna Davin, *Growing Up Poor: Home, School and Street in London 1870–1914* (London, 1996), pp. 205–6.

11 Ibid., pp. 205–6.

12 Ibid., p. 202.

13 Ibid., p. 215.

14 William Booth, *In Darkest England and the Way Out* (London, 1890), pp. 62–3.

15 Quoted in Gareth Stedman Jones, *Outcast London* (Harmondsworth, 1976), pp. 127–30.

16 Carolyn Steedman, *Childhood, Culture and Class in Britain: Margaret McMillan 1860–1931* (London, 1990), esp. pp. 62–120.

17 Edith Nesbit, *Five Children and It* (1902; Harmondsworth, 1959), p. 20.

18 Canon and Mrs S. A. Barnett, *Towards Social Reform* (London, 1909), p. 310.

19 B. Seebohm Rowntree, *Poverty*, 4th edn (London, 1902), p. 49.

20 Ibid., p. 128.

21 Hugh Cunningham, *Children and Childhood in Western Society since 1500*, 2nd edn (Harlow, 2005), p. 175; A. L. Bowley and A. R. Burnett-Hurst, *Livelihood and Poverty* (1915; New York and London, 1980), pp. 43–5; David Vincent, *Poor Citizens: The State and the Poor in Twentieth-Century Britain* (Harlow, 1991), p. 74.

22 John Macnicol, *The Movement for Family Allowances, 1918–45: A Study in Social Policy Development* (London, 1980).

23 Women's Group on Public Welfare, *Our Towns* (Oxford, 1943), pp. 104–5.

24 Davin, *Growing Up Poor*, pp. 117–18.

25 Denise Riley, *War in the Nursery: Theories of the Child and Mother* (London, 1983).

26 Mark Jackson, '"Grown-up children": understandings of health and mental deficiency in Edwardian England', in Marijke Gijswijt-Hofstra and Hilary Marland (eds), *Cultures of Child Health in Britain and the Netherlands in the Twentieth Century* (Amsterdam, 2003), pp. 149–168.

27 Gloria Wood and Paul Thompson, *The Nineties: Personal Recollections of the Twentieth Century* (London, 1993), p. 39.

28 Iona and Peter Opie, *The Lore and Language of Schoolchildren* (1959; London, 1977), p. 182.

29 Robert Woods and Nicola Shelton, *An Atlas of Victorian Mortality* (Liverpool, 1997), pp. 65–92; Anne Hardy, 'Rickets and the rest: child-care, diet and the infectious children's diseases, 1850–1914', *Social History of Medicine*, 5 (1992), pp. 389–412.

30 Davin, *Growing Up Poor*, p. 139.

31 Cunningham, *Children and Childhood*, pp. 173–5.

32 Deborah Dwork, *War is Good for Babies and Other Young Children: A History of the Infant and Child Welfare Movement in England 1898–1918* (London, 1987), p. 211.

33 Hugh Cunningham, *The Children of the Poor: Representations of Childhood since the Seventeenth Century* (Oxford, 1991), pp. 222–4.

34 John Macnicol, 'The evacuation of schoolchildren', in Harold L. Smith (ed.), *War and Social Change: British Society in the Second World War* (Manchester, 1986), pp. 3–31; Travis L. Crosby, *The Impact of Civilian Evacuation in the Second World War* (London, 1986).

35 Steve Humphries and Pamela Gordon, *A Labour of Love: The Experience of Parenthood in Britain 1900–1950* (London, 1993), pp. 227–8.

36 Humphries, *Hooligans or Rebels?*, p. 211; Lynn Abrams, *The Orphan Country: Children of Scotland's Broken Homes from 1845 to the Present* (Edinburgh, 1998), pp. 3, 31, 79.

37 June Rose, *For the Sake of the Children: Inside Dr Barnardo's: 120 Years of Caring for Children* (London, 1987), pp. 174–6.

38 Jeremy Seabrook, *Working-Class Childhood: An Oral History* (London, 1982), pp. 106–8.

39 Humphries, *Hooligans or Rebels?*, pp. 221–2.

40 Abrams, *Orphan Country*, p. 60.

41 Ibid., pp. 50–1.

42 Steve Humphries and Pamela Gordon, *Forbidden Britain: Our Secret Past 1900–1960* (London, 1994).

43 Harry Hendrick, *Child Welfare: Historical Dimensions, Contemporary Debate* (Bristol, 2003), pp. 133–40.

44 Humphries, *Hooligans or Rebels?*, p. 60.

45 Lynd, *English Children*, p. 8.

46 Anna Freud and Dorothy T. Burlingham, *War and Children* (1943; Westport, CT, 1973), pp. 181–3.

47 Dwork, *War is Good for Babies*, pp. 135–8, 211.

48 Quoted in Cunningham, *Children of the Poor*, p. 220.

49 John and Elizabeth Newson, 'Cultural aspects of childrearing in the English-speaking world', in M. Richards (ed.), *The Integration of a Child into a Social World* (Cambridge, 1974), p. 61.

50 Humphries and Gordon, *Labour of Love*, pp. 51–2.

51 Newsons, 'Cultural aspects', pp. 60–1.

52 Humphries and Gordon, *Labour of Love*, pp. 61–2.

53 Ibid., p. 73.

54 Ibid., pp. 68–70.

55 Newsons, 'Cultural aspects', pp. 62–3.

56 Humphries and Gordon, *Labour of Love*, pp. 74–5.

57 Stephen Kern, 'Freud and the birth of child psychiatry', *Journal of the History of the Behavioral Sciences*, IX (1973), pp. 360–8.

58 Deborah Thom, 'Wishes, anxieties, play and gestures: child guidance in inter-war

England', in Roger Cooter (ed.), *In the Name of the Child: Health and Welfare, 1880–1940* (London, 1992), pp. 200–19.

59 'A Lover of my Country', an article by an anonymous contributor to *Outlook*, 19 Sept. 1908, quoted in Deborah Thom, 'The healthy citizen of empire or juvenile delinquent? Beating and mental health in the UK', in Gijswijt-Hofstra and Marland (eds), *Cultures of Child Health*, pp. 191.

60 Ibid., pp. 190–204.

61 *Daily Herald*, 3 Sept. 1938.

62 Cathy Urwin and Elaine Sharland, 'From bodies to minds in childcare literature: advice to parents in inter-war Britain', in Cooter (ed.), *In the Name of the Child*, pp. 174–99.

63 Harry Hendrick, 'Children's emotional well-being and mental health in early post-Second World War Britain: the case of unrestricted hospital visiting', in Gijswijt-Hofstra and Marland (eds), *Cultures of Child Health*, pp. 213–42.

64 Opies, *Lore and Language*, p. 130.

65 Michael Anderson, 'The social implications of demographic change', in F. M. L. Thompson (ed.), *The Cambridge Social History of Britain 1750–1950*, 3 vols (Cambridge, 1990), vol. 2, pp. 40–1.

66 Wally Seccombe, *Weathering the Storm: Working-Class Families from the Industrial Revolution to the Fertility Decline* (London, 1993).

67 Asa Briggs, *The History of Broadcasting in the United Kingdom*, 5 vols (London, 1961–95), vol. I, p. 260; M. Pegg, *Broadcasting and Society, 1918–1939* (London, 1983), p. 116.

68 Sharp, *The London Child*, p. 87.

69 Richard Hoggart, *The Uses of Literacy* (1957; Harmondsworth, 1958), pp. 48–9.

70 Lynn Jamieson, 'Limited resources and limiting conventions: working-class mothers and daughters in urban Scotland, c. 1890–1925', in Jane Lewis (ed.), *Labour and Love: Women's Experience of Home and Family, 1850–1940* (Oxford, 1986), p. 60.

71 John R. Gillis, *For Better, For Worse: British Marriages, 1600 to the Present* (Oxford, 1985), p. 272.

72 Arnold Freeman, *Boy Life and Labour: The Manufacture of Inefficiency* (London, 1914), pp. 113–16.

73 Ibid., p. 135.

74 Jeffrey Richards, *The Age of the Dream Palace: Cinema and Society in Britain 1930–1939* (London, 1984), pp. 67–85.

75 G. Stanley Hall, *Adolescence*, 2 vols (1904; New York, 1921), vol. I, p. xiv.

76 John Springhall, *Youth, Empire and Society: British Youth Movements, 1883–1940* (London, 1977).

77 Robert Roberts, *A Ragged Schooling: Growing Up in the Classic Slum* (Manchester, 1976), pp. 94–5.

78 Opies, *Lore and Language*, p. 373.

CHAPTER SIX
Post-war Childhood

1 Elizabeth Roberts, *Women and Families: An Oral History, 1940–1970* (Oxford, 1995), p. 257; Lawrence Stone, *Road to Divorce: England 1530–1987* (Oxford, 1990), p. 412.

2 Stone, *Road to Divorce*, pp. 401–22, 435–6; Muriel Nissel, 'Families and social change since the Second World War', in R. N. Rapoport, M. P. Fogarty and R. Rapoport (eds), *Families in Britain* (London, 1982), pp. 95–119.

3 David Buckingham, *After the Death of Childhood* (Cambridge, 2000), pp. 63–9; *Social Trends* No. 36 (2006), pp. 22–8.

4 Michael Young and Peter Willmott, *Family and Kinship in East London* (1957; Harmondsworth, 1962), p. 28.

5 David Fowler, *The First Teenagers: The Lifestyle of Young Wage-Earners in Interwar Britain* (London, 1995); Bill Osgerby, *Youth in Britain since 1945* (Oxford, 1998), esp. pp. 30–49.

6 Viviana A. Zelizer, *Pricing the Priceless Child: The Changing Social Value of Children* (New York, 1985).

7 Women's Group on Public Welfare, *Our Towns* (Oxford, 1943), p. 22.

8   John and Elizabeth Newson, *Seven Years Old in the Home Environment* (London, 1976), pp. 237, 243.

9   Diana Leonard, *Sex and Generation: A Study of Courtship and Weddings* (London, 1980), p. 52.

10 Newsons, *Seven Years Old*, pp. 230, 233.

11 Ibid., p. 246.

12 Leonard, *Sex and Generation*, pp. 58–9.

13 John and Elizabeth Newson, *Infant Care in an Urban Community* (London, 1963), pp. 223, 231.

14 Elizabeth Roberts, *A Woman's Place: An Oral History of Working-Class Women 1890–1940* (Oxford, 1984), p. 13.

15 Ibid., p. 17.

16 Robert Roberts, *A Ragged Schooling: Growing Up in the Classic Slum* (Manchester, 1976), pp. 50–1.

17 Newsons, *Infant Care*, p. 228.

18 John and Elizabeth Newson, *Four Years Old in an Urban Community* (London, 1968), pp. 390–1.

19 Ibid., pp. 415, 417.

20 Newsons, *Seven Years Old*, pp. 364–5.

21 Jeremy Seabrook, *Working-Class Childhood: An Oral History* (London, 1982), p. 239.

22 Virginia Morrow, 'Rethinking childhood dependency: children's contributions to the domestic economy', *Sociological Review*, 44 (1996), p. 73.

23 G. Jones, 'The cost of living in the parental home', *Youth & Policy*, 32 (1991), pp. 19–28.

24 Jo Manton, *Mary Carpenter and the Children of the Streets* (London, 1976), p. 146.

25 Madeleine Leonard, 'Child work in the UK 1970–1998', in Michael Lavalette (ed.), *A Thing of the Past? Child Labour in Britain in the Nineteenth and Twentieth Centuries* (Liverpool, 1999), pp. 181, 183.

26 Miri Song, *Helping Out: Children's Labour in Ethnic Businesses* (Philadelphia, PA, 1999), quoting p. 52.

27 Morrow, 'Rethinking childhood dependency', pp. 67–8.

28 Ibid., p. 73

29 *Guardian*, 13 April 2005.

30 Morrow, 'Rethinking childhood dependency', p. 70; *Guardian*, 13 April 2005.

31 Martin Woodhead, Rachel Burr and Heather Montgomery, 'Adversities and resilience', in Heather Montgomery, Rachel Burr and Martin Woodhead (eds), *Changing Childhoods: Local and Global* (Chichester, 2003), p. 27.

32 Hugh Cunningham, 'The rights of the child from the mid-eighteenth to the early twentieth century', *Aspects of Education*, no. 50 (1994), pp. 2–16.

33 A. S. Neill, *Summerhill* (1962; Harmondsworth, 1968), p. 20.

34 John Holt, *Escape from Childhood* (1974; Harmondsworth, 1975), pp. 22–3.

35 David Archard, *Children: Rights and Childhood* (London, 1993); M. D. A. Freeman, *The Rights and Wrongs of Childhood* (London, 1983); M. D. A. Freeman (ed.), *Children's Rights: A Comparative Perspective* (Aldershot, 1996); M. D. A. Freeman, *The Moral Status of Children: Essays on the Rights of the Child* (The Hague, 1997); Colin Wringe, *Children's Rights: A Philosophical Study* (London, 1981).

36 Iona and Peter Opie, *The Lore and Language of Schoolchildren* (1959; London, 1977), p. 23.

37 Iona and Peter Opie, *Children's Games in Street and Playground* (Oxford, 1969), p. 10.

38 Ibid., pp. 264, 269–70.

39 Opies, *Lore and Language*, p. 107.

40 Allison James, 'Confections, concoctions and conceptions', in Bernard Waites, Tony Bennett and Graham Martin (eds), *Popular Culture: Past and Present* (London, 1982), pp. 294–307.

41 Opies, *Children's Games*, p. 15.

42 Ibid., p. 16.

43 Mayer Hillman, John Adams and John Whitelegg, *One False Move: A Study of Children's Independent Mobility* (London, 1990), p. 106.

44 Neil Postman, *The Disappearance of Childhood* (1982; London, 1983).

45 Buckingham, *After the Death of Childhood*.

46 Ibid., p. 65; Stephen Kline, *Out of the Garden: Toys and Children's Culture in the Age of TV Marketing* (London, 1993); *Guardian*, 10 June 2005.

47 Humphrey Carpenter, *Secret Gardens: A Study of the Golden Age of Children's Literature* (London, 1987), pp. 210–23.

48 Peter Barnes and Mary Jane Kehily, 'Play and the cultures of childhood', in Mary Jane Kehily and Joan Swann (eds), *Children's Cultural Worlds* (Chichester, 2003), p. 23; Opies, *Children's Games*, pp. 32–4.

49 Harry Hendrick, *Child Welfare: Historical Dimensions, Contemporary Debate* (Bristol, 2003), p. 250.

50 Ibid., p. 139.

51 Hendrick, *Child Welfare*, pp. 181, 184; Heather Montgomery and Rachel Burr, 'Children, poverty and social inequality', in Montgomery et al., *Changing Childhoods*, pp. 80–5; *Guardian*, 10 March 2006.

52 Hendrick, *Child Welfare*, p. 174.

53 Quoted ibid., p. 186.

54 Montgomery and Burr, 'Children, poverty and social inequality', p. 50.

55 Heather Montgomery, 'Children and violence', in Montgomery et al., *Changing Childhoods*, p. 146; www.rights4me.org.uk

56 Lynn Abrams, *The Orphan Country: Children of Scotland's Broken Homes from 1845 to the Present* (Edinburgh, 1998), p, 198.

57 For these and other cases, see David Batty, 'Catalogue of cruelty', www.society.guardian.co.uk/children/story

58 Hendrick, *Child Welfare*, pp. 194–6; Abrams, *Orphan Country*, pp. 234–8.

59 Quoted in Donald Mackinnon, 'Children and school', in Janet Maybin and Martin Woodhead (eds), *Childhoods in Context* (Chichester, 2003), p. 168.

60 Roberts, *A Woman's Place*, pp. 19–20.

61 Hillmann et al., *One False Move*, pp. 1–2; *Guardian*, 20 Sept. 2004. www.archive.official-documents.co.uk

62 www.rights4me.org.uk

63 Opie, *Lore and Language*, pp. 370–1.

64 Barbara Tizard and Ann Phoenix, *Black, White or Mixed Race? Race and Racism in the Lives of Young People of Mixed Parentage*, revised edn (London, 2001), p. 159.

65 Ibid., p. 163.

66 Ibid., p. 165.

67 *Guardian*, 28 Feb. 2006; *Observer*, 29 May 2005.

68 Hendrick, *Child Welfare*, pp. 191, 239–42.

69 Ibid., pp. 226–31.

Further Reading

This brief survey makes no attempt to be comprehensive. It is intended as a guide to those who may wish to pursue one or more of the themes explored in this book, and it concentrates on books that are likely to be relatively easy to access. Periodical articles in academic journals, where much of the most interesting research is first published, are excluded. Anyone interested in more detailed research will find some guidance from the endnotes to each chapter.

British experience is placed in a continental European, and, where appropriate, North American context, in Shulamith Shahar, *Childhood in the Middle Ages* (London, 1992), Danièle Alexandre-Bidon and Didier Lett, *Children in the Middle Ages, Fifth to Fifteenth Centuries* (Notre Dame, IND, 1999), Colin Heywood, *A History of Childhood: Children and Childhood in the West from Medieval to Modern Times* (Cambridge, 2001), and Hugh Cunningham, *Children and Childhood in Western Society since 1500*, 2nd edn (Harlow, 2005).

There is no book covering childhood in Britain for the whole period. The closest approximation is Ivy Pinchbeck and Margaret Hewitt, *Children in English Society*, 2 vols (London, 1969–73) which starts with the Tudors – and is, as the title suggests, confined to England. Its emphasis is on social policy.

Medieval Britain Nicholas Orme, *Medieval Children* (New Haven, CT and London, 2001) is an unrivalled source and interpretation for the Middle Ages. Sally Crawford, *Childhood in Anglo-Saxon England* (Stroud, 1999) carefully weighs up the archaeological and written evidence for her period. Nicholas Orme, *English Schools in the Middle Ages* (London, 1973) and Jo Ann Hoeppner Moran, *The Growth of English Schooling 1340–1548: Learning, Literacy, and*

Laicization in Pre-Reformation York Diocese (Princeton, NJ 1985) are the key books on schooling. Other topics can be followed in J. A. Burrow, *The Ages of Man: A Study in Medieval Writing and Thought* (Oxford, 1986); Edith Rickert (ed.), *The Babees' Book: Medieval Manners for the Young* (London, 1933); Barbara A. Hanawalt, *The Ties That Bound: Peasant Families in Medieval England* (Oxford, 1986), and *Growing Up in Medieval London: The Experience of Childhood in History* (Oxford, 1993).

Early Modern Britain, 1500—1800 Lawrence Stone, *The Family, Sex and Marriage in England 1500–1800* (London, 1977) has been controversial but remains valuable. It should be supplemented by Ralph A. Houlbrooke, *The English Family 1450–1700* (London, 1984), Linda Pollock, *Forgotten Children: Parent-Child Relations from 1500 to 1900* (Cambridge, 1983), and Anthony Fletcher, *Gender, Sex and Subordination in England 1500–1800* (New Haven, CT and London, 1995). The Puritans can be studied in C. John Sommerville, *The Discovery of Childhood in Puritan England* (Athens, GA and London, 1992), and John Philip Morgan, *Godly Learning: Puritan Attitudes Towards Reason, Learning, and Education, 1560–1640* (Cambridge, 1986). David Cressy, *Education in Tudor and Stuart England* (London, 1975) is a valuable source book, and Rosemary O'Day, *Education and Society 1500–1800: The Social Foundations of Education in Early Modern Britain* (London, 1982) provides the best overall survey of her topic. Keith Thomas's lecture, *Rule and Misrule in the Schools of Early Modern England* (Reading, 1976) sheds invaluable light on an obscure theme. Ilana Krausman Ben-Amos, *Adolescence and Youth in Early Modern England* (New Haven, CT and London, 1994) is the best guide to the later childhood years. Social policy is elucidated in Paul Slack, *Poverty and Policy in Tudor and Stuart England* (London, 1988). Ruth K. McClure, *Coram's Children: The London Foundling Hospital in the Eighteenth Century* (New Haven, CT and London, 1981) is an absorbing case study.

The Victorians James Walvin, *A Child's World: A Social History of English Childhood 1800–1914* (Harmondsworth, 1982) is the best overall interpretation. Eric Hopkins, *Childhood Transformed: Working-Class Children in Nineteenth-Century England* (Manchester, 1994) is an excellent survey. Valuable studies with a narrower focus include Heather Shore, *Artful Dodgers: Youth and Crime in Early Nineteenth-Century London* (Woodbridge, Suffolk, 1999); Louise A.

Jackson, *Child Sexual Abuse in Victorian England* (London, 2000); Peter Kirby, *Child Labour in Britain, 1750–1870* (Basingstoke, 2003); Gillian Wagner, *Barnardo* (London, 1980); Joy Parr, *Labouring Children: British Immigrant Apprentices to Canada, 1869–1924* (London, 1980); Phil Gardner, *The Lost Elementary Schools of Victorian England* (London, 1984); Anna Davin, *Growing Up Poor: Home, School and Street in London 1870–1914* (London, 1996); J. S. Hurt, *Elementary Schooling and the Working Classes 1860–1918* (London, 1979), Carol Dyhouse, *Girls Growing Up in Late Victorian and Edwardian England* (London, 1981); John Tosh, *A Man's Place: Masculinity and the Middle-Class Home in Victorian England* (New Haven, CT and London, 1999), J. R. de S. Honey, *Tom Brown's Universe: The Development of the Victorian Public School* (London, 1977); Pamela Horn, *The Victorian and Edwardian School Child* (Stroud, 1989).

The Twentieth Century Oral history becomes a valuable resource from the late nineteenth century, and a number of books have been based on it. Leading examples include Thea Thompson (ed.), *Edwardian Childhoods* (London, 1981); Stephen Humphries, *Hooligans or Rebels? An Oral History of Working-Class Childhood and Youth 1889–1939* (Oxford, 1981); Gloria Wood and Paul Thompson, *The Nineties: Personal Recollections of the Twentieth Century* (London, 1993); Steve Humphries and Pamela Gordon, *A Labour of Love: The Experience of Parenthood in Britain 1900–1950* (London, 1993); Jeremy Seabrook, *Working-Class Childhood: An Oral History* (London, 1982); and two books by Elizabeth Roberts, *A Woman's Place: An Oral History of Working-Class Women 1890–1940* (Oxford, 1984), and *Women and Families: An Oral History, 1940–1970* (Oxford, 1995). There are valuable essays on changing ideas and policies in Roger Cooter (ed.), *In the Name of the Child: Child Health and Welfare, 1880–1940* (London, 1992); Marijke Gijswijt-Hofstra and Hilary Marland (eds), *Cultures of Child Health in Britain and the Netherlands in the Twentieth Century* (Amsterdam and New York, 2003); and Jon Lawrence and Pat Starkey (eds), *Child Welfare and Social Action in the Nineteenth and Twentieth Centuries: International Perspectives* (Liverpool, 2001). Harry Hendrick, *Child Welfare: Historical Dimensions, Contemporary Debate* (Bristol, 2003) is the best single volume on social policy, and Lynn Abrams, *The Orphan Country: Children of Scotland's Broken Homes from 1845 to the Present* (Edinburgh, 1998) is an excellent case study. Stephen Kline, *Out of the Garden:*

Toys and Children's Culture in the Age of TV Marketing (London, 1993) and David Buckingham, *After the Death of Childhood: Growing Up in the Age of Electronic Media* (Cambridge, 2000) are excellent guides to the media and childhood. John Springhall, *Youth, Empire and Society: British Youth Movements, 1883–1940* (London, 1977) is the best overall survey of the topic.

General Christina Hardyment, *Dream Babies: Child Care from Locke to Spock* (London, 1983) is an excellent guide through advice literature. Linda Pollock, *A Lasting Relationship: Parents and Children Over Three Centuries* (Hanover and London, 1987) is an invaluable selection of primary sources from 1600 to 1900. John Burnett (ed.), *Destiny Obscure: Autobiographies of Childhood, Education and Family from the 1820s to the 1920s* (Harmondsworth, 1982) draws on many unpublished autobiographies. The work of Iona and Peter Opie is crucial for understanding children's cultural world: *The Lore and Language of Schoolchildren* (London, 1959), *Children's Games in Street and Playground* (London, 1969), and *The Singing Game* (London, 1985) delve deeply into the past as well as recording what is happening in the second half of the twentieth century. Anne Higonnet, *Pictures of Innocence: The History and Crisis of Ideal Childhood* (London, 1998) is a stimulating discussion of images of children. Also valuable is J. C. Steward, *The New Child: British Art and the Origins of Modern Childhood 1730–1830* (Berkeley, CA, 1995). There is now a substantial amount of scholarly writing on children's literature. Peter Coveney, *The Image of Childhood* (Harmondsworth, 1967) remains stimulating. S. F. Pickering, Jr, *John Locke and Children's Books in Eighteenth-Century England* (Knoxville, TN, 1981), the essays in J. H. McGavran (ed.), *Romanticism and Children's Literature in Nineteenth-Century England* (Atlanta, GA, 1991), and Humphrey Carpenter, *Secret Gardens: A Study of the Golden Age of Children's Literature* (London, 1987) are good introductions to their periods.

Index

Picture Credits

BBC Books would like to thank the following for providing images for the plate sections and for permission to reproduce copyright material. While every effort has been made to trace and acknowledge copyright holders, we would like to apologize should there have been any errors or omissions.

Plate

1   Reproduced from *Childhood in Anglo-Saxon England* (Sutton Publishing, 1999)
2   Bodleian Library, University of Oxford
3   Bodleian Library, University of Oxford
4   Bodleian Library, University of Oxford
5   The British Library, London
6   The National Gallery of Art, Washington DC / The Bridgeman Art Library
7   Getty Images
8   The National Portrait Gallery, London
9   Reproduced from *English Art 1553–1625*, Plate 86b (Oxford University Press, 1962)
10 The National Gallery, London / The Bridgeman Art Library
11 Plymouth City Museum and Art Gallery
12 Derby Museum
13 V&A Images / Victoria and Albert Museum

14 © Fitzwilliam Museum, University of Cambridge /
The Bridgeman Art Library

15 All rights reserved. The Metropolitan Museum of Art,
New York

16 Getty Images

17 Mary Evans Picture Library

18 © Harrogate Museums and Art Gallery, North Yorkshire /
The Bridgeman Art Library

19 Private Collection / The Bridgeman Art Library

20 Reproduced with the permission of Punch Ltd. www.punch.co.uk

21 Reproduced from *Children's Pleasures* (Dean of London, 1996)

22 The Scout Association

23 The Bridgeman Art Library

24 © Barnardo's

25 Reproduced from *Hooligans or Rebels?* (Blackwell Publishers, 1995)

26 Farnworth Library, Bolton

27 Reproduced from *Hooligans or Rebels?* (Blackwell Publishers, 1995)

28 © Museum of London

29 Prudential plc Group Archives

30 Corbis

31 Getty Images

32 Courtesy Iona Opie. Reproduced with permission.

The Voices of Children
A Play by Michael Morpurgo

Present day. The communal gardens in an apartment block in west London.

Centre stage is a great, uprooted oak tree, the massive root system facing the audience. Beneath the roots is a large crater.

A children's birthday party is in full swing (the children aged between seven and ten). There's a game of musical chairs going on without the chairs. Some 25 children are there, all in historical costumes of various periods from Anglo-Saxon through medieval to Victorian, except for two: **Hugh** *aged eight, dressed as Bart Simpson, and his sister* **Beaty**, *dressed as Marge Simpson. Both are wearing easily identifiable cut-out cardboard hairpieces. They are dancing in a circle with the others (***Hugh*** obviously unwilling) to the strains of Boney M. The mood is wild. The music stops. Last to sit down is* **Hugh** *because he isn't paying attention.*

Children (*cry out in unison*). 'Hugh! Hugh!'

Hugh *is out. He stomps off, fed up. The dancing circle continues with the music and then unravels, leaving* **Hugh** *alone with the tree. He sits down on the edge of the crater, disconsolate, chucking stones at the roots. We hear the music stop again.* **Beaty** *joins him, really fed up.*

Hugh   I wasn't trying anyway.

Beaty   Nor me.

Hugh	(*still chucking stones*). I could kill her.
Beaty	Who?
Hugh	Mum. I told her, didn't I? Historical. The costumes for the party had to be historical. But she always knows best, doesn't she?
Beaty	Tell me about it.
Hugh	(*mimicking his mother sarcastically*). 'Oh, no, Hugh. I talked to Jamie's grandma about it, and she definitely said hysterical not historical. And hysterical, dear, means funny, if you didn't know. And Bart Simpson's funny – you're always telling me.' And then she goes and makes me wear this ... thing. (*He whips off his hairpiece and hurls it into the crater, and **Beaty** does the same in solidarity*.) I'll kill her.
Beaty	You're not allowed.
Hugh	And that's another thing. Why should she tell me what to wear anyway? They're always making the rules. Dad's just as bad. It's all they do, sit around making rules and drinking cups of coffee.
Beaty	We've got to have rules. It's like the days of the week. Monday and Tuesday and that. You wouldn't know when to go to school else. They are sort of like birthdays. You can't grow older unless you have birthdays, can you?
Hugh	Who wants to be old anyway? You get all wrinkly and you get hairs in your ears like grandpa. No, thank you! You know what I want? I want to stay eight years old for ever, and make up my own rules. And the first rule will be that I make the rules.

Beaty	(*not listening. She is looking at the fallen oak tree*). It's sad.
Hugh	What is?
Beaty	That tree. It got old, didn't it. I really loved it. It was the oldest in London, mum said. Been here for ever.
Hugh	Couldn't have been for ever. Nothing's for ever, is it? (*He's gazing at the upturned roots.*) There's hundreds and hundreds of roots. Which was the first, I wonder?
Beaty	And who planted it?

*Enter silently, and without them noticing, a sturdy-looking 11-year-old Anglo-Saxon boy, **Cedd**. He is scantily clad in furs. **Cedd** will serve as the narrator throughout the play, donning different period costumes on stage as the centuries pass.*

Cedd	I did. I planted it. (*He bends down and picks up an acorn.*) With this. Then when I died they buried me beside it because it was my tree. (*He scoops up a handful of earth, and lets it pour through his fingers.*) Not a lot of me left, is there?
Hugh	(*terrified, like his sister, at the implication of what has just been said. They have backed away, **Hugh** hiding behind **Beaty** for protection*). Who's he?
Beaty	(*whispering*). He wasn't at the party?
Hugh	Is he a ghost or what?
Beaty	Think so, and he hasn't got much clothes on either. Looks like Stig of the Dump.
Cedd	You should plant another one.

Beaty	Why us?

Cedd	Because it was my tree and you are my descendants, my relations. You came from me, just like this tree came from an acorn. (*To* **Beaty**) You could plant it together (*to* **Hugh**) and you could put the acorn in, dig the hole for it too. I always had to do the digging when I was your age. They always give us boys the dirty jobs, don't they?

Hugh	(*less fearful now, glad of the proffered solidarity*). Huh, tell me about it.

Cedd	All right, I will. You'd better sit down though, because it's quite a story.

Beaty *and* **Hugh** *are nonplussed by this response, but they sit on the edge of the crater. Just as they do so, on to the stage come all the 'party' children, ghosts now every one of them, and moving slowly.* **Beaty** *and* **Hugh** *are alarmed. They can see the transition and know what it means.*

It's my story, and your story and their story too. They were there. They'll tell you all about it. They'll tell it as they found it, as they saw it, as it happened. And they are all your ancestors, like me. But it's the story of all the children who have known this land and breathed this air. It begins with me. I was digging a grave. My own little sister's grave. She was called Hedda.

From the chorus comes a diminutive Anglo-Saxon girl, **Hedda**, *very frail and pale. As with all the children from the chorus who come forward, she speaks directly to the audience.*

Hedda	I am full yong.
	I was born yesterday.
	Death is ful hasty
	On me to been wreke.

Hedda *rejoins the chorus.*

Children   (*singing*).
Matthew, Mark, Luke and John,
Bless the bed that I lie on.
Four corners to my bed,
Four angels round my head.
One to watch, and one to pray,
And two to bear my soul away.

The verse is repeated.

Cedd   (*wearing a medieval costume now*). More than anything it
was hunger and cold that took us young, took us from our
families, took us from this world. Every mother, every father,
every sister, every brother, knew the pity of it. It went on like
this for hundreds of years, a massacre of the innocents. We
had a day of our very own, a day to remember how King
Herod had killed all the innocent children, but it was a day
when we remembered all the children. Childermas it was
called, 28 December every year, one day when we could be
just who we wanted to be. It was a day when we could say
what we liked, a day a boy could be a bishop, and even give
a sermon, like John did in Gloucester Cathedral in front of
hundreds of people. He told them.

John, *escorted by two other children comes forward from the chorus. He's in
tattered clothes. His escorts dress him up like a bishop, and give him a bishop's
mitre and crook. The mitre is too big and slips down over his face. They try again
to put it on but it won't stay up. So they hold it up for him as he gives his sermon.
He does this with bishop-like pomposity, but he means every word.*

John   Young babes and little children are simple, without gyle,
innocent, without harme and all pure without corruption.
You shall perceive in them no manner of malice, no envy,
no disdayne, no hurtfulness, no synfull affection, no pride,

no ambition, no singularities, no desire of honour, of riches, of carnality, of revenging, of quitting evil for evil.

Children *sing 'The Coventry Carol'.*

Cedd   The trouble was, once the day was over, we were treated just the same as we had been before, worked to the bone, beaten whenever they felt like it. But once out of sight we could be children again. We could wander where we wanted, do what we pleased, play blind man's buff and hide and seek – and football too.

Hugh   Football!?

Cedd   They made it out of a pig's bladder. Alexander and Peter will tell you how it was.

Two quite well-to-do medieval children, **Alexander** *and* **Peter**, *step forward to declaim alternate couplets in this poem, each miming, quite comically, the other's couplet.*

Alexander   Eache time and season hath its delites and joys
                   Loke in the streets beholde the little boys

Peter   How in fruit season for joy they sing and hop
                   In Lent is eache one full busy with his top

Alexander   And now in winter for all the grievous colde
                   All rent and ragged a man may them beholde

Peter   They have great pleasour, supposing well to dine
                   When men be busied in killing of fat swine

Alexander   They get the bladder and blowe it great and thin
                   With many beanes and peasen put within

| Peter | It ratleth, soundeth and shineth clere and fayre |
| | When it is throwen and caste up in the ayre |

| Alexander | Eache one contendeth and hath a great delite |
| | With foote and with hande the bladder for to smite. |

| Cedd | Girls didn't play football. They didn't have nearly so much fun as boys did. |

| Beaty | Tell me about it! |

| Cedd | (*not understanding this phrase*). Abigail knows all about it, don't you, Abigail? She was made to learn this and recite it often, so she'd be a good girl, weren't you, Abigail? |

Abigail *comes forward demurely.*

Abigail	(*speaking very properly*).
	In temperate and patient innocence
	With modesty of bearing and of dress
	And showed in speech a modesty no less.
	She used no fancy term in affectation
	Of learning, but according to her station
	She spoke in all and everything she said
	She showed she was good and gently bred.

| Cedd | And did you show you were good and gently bred? |

| Abigail | (*screaming with frustration and rage and stamping her foot*). No! No! No! (*She runs off the stage.*) |

| Beaty | Good for you. |

| Cedd | But there were rules for boys and girls alike. |

Geoffrey *and* **Catherine** *come forward.*

Geoffrey *and* **Catherine** (*speaking in unison in rather schoolmarm voices*).

> Child, climb not over house nor wall,
> For no fruit, birds or ball.
>
> Child, over men's houses no stones fling
> Nor at glass windows no stones sling
>
> And, child, when thou goest to play
> Look thou come home by light of day.

Cedd Then, as if there weren't enough rules already, someone went and invented school. No-one wanted to go. I mean, why did they do that?

Hugh Dunno. I think they are still trying to work that out.

Michael *comes forward looking doleful, rubbing his backside.*

Michael
> My master looketh as he were mad,
> 'Where hast thou been, thou sorry lad?'
> 'Milking ducks, as my mother bade'
> It was no marvel that I were sad.
>
> My master peppered my tail with good speed
> He would not leave till it did bleed
> Much sorrow have he for his deed.
> I would my master were a hare
> And all his books greyhounds were
> And I myself a jolly hunter
> To blow my horn I would not spare
> For if he were dead I would not care!

Beaty	(*aside to* **Hugh**). They speak funny, don't they?
Hugh	That's 'cos they always spoke in poetry in those days. He's getting changed again. Looks like a Tudor now. I done the Tudors in school – the Armada and that.
Cedd	(*changed into Elizabethan costume*). I've always liked stories, Bible stories, saints' stories, Robin Hood – if anyone should've been a saint, it was him, helping the poor like he did. But riddles were my favourite. Here, can you work this one out? Ready?
Beaty and **Hugh**	(*together*). Ready.
Cedd	Two legs sat upon three legs With one leg in his lap. In comes four legs And runs away with one leg. Up jumps two legs, Catches up three legs, Throws it after four legs And makes him bring back one leg.

(**Beaty** *and* **Hugh** *are stumped.*)

You do go to school, do you? (*They nod.*) Well, they didn't teach you much then, did they? Watch this.

Riddle is now acted out by the children. **Simon** *comes on with a three-legged stool, sits on it. He has a leg of mutton in his lap. Dog comes in (***Abigail** *on four legs) snatches leg of mutton and runs off stage.* **Simon** *throws stool off stage at dog who comes back on, tail between legs, and brings back bone, licked clean. Dog tries to look happy and contrite at the same time.*

Cedd	See? Good, eh?

Beaty	Were they really all our relations?
Cedd	Every one of them, including the dog. (*Suddenly serious.*) They couldn't all play silly games though. Lots of our relatives never lived to grow up. Nehamiah, she died when she was very little. (**Nehamiah** *comes on – in nightclothes, supported by her father.*) These were the last words she ever spoke.
Nehamiah	Father, I go abroad tomorrow and bring you a plum pie. (*As she leaves him reluctantly, she lets go his hand.*)
Father	Such a child I never saw, for such a child I bless God. Thou gavest her to us, thou hast taken her from us, blessed be the name of the Lord.
Cedd	(*shrugging on another costume, that of a boy of the Civil War, with a sword at his side*). What do you think? (*He gives a twirl.*)
Beaty	Cool.
Hugh	When are we now?
Cedd	Just after the Civil War, after they'd chopped off Charles I's head. The royalists wore better clothes, but the Puritans won and, unfortunately, they were very keen on schools. So even more of us had to go to school now. (**William** *comes on, a boy, a Puritan.*) But William was a farm boy, so he got lucky sometimes.
William	From the age of ten or twelve years, we were very much better off the schoole, espetialy in the spring and summer season, plow time, turfe time, hay time and harvest, looking after the sheep, helping at plough, making hay and shearing, two of us at 13 or 14 years of age being equal to one man

shearer so we made small progress in Latin, for what we got in winter we forgot in summer. We got what writing we had in winter (*sees schoolmaster coming*) – look out. *Cave.* Here's the master. I'm off.

Alexander, *dressed as a schoolmaster, hurries on, shaking his cane in fury after* **William**. *Suddenly seeing the audience, he remembers the dignity of his position. He mimicks a teacher.*

Alexander   Obedience is one of the capital benefits arising from a public education, to break the ferocity of human nature, to subdue the passions and to impress the principles of religion and morality – this is the first object to be attended to by all schoolmasters who know their duty. William! (*He goes off stage.*) William! Come back this minute, you rascal you!

Cedd   (*in eighteenth-century coat and hat now.*) But to be honest those children who were in school were the lucky ones – despite schoolmasters like him. You won't want to see this but you have to. It's part of the story.

A poor mother comes on, carrying a baby in her arms. She looks around and puts the baby down, kisses it, then runs off, weeping.

Many children were very poor, and poor meant hungry. Another mouth to feed was a mouth too many. Some were left in church porches. Worse still, some became beggars and a few even ended up as slaves. Slaves! Can you believe it?

Two street children come on, **William** *and* **Joan**. *One crouches to pick up the baby.*

Hugh   Who are they?

Cedd   Children who never lived to laugh and play. Listen.

William	Is this a holy thing to see
	In a rich and fruitful land,
	Babes reduced to misery
	Fed with cold and usurous hand?

Joan	Is that trembling cry a song?
	Can it be a song of joy?
	And so many children poor?
	It is a land of poverty.

William and **Joan** (*together*).

And their sun does never shine
And their fields are bleak and bare
And their ways are filled with thorns
It is eternal winter there.

Beaty	They make me feel so sad. Are they our relations too?

Cedd	We all are.

Hugh	Were we always poor?

Cedd	No, but even if you weren't poor, children could have a hard time of it. Rules again. Rules, rules. Elizabeth was your great-great-grandmother – doesn't look like it, does she?

Elizabeth *comes forward, middle class in her early teens, confident.*

Elizabeth	The milk rebellion was crushed immediately. In his dressing-gown, with his whip in his hand, father attended our breakfast ... That disgusting milk! He began with me; my beseeching look was answered by a sharp cut, followed by as many more as were necessary to empty the basin. And bathtime was worse still. A large tub stood in the kitchen court, the ice on top of which had often to be

broken before our horrid plunge into it. We were brought down from the very top of the house, four pairs of stairs, with only a cotton cloak over our night-gowns, just to chill us completely before the dreadful shock. How I screamed, begged, prayed, entreated to be saved, half the tender-hearted maids in tears besides me, all to no use. Millar, our nurse, had her orders.

Cedd   But once she got outside away from her father, away from the rules ...

*There follows a game of 'drop handkerchief'. Children (including **Elizabeth**), alternating girl/boy circle around in a ring. **Elizabeth** drops the handkerchief behind **Piers**'s Back. She runs off. **Piers** picks it up and is held by the girls on either side so **Elizabeth** can get away. He breaks free finally. She rejoins the ring just as he catches her. They go to the centre of the ring and kiss.*

That's Piers. And if you want to know, he became a relation as well, a little bit later.

The children, *in nine couples, now come forward and recite a couplet each, before the next couple takes their place.*

First couple   The Sun does arise
                     And make happy the skies

Second couple   The merry bells ring
                     To welcome the Spring

Third couple   The skylark and thrush
                     The birds of the bush

Fourth couple   Sing louder around
                     To the bells' cheerful sound

Fifth couple	While our sports shall be seen
	On the Echoing Green.
Sixth couple	Old John, with white hair
	Does laugh away care
Seventh couple	Sitting under the oak
	Among the old folk.
Eighth couple	They laugh at our play
	And soon they all say
Ninth couple	'Such, were the joys
	When we all, girls and boys

Children (*all together*).

In our youth time were seen
On the Echoing Green.'

Beaty   Were they Victorians? We've done Victorians in class,
Oliver Twist and all that stuff.

Cedd   (*donning a Victorian hat and coat*). We're coming to them
now. And you won't like what you are going to hear. There
never was a worse time than this for children. Children
should be seen and not heard. That's how they were treated
up at the big houses. And that was bad enough. (**George**
*comes on carrying his sweep's brushes over each shoulder,
blackened, coughing, exhausted.*) For the poor children,
the working children, it was a lot worse. This is George.
He died when he was 11.

George   I was a climbing boy, I was. I was apprentice to a master
sweep. In Cambridge it was. The last chimney I did was at
Fulbourne Hospital. I didn't want to go up again. I was bad

in my chest, see. But they made me. They pricked the soles of my feet to make me go up. They set straw alight under me. I had to go up, didn't I? When I died they opened me up and they found all my lungs and my windpipe was full of black powder. I suffocated to death, couldn't breathe. It was good to die. Didn't suffer no more after that.

Cedd   There were thousands of climbing boys like George. Wherever they wanted cheap labour they used children – in the factories and the mills, down the mines, in the dirt and the dark, like Sarah – oh, yes, girls too went down the mines.

Six children come in pushing a coal cart, all bent to their work, all blackened, all barely able to keep going. They stop and lean on the cart. One of them, **Sarah,** *straightens herself slowly.*

Sarah   I work in the Gauber pit. I have to work without a light and I'm scared. Sometimes I sing when I've a light, but not in the dark. I dare not sing then. I don't like being in the pit. I'm very sleepy when I go sometimes in the morning. I go to Sunday school and read *Reading Made Easy*. I would like to be at school far better than in the pit.

Cedd   Do you know the saddest story I ever heard? It was about a factory girl who had to get up early every morning to go to work. One morning she was sick, too weak to get up. She was lying in her father's arms. She woke up and the first thing she thought was that it must be time to go to work. 'Father, is it time?' she said. 'Father, is it time?' Then she sank back in his arms and died.

The sound of a drum and marching feet. A protest march of ragged factory children, carrying banners reading 'Father is it time?', 'Behold and Weep!'

Factory children (*shouting*). 'No more! No more! No more!'

Suddenly the children are still and silent. A single child, **Clare***, steps forward.*

Clare	The young lambs are bleating in the meadows, The young birds are chirping in the nest, The young fawns are playing with the shadows, The young flowers are blowing towards the West. But the young, young children, O, my brothers, They are weeping bitterly! They are weeping in the playtime of the others, In the country of the free.

Children pick up the echo of the last word and chant it in time with the drumbeat of the protest march, punching the air as they go off.

Children	(*chanting*). 'Free! Free! Free! Free! Free!'

Hugh *and* **Beaty**, *deeply upset and angry, jump up and join in the chanting as the children leave.*

Cedd	There's more. (**Hugh** *and* **Beaty** *sit down again*.) There were the street children like Jim. It was a cold winter's night and it was late. Look.

Enter **Jim***, in rags, from stage left. He sits down hugging his knees, shivering.* **Dr Barnardo** *(a child dressed up) comes from stage right. He notices* **Jim** *and goes over to him.*

Dr Barnardo	Come, my lad, had you not better get home? It's very late. Mother will be coming for you.
Jim	Please, sir, let me stop.
Dr Barnardo	Why do you want to stay?
Jim	Please, sir, do let me stay. I won't do no harm.

Dr Barnardo	Your mother will wonder what kept you so late.
Jim	I ain't got no mother.
Dr Barnardo	Haven't got a mother, boy? Where do you live?
Jim	Don't live nowhere.
Dr Barnardo	Do you mean to say, my boy, that you have no home, that you have no mother or father?
Jim	That's the truth on't, sir. I ain't telling you no lie about it.
Dr Barnardo	But where did you sleep last night?
Jim	Down Whitechapel, sir, in one of them carts as is filled with 'ay. I won't do 'arm, sir, if you let me stay.
Dr Barnardo	Are there other children sleeping out like you?
Jim	Oh, yes, lots, 'eaps on 'em, sir. More 'n I could count.
Dr Barnardo	You come along with me, lad. I'll find you somewhere warm, somewhere you can stay, and a good hot meal too.
Jim	Honest?
Dr Barnardo	Honest. (*He helps Jim up and they leave.*)
Cedd	That was Dr Barnardo. He looked after thousands of street children just like Jim.
Beaty	So there were some good people?
Cedd	Lots of them, luckily for you. If there hadn't been, like as not you'd be living on the streets or working in factories

still. Things got better all right. But not in a hurry. Look at your great-grandfather now, James he was called. He was 13, first day at work.

James *comes on, sees the audience, and stops to tell them. He's very pleased with himself – dressed in his new working clothes.*

James	Said goodbye to my schooling at Spotland Board School. Off to work at Heaps – 55 and a half hour working week for 10 shillings and sixpence, a fortune for Mother. Mother rigged me out in this at a total cost of 15 shillings. Not bad, eh? (*Does a turn.*) Corduroy trousers, leather braces. Brown cap, got a button on top and the scarf to keep the wind out. Proper little man, Mother called me. And she's right. I'm a breadwinner now and proud of it. Got to go. Mustn't be late on my first day. (*Lifts his cap and runs off.*)
Beaty	(*gazing after him*). Dreamy. Looks like Leonardo DiCaprio in that ship film, y'know, *Titanic*.
Hugh	Looks a lot like me, I reckon.
Beaty	(*scoffing*). You!
Hugh	Well, he is my great-grandfather.
Beaty	He's mine too.
Cedd	(*pulls on a jacket and flat cap like **James**'s*). He married your great-grandmother young, very young. They had a baby. He went off to fight in the First World War. Never came back. Nearly a million of them never came back. That was the First World War.

Children *come on stage, dancing. The chant raucously, as in street singing, as they dance.*

Children   When the war is over and the Kaiser's dead
He's no gaun tae Heaven wi' the eagle on his head
For the Lord says, 'No!' He'll have tae go below
For he's all dressed up and nowhere tae go.

Cedd   Then a few years later they had a Second World War

Children *begin doing a conga around the stage.*

Children   *(singing – same tune as before).*
When the war is over Hitler will be dead
He hopes to go to Heaven with a crown upon his head
But the Lord says 'No!' You'll have to go below,
There's only room for Churchill, so cheery-cheery oh!

Sounds of siren going off and bombs falling.

Beaty   I thought you said things got better for kids.

Cedd   They did.

Beaty   There's nothing better about wars, is there? How can wars
ever be better?

Cedd   No, but sometimes wars can make people stop and think
a bit – only good thing about them. They know they have
to try to make things better for their grandchildren, look
after them better, feed them better.

A girl, **Charis,** *in pigtails, comes on hopscotching along the pavement on her way
back home from school, talking to herself.*

Charis   I hate school dinners. I hate school dinners.

                (*chanting*).
                Splishy splashy custard
                Dead dogs' eyes
                All mixed up with giblet pies
                Spread it on the butty nice and thick
                Swallow it down with a bucket of sick.

From behind, the **children** *echo her chant.* **Charis** *stops her hopscotching, spooked by the echo. She runs off.*

Hugh   Who was that?

Cedd   (*in modern clothes now, baseball cap, Chelsea shirt etc.*).
                Your mum.

Hugh and **Beaty** (*together*) Our mum!

Cedd   Yep. And then after her there was you and you, and after
                you ... That's how it happens, how things keep going.
                That's why you've got to plant that acorn I gave you. It's
                what we're here for, to keep things going, make new life,
                and make things better, if we can.

Beaty   Yes, and we will too.

Hugh   (*kneeling down*). Here? Do I plant it here?

Cedd   Where you like.

Hugh *hands the acorn to* **Beaty** *and digs with his hands on the edge of the crater. As he does so, the chorus of children from the ages emerges to form a semicircle around them.* **Hugh** *and* **Beaty** *do not notice.* **Beaty** *kneels now to plant the acorn, and they both fill in the hole, stand up and look down, as if waiting for the tree to grow.* **Hugh** *nudges* **Beaty**. *The semicircle has become a circle. He has noticed they* *are now surrounded by all the children. They feel a little threatened until* **Cedd**, *with them in the centre of the circle, reassures them.*

Cedd   They've come to say goodbye. We all have. But first they wanted to play a game with you. It's a game they know and you'll know. A game all children have always known. Blind man's buff.

Hugh   Can I ask you something? Why the shirt? Why Chelsea?

Cedd   They're the champions again, aren't they?

Hugh   How come you know so much?

Cedd   I don't know who's going to win next year, do I?

Hugh   I do. Manchester United.

Cedd   You up for blind man's buff? (*He holds out the blindfolds.*)

Hugh   Both of us at once?

Cedd   Why not? We can change the rules if we want to, can't we?

Cedd *ties the blindfolds on both* **Hugh** *and* **Beaty**. *Turns them round and round. They begin to grope forwards, arms, outstretched, finding each other first. The children in the circle laugh, loving the fun of it. The circle of historical children, hands joined, begins to turn. We hear the distant strains of Boney M. They move to the rhythm of it in a flowing dance, in time-synchronized steps.* **Cedd** *joins the circle, and after a while leads the children off, leaving* **Hugh** *and* **Beaty** *groping alone on stage.*

    The music is louder now as the children return, in the same costumes but as the party children, dancing excitedly, hysterically (hands not joined), as they form the dancing circle again. **Cedd** *is not among them.* **Beaty** *catches one of the children, and rips off her blindfold.* **Hugh** *does the same. They turn around and around wondering, wondering. The circle turns into disco dancing.* **Hugh** *and*

Beaty *walk through the dancers to the front of the stage, still wondering about all they've seen. The music dies away, the party children dance on – in silence now. From among them, from the crater, a young tree slowly rises. (A child as a tree.) The children see it, stop dancing and watch in wonder.* **Hugh** *and* **Beaty** *turn and see it too. The two join hands, backs to the audience. The children all back away, off stage, reverently, leaving the stage to the tree and* **Hugh** *and* **Beaty**. *Then they too leave the stage slowly. The tree stands alone.*

The End.